PRAISE FOR
WHEN THE LIGHT OF THE WORLD WAS SUBDUED,
OUR SONGS CAME THROUGH

"In another age, these Native poets would have been healers, visionaries, spiritual leaders. This collection proves they are all of these still. Their songs are elixir for our times, a prescription for what ails us as a people, nation, planet. The poets have come to our rescue."

—Sandra Cisneros, author of *The House on Mango Street*
and *A House of My Own*

"I once thought to read a modest poem at a Native gathering, but retreated because the poetry was so deep, meaningful, and beautiful. And those were just regular Native folks! In this book are to be found the irregulars, the professionals, the masters of words, the singers of oratory and evocation, drawn across time and space. *When the Light of the World Was Subdued, Our Songs Came Through* demonstrates, again, that the pains and joys of Indian Country have authored a literature that is world historical in its goodness and intelligence."

—Philip J. Deloria, Harvard professor of history
and author of *Playing Indian*

"This anthology is revelatory and stunning. With judicious historical context, source poems in indigenous languages, and outstanding selections of contemporary poems, it shows the remarkable strength and diversity of Native poetry, which vitalizes all of American poetry. It is essential reading."

—Arthur Sze, National Book Award–winning author of *Sight Lines*

WHEN THE
LIGHT OF THE WORLD
WAS SUBDUED,
OUR SONGS CAME THROUGH

ALSO BY JOY HARJO

An American Sunrise

Conflict Resolution for Holy Beings

Crazy Brave: A Memoir

Soul Talk, Song Language: Conversations with Joy Harjo

For a Girl Becoming

She Had Some Horses

How We Became Human: New and Selected Poems

A Map to the Next World

The Good Luck Cat

Reinventing the Enemy's Language:
Contemporary Native Women's Writing of North America

The Spiral of Memory

The Woman Who Fell from the Sky

Fishing

In Mad Love and War

Secrets from the Center of the World

What Moon Drove Me to This?

The Last Song

MUSIC ALBUMS

Red Dreams: A Trail Beyond Tears

Winding Through the Milky Way

She Had Some Horses

Native Joy for Real

Letter from the End of the Twentieth Century

PLAYS

We Were There When Jazz Was Invented

Wings of Night Sky, Wings of Morning Light

ALSO BY LEANNE HOWE

Savage Conversations

Famine Pots: The Choctaw Irish Gift Exchange 1847–Present

*Singing Still: A Libretto for the 1847 Choctaw Gift
to the Irish for Famine Relief*

Choctalking on Other Realities

*Seeing Red—Hollywood's Pixeled Skins:
American Indians and Film*
(editor, with Harvey Markowitz and Denise Cummings)

Miko Kings: An Indian Baseball Story

Evidence of Red

Shell Shaker

PLAYS

Big PowWow (with Roxy Gordon)

Indian Radio Days (with Roxy Gordon)

ALSO BY JENNIFER ELISE FOERSTER

Leaving Tulsa

Bright Raft in the Afterweather

WHEN THE
LIGHT OF THE WORLD
WAS SUBDUED,
OUR SONGS CAME THROUGH

A Norton Anthology of Native Nations Poetry

EDITORS

Joy Harjo · *Executive Editor*

LeAnne Howe · *Executive Associate Editor*

Jennifer Elise Foerster · *Associate Editor*

W. W. NORTON & COMPANY
Independent Publishers Since 1923

For information about special discounts for bulk purchases, please contact
W. W. Norton Special Sales at specialsales@wwnorton.com or 800-233-4830

Manufacturing by LSC Communications, Harrisonburg
Book design by Judith Stagnitto Abbate / Abbate Design
Production manager: Lauren Abbate

Library of Congress Cataloging-in-Publication Data

Names: Harjo, Joy, editor. | Howe, LeAnne, editor. | Foerster, Jennifer Elise, editor.
Title: When the light of the world was subdued, our songs came through : a Norton
    anthology of Native nations poetry / editors, Joy Harjo, LeAnne Howe, Jennifer
    Elise Foerster.
Description: First edition. | New York, N. Y. : W. W. Norton & Company, 2020.
Identifiers: LCCN 2020019323 | ISBN 9780393356809 (paperback) |
    ISBN 9780393356816 (epub)
Subjects: LCSH: American poetry—Indian authors. | Indians of North America—
    Poetry.
Classification: LCC PS591.I55 W47 2020 | DDC 811.008/897—dc23
LC record available at https://lccn.loc.gov/2020019323

W. W. Norton & Company, Inc., 500 Fifth Avenue, New York, N.Y. 10110
www.wwnorton.com

W. W. Norton & Company Ltd., 15 Carlisle Street, London W1D 3BS

1 2 3 4 5 6 7 8 9 0

A BLESSING

N. Scott Momaday

THIS ANTHOLOGY is a most welcome addition to American literature. The Native Americans have always been deeply invested in language. The songs, spells, and prayers of the Native oral tradition are among the world's richest examples of verbal art. The present collection is a comprehensive celebration of that tradition and that art.

PRAYER FOR WORDS

My voice restore for me.
Diné

Here is the wind bending the reeds westward,
The patchwork of morning on gray moraine:

Had I words I could tell of origin,
Of God's hands bloody with birth at first light,
Of my thin squeals in the heat of his breath,
Of the taste of being, the bitterness,
And scents of camas root and chokecherries.

And, God, if my mute heart expresses me,
I am the rolling thunder and the bursts
Of torrents upon rock, the whispering
Of old leaves, the silence of deep canyons.
I am the rattle of mortality.

I could tell of the splintered sun. I could
Articulate the night sky, had I words.

—N. SCOTT MOMADAY

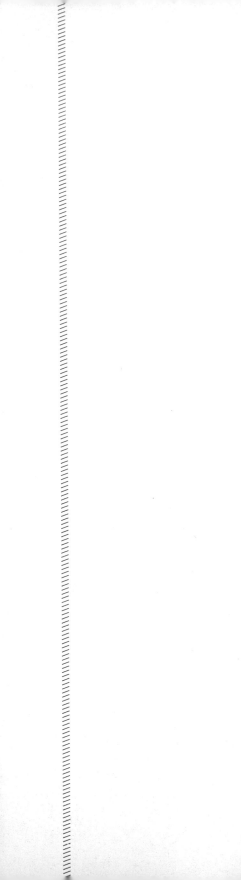

CONTENTS

PLAINS AND MOUNTAINS

PACIFIC NORTHWEST, ALASKA, AND PACIFIC ISLANDS

SOUTHWEST AND WEST

WHEN THE
LIGHT OF THE WORLD
WAS SUBDUED,
OUR SONGS CAME THROUGH

INTRODUCTION

Joy Harjo

W E BEGIN WITH THE LAND. We emerge from the earth of our mother, and our bodies will be returned to earth. We are the land. We cannot own it, no matter any proclamation by paper state. We are literally the land, a planet. Our spirits inhabit this place. We are not the only ones. We are creators of this place with each other. We mark our existence with our creations. It is poetry that holds the songs of becoming, of change, of dreaming, and it is poetry we turn to when we travel those places of transformation, like birth, coming of age, marriage, accomplishments, and death. We sing our children, grandchildren, great-grandchildren: our human experience in time, into and through existence.

The anthology then is a way to pass on the poetry that has emerged from rich traditions of the very diverse cultures of indigenous peoples from these indigenous lands, to share it. Most readers will have no idea that there is or was a single Native poet, let alone the number included in this anthology. Our existence as sentient human beings in the establishment of this country was denied. Our presence is still an afterthought, and fraught with tension, because our continued presence means that the mythic storyline of the founding of this country is inaccurate. The United States is a very young country and has been in existence for only a few hundred years. Indigenous peoples have been here for thousands upon thousands of years and we are still here.

When the first colonizers from the European continent stepped into our tribal territories, we were assumed illiterate because we did not communicate primarily with written languages, nor did we store our memory in books and on papers. The equating of written languages to literacy came with an oppositional world view, a belief set in place as a tool for genocide. Yet our indigenous nations prized and continue to value *the word*. The ability to speak in metaphor, to bring people together, to set them free in imagination, to train and to teach, was and is considered valuable, more useful than gold, oil, or anything else the newcomers craved. Many of our known texts, though preserved in orality, stand next to the top world literary texts, oral or written. The Diné Blessingway Chant, or Hózhóóní, is a poetic song text that is remembered word for word and is central to a ceremony for setting a community in the direction of beauty, or healing. The Pele and Hiʻiaka saga of two sisters is an epic poem that carries profound cultural significance to this day in the practice and fresh creation of ʻōlelo Hawaiʻi. Like the *Mahabharata* of the Hindu religion or the *Iliad* of ancient Greece, every culture, every tradition has its literature that guides and defines it—and the cultures indigenous to North America are no different.

What then distinguishes indigenous poetry from other world poetry traditions? Much depends on indigenous language constructs, which find their way into poems written in other languages, as in English here. My own poem "She Had Some Horses" would not have been written without stomp dance, or without my having heard Navajo horse songs. So many poetry techniques are available, whether it's utilizing metaphor, syntactic patterning, or some other application of poetic tools; and those of us who read and listen to poetry want our ears and perception "bent" for unique insight and want to see how the impossible becomes momentarily possible in the arrangement of language and meaning. This is true of poetry in all languages. Each tribal entity and language group is different. English then has become a very useful trade language. We use it to speak across tribal nations, to people all over the world. Many of the poets here find a way to carry out established tribal form and content in English. Consider Louis Little Coon Oliver's "The Sharp-Breasted Snake" poem and its movement on the page. Some of the poets don't want that at all, and instead they create and work within generational urban cultural aesthetics. What is shared with all tribal nations in North America is the knowledge that the earth is a living being, and a belief in the power of language to create, to transform, and to establish change. Words are living beings. Poetry in all its forms, including songs, oratory, and ceremony, both secular and sacred, is a useful tool for the community. Though it is performative there is no separation of audience and performer.

Even as we continue to create and perform our traditional forms of poetry, we have lost many of these canonical oral texts due to destruction throughout the Western Hemisphere of the indigenous literary field by the loss of our indigenous languages. We were forced to forsake our languages for English in the civilizing genocidal process. We are aware of the irony, for many of us, of our writing in English. But we also believe English can be another avenue through which to create poetry, and poetry in English and other languages can live alongside texts created and performed within our respective indigenous languages. It is the nature of the divided world in which we live.

Many who open the doors of this text arrive here with only stereotypes of indigenous peoples that keep indigenous peoples bound to a story in which none of us ever made it out alive. In that story we cannot be erudite poets, scholars, and innovative creative artists. It is the intent of the editors to challenge this: for you to open the door to each poem and hear a unique human voice speaking to you beyond, within, and alongside time. This collection represents the many voices of our peoples, voices that range through time, across many lands and waters. May all readers of this anthology bear a new respect for the unique contributions of these poets of our indigenous nations.

We are more than 573 federally recognized indigenous tribal nations in the mainland United States; 231 are located in Alaska alone. That number doesn't include the indigenous peoples of Hawai'i, the Kanaka Maoli, whose nation numbers over 500,000, and the indigenous peoples of Guåhan and Amerika Sāmoa. We speak more than 150 indigenous languages. At contact with European invaders we were estimated at over 112 million. By 1650 we were fewer than six million. Today we are one-half of one percent of the total population of the United States. Imagine the African continent with one-half of one percent of indigenous Africans and you might understand the immensity of the American holocaust.

There is no such thing as a *Native American*. Nor is there a Native American language. We call ourselves *Mvskoke, Diné*, or any of the other names of our tribal nations. In many cases these names often translate as "the people." Within our communities we know each other as Bird, Wind, or Panther, or by other nomenclature determined by the particular tribal band, ceremonial ground, or family. Some of us grew up with the term *American Indian*, which came into use after the Italian explorer Christopher Columbus sailed into the region that came to be called the West Indies on his heavily financed trip to discover a shorter route for trade to India. *America* is a derivative of the name of the Italian explorer and cartographer Amerigo Vespucci. He proved that the West Indies and Brazil were not India but what became known as the New World. *Native American* became ubiquitous in the 1990s, employed by academics to replace *American Indian*. Only the youngest generations of Natives have begun to use that term. None of the original treaties signed with the federal government use the term *Native American*. *Native*, or *Indigenous*, or *Native Nations* are where we have settled in the editing of this collection. Many tribal nations have reclaimed or are reclaiming their original names. One of the first was the Papago, who now use their original name *Tohano O'odham*. Many tribes' names mean "enemy" in the language of their enemy. For example, *Sioux* is a French name adopted by the English that was derived from an Ojibwe name that meant "little snakes."

Because we respect indigenous nations' right to determine who is a tribal member, we have included only indigenous-nations voices that are enrolled tribal members or are known and work directly within their respective communities. We understand that this decision may not be a popular one. We editors do not want to arbitrate identity, though in such a project we are confronted with the task. We felt we should leave this question to indigenous communities. And yet, indigenous communities are human communities, and ethics of identity are often compromised by civic and blood politics. The question "Who is Native?" has become more and more complex as culture lines and bloodlines have thinned and mixed in recent years. We also have had to contend with an onslaught of what we call "Pretendians," that is, nonindigenous people assuming a Native identity. DNA tests are setting up other problems involving those who discover Native DNA in their bloodline. When individuals assert themselves as Native when they are not culturally indigenous, and if they do not understand their tribal nation's history or participate in their tribal nation's society, who benefits? Not the people or communities of the identity being claimed. It is hard to see this as anything other than an individual's capitalist claim, just another version of a colonial offense. We note that there are some poets who have cycled through varying tribal claims from their first appearance in print. Some claim identity by tenuous family story and some are perpetrating outright fraud. We do not want to assist in identity crimes.

Within these pages you will find 161 poets. There were many more poets we wanted to include, but we were limited by the available number of pages. The poets span four centuries, from the seventeenth to the present. The earliest recorded written poem by a Native person was composed as an elegy by "Eleazar," a senior at Harvard College in 1678, whose tribal identity remains unknown. He most likely died before graduating. We do not know anything about Eleazar's life. All we have is his poem, "On the death of that truly venerable man D. Thomas Thacher, who moved on to the Lord from this life, 18 of August, 1678," which is written in Latin. Three lines translated into English read:

. . . With righteous tears, and with weighty grief.
The mind is senseless, the mind is silent, now the hand refuses this just
Office . . .

The Boston minister Cotton Mather published the elegy in his most famous book, *Magnalia Cristi Americana* (1702). Mather commented on Eleazar's contribution:

> And because the Nation and Quality of the Author, will make the Composure to become a Curiosity, I will here, for an *Epitaph*, insert an Elegy, which was composed upon this Occasion (Thacher's death) by an *Indian Youth*, who was then a Student of Harvard College.

The most recent poems in the anthology center indigenous tribal traditions and knowing within contemporized oratorical forms, far from the confines of Puritanical constructions.

In this collection more than ninety nations are represented. This speaks to the powerful presence and practice of poetry within our communities. These poems range from ceremonial, like the opening to the anthology by the renowned Kiowa poet and writer N. Scott Momaday, to concrete constructions like Orlando White's "Empty Set" and Wayne Kaumualii Westlake's "Hawaiians Eat Fish." These poets range in age from high school students whose poems appeared in tribal and community newspapers in the late 1800s to the early 1900s, to young spoken-word artists, to the abovementioned poet Louis Little Coon Oliver, whose first book of poems was published after he turned eighty years old.

Just as we have familial ancestors, so we have poetry ancestors. We venture to claim that even poetry anthologies have ancestor anthologies. This collection of poetry has ancestors and would not be here without them. One of the oldest anthologies that set contemporary Native poetry into motion was *The Remembered Earth: An Anthology of Contemporary American Literature*, edited by Geary Hobson, first published in 1979 by Red Earth Press, then picked up by the University of New Mexico Press and published in 1981.

Ancestor anthologies include *Songs From This Earth on Turtle's Back*, edited by Joseph Bruchac, Greenfield Review Press, 1983; *That's What She Said, Contemporary Poetry and Fiction by Native American Women*, edited by

Rayna Green, Indiana University Press, 1984; *Harper's Anthology of Twentieth Century Native American Poetry*, edited by Duane Niatum, HarperOne, 1988; *Voices of the Rainbow: Contemporary Poetry by Native Americans*, edited by Kenneth Rosen, Arcade Publishing, 1993; *Returning the Gift: Poetry and Prose from the First North American Native Writers' Festival*, edited by Joseph Bruchac, University of Arizona Press, 1994; *Reinventing the Enemy's Language: Contemporary Native Women's Writings of North America*, edited by Joy Harjo and Gloria Bird, W.W. Norton, 1998; and *Sing: Poetry from the Indigenous Americas*, edited by Allison Hedge Coke, University of Arizona Press, 2012.

Recent relatives of this Norton anthology are *New Poets of Native Nations*, edited by Heid E. Erdrich (Anishinaabe–Turtle Mountain) and published in 2018 by Graywolf Press, which presents twenty-one Native poets first published in the twenty-first century; and *Native Voices: Indigenous Nations Poetry, Craft, and Conversations*, edited by Cmarie Fuhrman and Dean Rader and published by Tupelo Press in 2019.

Despite the contributions of the previously published Native poetry anthologies there are no other anthologies that attempt to address the historical arc of time and place of indigenous nations' poetry. There has never been a Norton anthology solely of Native poetry, though Gloria Bird and I previously edited the Norton anthology of contemporary Native women's literature noted above. One of the contributing editors of this book remarked during the process of editing that to have a Norton anthology of Native poetry means that finally we have a place in American poetry. We have always been here, beneath the surface of American poetic consciousness, and have questioned how there can be an American poetry without our voices.

I realized that the only way I could take on an historic comprehensive poetry anthology would be to recruit a circle of contributing editors and advisors. As a faculty member, then, at the University of Tennessee in Knoxville, I taught two courses of students who were enthused about learning more about Native poetry and appreciated the experience of assisting in all the tasks that go into assembling a Norton anthology. The first class of students came on at the beginning of the project and were helpful as the concept was developed, the contributing editing team was assembled, and the extensive evaluation of other Native literary texts and the development of the concept and shape of the anthology took place. The second class came on when most of the hard editing was completed. They assisted with gathering biographical information, making tribal lists, and other tasks. These invaluable assistants are listed as assistant editors. The university provided me with an assistant, Jeremy Michael Reed. His efforts in organization and research led to his being named a managing editor of the anthology. Allison Davis, a PhD student at the University of Tennessee, gave assistance in assembling, editing, and typing up the manuscript and was also named a managing editor. James Matthew Kliewer, LeAnne Howe's assistant at the University of Georgia, gave excellent service in editing, copying, and researching for the anthology.

LeAnne Howe, Choctaw, joined me as executive associate editor. We decided that the core selection and editing team would be made up of indigenous poets. When American Indian literature began as a recognized field of academic endeavor in the early 1970s, most if not nearly all the scholars in attendance were non-Native. We wanted to show how this field has developed. We had five teams of editors, a team for each geographical section featured, comprised of poets indigenous to that region. One of our contributing editors, Jennifer Elise Foerster, Mvskoke, proved invaluable in setting up and organizing the different stages of editing and assembling the anthology. We named her our associate editor.

Because land is central to culture and identity, we have organized this collection into five geographical regions. We employed the Muscogean directional path, which begins East to North and continues to the West and then to the South. Each tribal nation is very different in orientation, ritual, and practices.

The first section then is "Northeast and Midwest," which includes the states of Maine, Vermont, New Hampshire, Massachusetts, Connecticut, Rhode Island, Delaware, Maryland, Pennsylvania, New York, New Jersey, Ohio, Indiana, Illinois, Minnesota, Wisconsin, Michigan, Missouri, and Iowa. This geographical area is characterized by rivers and lakes carved by glaciers. The first colonizers were the English. The Puritanical influence from the early beginnings of countryhood have continued to mark American culture and law.

The poems from this region begin with a timeless dream song of the Anishinaabeg translated into English in the early 1900s and close with a poem by b: william bearhart, born in 1979, that references an Andy Warhol painting of Geronimo he saw in a gallery in Las Vegas.

We continue on the circle to "Plains and Mountains," which include the states of North Dakota, South Dakota, Nebraska, Kansas, Oklahoma, Texas, Montana, Wyoming, Nevada, and parts of Utah and Colorado. These lands contain the heart of the Northern Hemisphere (excluding Canada, of course), vast plains rimmed by lakes and mountains. These lands bore many road and railroad paths crossing indigenous territories as European immigrants moved west. The poems of Elsie Fuller, born in 1870, and Zitkála-Ša (also known as Gertrude Simmons Bonnin), born in 1876, open this section. It closes with a poem by Duckwater Shoshone, Southern Ute, and Pyramid Lake Paiute Nation citizen Tanaya Winder, born in 1985, that is informed by the tragic loss of a beloved by suicide—which is epidemic among our tribal nations.

"Pacific Northwest, Alaska, and Pacific Islands" includes, of course, Alaska and Hawai'i, along with western Montana, Idaho, Washington, and Oregon. It comprises the largest geographical area and has been the most challenging to represent. These lands veer from the Arctic Circle, to islands in the Pacific—Guåhan and Amerika Sāmoa—that are more than two thousand miles from any large land base, to the northwestern mainland jutting out into the Pacific. Portions of these lands were explored by Captain James Cook, or were colonized by Christian missionaries and by the larger fur-trapping companies like the Hudson's Bay Company. The poems in this section begin with the first *wā* (epoch) in the *Kumulipo*, a Hawaiian Creation chant, translated by Queen Lili'uokalani in 1897. She was dethroned by U.S. businessmen who wanted the lands for commerce. There are also excerpts from a speech by Chief Seattle made in 1854, translated by the beloved Vi Hilbert, and "Prayer Song Asking for a Whale," told in St. Lawrence Island Yup'ik by Lincoln Blassi, who was born in 1892. The last poems are by spoken-word poet Jamaica Heolimeleikalani Osorio, Native Hawaiian/Kanaka Maoli born in 1991; Michael Wasson, born in 1990, of the Nimíipuu, Nez Perce, whose "A Poem for the Háawtnin & Héwlekipx [The Holy Ghost of You, The Space & Thin Air]" is a kind of prayer before prayer; and Ishmael Hope, 1981, Tlingit and Iñupiaq, whose "Canoe Launching Into The Gaslit Sea" emerges directly from the oral traditions to entreat the people to come together.

"Southwest and West" includes the states of New Mexico, Arizona, Utah, Nevada, and California, along with southwestern Colorado. The lands include the bones and arches of muscle in all its mineral color, high pines and desert, all the way to the Pacific Ocean. The Spanish were some of the first European colonizers. These poems open with "The Indian Requiem" by Arsenius Chaleco, Yuma, born in 1889. Many poems of this time fell into the "vanishing Indian" trope. His poem makes a turn to include the vanishing white man. This section closes with a poem by Diné poet Jake Skeets, born in 1991, called "Drunktown," which ventures into the painful territory of a border town that slinks violently alongside Native lands. The inhabitants live off Native art and image while treating Native citizens with utmost contempt.

We come around to the final section, "Southeast," which includes Virginia, Kentucky, Tennessee, North Carolina, South Carolina, Georgia, Florida, Alabama, Mississippi, Louisiana, and Arkansas. This area suffered from the exploration of the Spaniard Hernando de Soto and his party in 1539–1543, and from other Spanish explorers, then from the encroachments and wars waged among the English, the French, and the Americans. Because these lands were rich in resources and strategically located for trade and national expansion, the land grabs were ferocious. Andrew Jackson and his predecessors removed most of the indigenous populations to Indian Territory: land west of the Mississippi, primarily present-day Oklahoma, that was deemed by the U.S. government as land "reserved" for relocation. Despite the long history of written literature among many of the Southeastern nations, we noticed we had the fewest poems from this region. One of the first poems presented for the Southeast is "Sequoyah" by Joshua Ross, Cherokee Nation of Alabama, born in 1833. The poem honors the man who invented the Cherokee syllabary. The section closes with a poem by Lara Mann, Choctaw, born in 1983, who returns us to the Nanih Waiya cave of our rebirth: "We had to come/ to our Source, go in, come back out renewed."

This makes a circle, and we once again face East, which is the direction of beginning. And it will begin again, with the next generations of poets, the children, grandchildren, and great-grandchildren of those poets speaking here within these pages. We note that the tribal nations of the states bordering Canada and Mexico often extend beyond those political borders, just as the borders of the states themselves as they are known do not contain or adequately define tribal areas. Because of the limitations of the size of this anthology we could not include our Canadian and Mexican relatives. Many tribal nations had winter and summer homes across what are now state lines or country borders. Many are now located far from their original homelands.

Each of these tribal nations has its own rich literary traditions. There are many more poets of tribal nations than are represented in this anthology, but we are limited by space, resources, and language. *When the Light of the World Was Subdued, Our Songs Came Through* is only a slivered opening into a vast literary field.

Within this anthology are many inconsistencies in the spelling and naming in tribal languages and in English native-related terms. The lack of uniformity is generally due to geographical location in tribal areas, shifting dialects, education, generation, and personal preference.

We apologize to specific oral texts with their roots in deep culture for their placement in English in a collection that will find its way into many hands, many places. We ask permission for your presence here, to teach, to show that you are a part of a massive cultural literature that still exists, in the tongues, minds, hearts, and memory of the people, of these lands. We ask your forgiveness if we have inadvertently caused any harm in this transmission.

We give thanks to those who kept culture going, kept the arts and poetry going. Until 1978, cultural tribal-nation expression was outlawed. It wasn't until the passing of the American Indian Religious Freedom Act in 1978 that we were free to practice our indigenous cultures in the United States. This act included but did not limit access to sacred sites, freedom to worship through ceremonial and traditional rites, and use and possession of sacred objects. We did not have organized religion, per se; rather the whole earth is a sacred site. A poem can be considered a sacred site, in which so much of our culture is stored, made into form to be acknowledged, given a place, even a place to hide. Many of our oldest and most traditional poems and songs contain maps of the stars, road maps, or precepts of spiritual knowledge.

We acknowledge the source of poetry, those who agreed to create the poetry in which to hold meaning with words, and those poets who kept and keep it going, despite history.

Mvto, Yakoke, thank you to all who brought this collection together, from far back in time, to the present.

NORTHEAST
AND MIDWEST

Writing a Poetry of Continuance

Kimberly M. Blaeser

THE BILINGUAL and multidimensional dream song of the Anishinaabeg that opens these selections from Native poets of the Northeast and Midwest effectively introduces the preoccupations of many of the poems in this section. The dream song arises from an intimacy with the watery landscape of the Anishinaabeg, invests itself in a reality beyond the page alone, embodies tribally specific perspectives, and voices a long-standing spirituality, all of which—grounding in place, non-static rendering, cultural knowledge, and spiritual allusiveness—informs the work of many of the thirty writers represented here, including both early and contemporary poets. Place in Indigenous literature, of course, ultimately includes various historical and contemporary conflicts involving land, water, and other regional resources like minerals and timber, and it includes the complex realities of Native urban lifestyles. These thematic concerns appear in the work of the more than fifteen tribal nations represented from the region, even as individual poetic works distinguish themselves in form, voice, philosophical stance, or unique details culled from the wide-ranging knowledge and experience of the individual writers.

The earliest poets in these pages lived and wrote as long ago as the nineteenth century. Jane Johnston Schoolcraft's oeuvre of approximately fifty poems was written beginning in about 1815 and Emily Pauline Johnson penned her work primarily in the 1880s. These two Native women found themselves "translating" their culture experience and knowledge as well as their language into the English poetic forms and vernacular of the time. That translation of "an other" cultural experience continues through the writings of the early boarding school students, in the formal translations of tribal writing and the bilingual presentations of poems, as well as through the ongoing contemporary attempts to interpret the devastating history, contemporary legacy, and manifestations of cultural genocide through an Indigenous or tribally specific lens. The poems, too, wield attempts to reclaim a cultural aesthetic and the right to artistic self-determination.

In these many ways, the backdrop of colonization permeates much of the writing here. Poems like the early William Walker Jr.'s "Oh, Give Me Back My Bended Bow" render the tensions between tribal identities and mainstream expectations—here manifested as the physical accoutrements, literal places, and everyday preoccupations of a life ("bended bow," "o'er hills," and "the otter's track" versus "ancient pages," "antiquated halls," and "Grecian poet's song"). But later work by the likes of Gerald Vizenor, Roberta Hill, Linda LeGarde Grover, or Laura Da' likewise embody effects of manifest destiny, assimilation policies, and stereotypic misrepresentation. Vizenor, for example, writes of "half truths/ peeling like blisters of history"; Hill describes a reality where "We stand on the edge of wounds, hugging canned meat"; LeGarde Grover depicts the brutal reeducation policies of tribal boarding schools—"We will not spare the rod./ We will cut your hair. We will shame you."—and Da' addresses the literal erasure of Native knowledge, identity, and sovereignty through such things as the rampant renaming and remapping of tribal homelands.

An equally prevalent approach to writing Native America displayed in these pages is the simple and eloquent assertion of tribal realities: Poets write life as "exotic curiosities" (Gail Tremblay), as "neon acrylic brush strokes on a screen printed image" (b: william bearhart). They enact Native stories of origin and Native stories of ghost "suppers for the dead" (Gordon Henry Jr.). Landscapes and their inhabitants fill the poems like "teeth marks on birch bark" (Kimberly M. Blaeser). Performative poetics embody the sonic realities of oral cultures in works like Peter Blue Cloud's dual-voiced poem "Rattle," or the bilingual poems of Ray Young Bear. Selections engage in word play and trickster humor, include allusive visual texts, and stretch the boundaries of expected "Indian" identities or Native poetries. Whether the poem claims "I am a citizen of two nations: Shawnee and American" (Laura Da') or "We are the Lou Reed Skins, the Funky Skins, the Cowboy Skins" (Alex Jacobs), each of these lines places us in the immediacy of being Indigenous. Here are poems that know the Thunderers, that know the "rez car" (Jim Northrup), stories invoking the sweetgrass smell of baskets (Salli M. Kawennotakie Benedict), tribal songs that recall the mythic dive of water animals, and poems that "swim within this stream /of catastrophic history" (Denise Sweet) "Knowing, how our own song/ completes the chorus" (James Thomas Stevens).

The homeland or geography of the poets, and thus of the poems themselves, varies greatly, encompassing as it does the Northeast coast, the Great Lakes and a multitude of other freshwater lake regions, rich riverways (including the headwaters of the Mississippi), the hills and mountains of the Appalachian region, the northern woodlands, and the prairies. This is both canoe country and the locale for immense cargo ships. This is voyageur territory once rich with copper, timber, iron ore, fish, fur-bearing animals, and other resources—a homeland prized enough to be fought over more than once. Elements of subsistence economies continue across the regions as do the efforts to protect these traditional activities: gathering of *manoomin* (wild rice) in fall; the ritual planting of the "three sisters" (corn, beans, and squash); sugarbush/maple syrup camps in spring; trapping, hunting, fishing, leeching, spearing, and the gathering of clams and other seafood; and the harvest of nuts, berries, and medicinal plants—all these activities remain a part of the seasonal cycle that informs the identity of the tribes, builds connections across the generations, and supplements wage-earning jobs. Therefore, they remain a part of the fabric of the poems. The language of place present in these works also involves the tribal villages and reservations; involves Métis culture and the merging of Native culture with other immigrant groups like German, Swedish, and Norwegian inhabitants; and involves both small-town economies and the large urban areas where more than half of tribal members now live. Through the centuries, these territories have been the site of major Indigenous political organizations and resistance movements. Here the Haudenosaunee Confederacy developed a much lauded and studied cooperative government, one that today still issues its own passport. Here in the shadow of Fort Snelling, the American Indian Movement (AIM) was born on the Minneapolis streets in the 1960s and gave rise to a new wave of Native activism across the nation. As Steve Pacheco's poem "History" acknowledges, the intent or implied gesture of these works is "for history to surround us."

The complex "placement" of both poets and poems in the Northeast and Midwest regions is also tied to migrations—not only the migratory patterns of birds and animals, but the original migration stories of tribes like the Anishinaabe, who followed the "migis" shell from the St. Lawrence River to their current homelands in the Great Lakes. Or like the Oneida, who originated in what is now upstate New York and now inhabit both

Northeastern and Midwestern regions of the United States as well as locations in Ontario, Canada. Indeed, the original homelands of several of the individual tribal nations once spread across what is now the U.S.–Canadian border. With families, languages, and clans arbitrarily separated by a political boundary, Native people sometimes "commute" for ceremonies. The references of the poems, too, may extend to the First Nations' 1990 Oka standoff in Quebec as readily as to U.S. references like the war in Vietnam. Equally as important in the experience of the poets are their migrations to and from cities for employment and education, or their migrations to and from reservations and homelands for important gatherings. Kimberly Wensaut, for example, traces the literal and symbolic migrations "in our seasonal souls" and ironically embodies the tensions of dual existence as a "Prodigal Daughter." Poems like Marcie Rendon's playful "What's an Indian Woman to Do?" both worry the edges of mixed identity and strongly claim Indigenous belonging.

Also addressed in the poems or understood as their backdrop are major historical events: past intertribal warfare, forced removals to reservations, tragedies like the internment of Dakota women, children, and old men together with the mass hanging of Dakota warriors, or tragedies like the Chippewa Trail of Tears. Just as the land itself is marked with burial grounds, effigy mounds, abandoned missions, old boarding schools, Indian Health Service (IHS) hospitals, contemporary powwow grounds, tribal colleges, casinos, and impressive new tribal buildings housing everything from tribal courts to cultural centers, so, too, does the fabric of the poems include allusive gestures to these many layers of history, to the embedded knowledge of place, and to the material culture of the individual tribes. They refer as well to all manner of contemporary realities from language recovery to 49 songs, Indian kitsch to tribal protests, and intellectual sovereignty to sacred lands.

Ultimately, these poems reject the placating fantasy of Henry Wadsworth Longfellow's popular "Song of Hiawatha" (supposedly set on the shores of the Great Lakes), reject the bromide of the noble and disappeared savage. The Indigenous poetics in these pages tune themselves differently—to a survivance truth both painful and celebratory. The poems look steadily at a dark history. They critique laws and rhetoric that enforce settler colonialism or the racism of "manifest manners"—a term coined by Anishinaabe scholar Gerald Vizenor referring to the continued legacy of manifest

destiny as it is exhibited in the everyday actions of individuals or insti-
tutions. But sometimes these poems approach this "woke" state through
humor, symbolism, or the seemingly random accumulation of the everyday.
They invoke buried Iroquoian and Algonquian languages and non-Western
teachings. They hold up a mirror to loss and unexpectedly translate the
small reflection it makes as hopeful. In the words of poet Karenne Wood,
"This is to say we continued."

THE WATER BIRDS WILL ALIGHT
Sung by Gegwejiwebinan

THIS SONG was recorded by ethnologist Frances Densmore, who worked with Mide (Midewiwin or Grand Medicine Society) singers from White Earth, Leech Lake, and Red Lake nations between 1907 and 1909. Densmore did not speak Ojibwe fluently and relied on local interpreters, primarily Mary Warren English.

Gegwejiwebinan gave an English translation of his name, "Trial Thrower." Translator and scholar Margaret Noodin notes that Anishinaabeg names often carry stories. The spelling of his name used by Frances Densmore is GEG WE'DJWE'BĬNÛN'.

Kegĕt'
Indábunisin' dangûg
Bĭnes'iwug'
Ekwa'yaweyân'

                                      [From the Densmore publication]

Surely
Upon the whole length of my form
The water birds will alight

                             [As translated by Mary Warren English]

Geget indabooniisaandaagoog Binesiwag akwaa-ayaayaan

                           [Contemporary Anishinaabemowin spelling]

It is certain they land on me the thunderbirds across my existence

                           [Literal traslation by Margaret Noodin]

"This literal translation shows you that Mary was creating a new English version with different syntax and she or Densmore either erased a line break or inserted all the other line breaks. I would view the entire song as one sentence. You would have to listen for breath spaces or find rhyme patterns to catch the actual breaks in a line." (*Margaret Noodin*)

ELEAZAR *(?–1678), tribal affiliation unknown.* Beyond his name, Eleazar, not much is known, though he most likely would have been an East Coast tribal member. He entered Harvard in 1675 and later contracted smallpox and died before he could graduate. Eleazar is listed on a plaque unveiled at the university on May 3, 1997, in honor of the early Native Harvard students. "Eleazar's Elegy," written in 1678 in Latin, models itself after the classical form, drawing on language from Ovid, among other authors. Cotton Mather published this poem in *Magnalia Christi Americana*, his ecclesiastical history of New England. The translation offered here is by Cassandra Hradil, based on earlier translations by Sally Livingston and Vanessa Dube, and in consultation with Lisa Brooks.

ELEAZAR'S ELEGY FOR THOMAS THACHER

In death of a man to be truly
honored, D. Thomas Thacher, who
to the lord from this life passed,
18.8.1678.

I will try to remember and retell,
with sad grief,
him, whom with tears the times
reclaim, our bright man.
Thus the mother mourned
Memnon, mourned Achilles,
with just tears, and with heavy
grief
the mind is struck senseless, the
lips are silent,
now the palm refuses funeral rites;
Duty: what? Does sad Apollo deny
help?
But I will try to speak your praises,
Thacher,
praises of your virtue, which flies

above the stars.
To masters consulted about
important affairs, and to men of
the cloth
your virtue was known, and sacred
was your faith.
You live after death; you are happy
after your fate; do you lie at ease?
But surely among the stars in glory
you rest.
Your mind now returns to the sky; victory has been shared:
now Christ is yours, and what he has earned yours.
This will be the end of the cross; the end of the great evil;
beyond which it will not step further.
You, cross, remain in vain; the bones lie silent in the grave;
death is ended; lovely life returns to life.
To whom the final trumpet will give sound through the dense clouds,
when, returning to the lord, you bear the iron scepters.
Then you will ascend the skies, where the fatherland of the pious truly is;
now Jesus approaches you before this fatherland
there you truly will rest; there bounty without end;
joys and music not borne back to humans.
The dust holds your body, but upon the earth your name will not end,
renowned in the days and times that will be,
your soul having flown from your limbs, it walks the steep heavenly vault,
deathless, intertwined with immortal winds.

 JANE JOHNSTON SCHOOLCRAFT (BAMEWAWAGE ZHIKAQUAY) *(1800–1842)*, *Ojibwe,* was born to an Ojibwe mother and a Scots-Irish father. She grew up speaking both Ojibwemowin and English, and at fifteen, she began writing poetry in both languages. Jane's poems were published in the magazine she coedited with her husband, Henry Schoolcraft, *The Muzzeniegun, or Literary Voyager.* Schoolcraft is considered to be the first known Native woman writer.

Like others writing in Ojibwemowin, Jane Johnston Schoolcraft created an Ojibwemowin version and an English version of her poems. The English version takes on the characteristic rhyme and meter of poetry published during her era, which is distinctly different from her writing of Ojibwemowin verse. Schoolcraft's Ojibwemowin and English versions of the poems below were published in Robert Dale Parker's *The Sound the Stars Make Rushing Through the Sky: The Writings of Jane Johnston Schoolcraft*. The literal translations following each line are provided by translator Margaret Noodin.

To the Pine Tree

on first seeing it
on returning from Europe

Zhingwaak! Zhingwaak! Ingii-ikid,—Pine! Pine! I said,
Weshki waabamag zhingwaak—the one I see, the pine
Dagoshinaan neyab, endanakiiyaan.—I return back, to my homeland.
Zhingwaak, zhingwaak nos sa!—The pine, the pine my father!
Azhigwa gidatisaanan—Already you are colored
Gaagige wezhaawashkozid.—Forever you are green

Mii sa naa azhigwa dagoshinaang—So we already have arrived
Bizindamig ikeyaamban—Listen to him/her in that direction
Geget sa, niminwendam—Certainly I am happy
Miinwaa, waabandamaan—And I see
Gii-ayaad awiiya waabandamaan niin—He was there I saw it myself
Zhingwaak, zhingwaak nos sa!—The pine, the pine my father!
Azhigwa gidatisaanan.—Already you are colored.

Gaawiin gego, gaa-waabanda'iyan—Nothing, you did show me
Dibishkoo, ezhi-naagwasiinoon—like it, the way it looks
Zhingwaak wezhaawashkozid—Pine you are green
Wiin eta gwanaajiwi wi—he is only that beautiful
Gaagige wezhaawashkozid.—Forever he is the green one

[Translation by Margaret Noodin]

The pine! The pine! I eager cried,
The pine, my father! See it stand,
As first that cherished tree I spied,
Returning to my native land.
The pine! The pine! Oh lovely scene!
The pine, that is forever green.

Ah beauteous tree! Ah happy sight!
That greets me on my native strand
And hails me, with a friend's delight,
To my own dear bright mother land
Oh 'tis to me a heart-sweet scene,
The pine—the pine! That's ever green.

Not all the trees of England bright,
Not Erin's lawns of green and light
Are half so sweet to memory's eye,
As this dear type of northern sky
Oh 'tis to me a heart-sweet scene,
The pine—the pine! That ever green.

ON LEAVING MY CHILDREN JOHN AND JANE AT SCHOOL, IN THE ATLANTIC STATES, AND PREPARING TO RETURN TO THE INTERIOR

Nii'aa nindinendam—Oh I am thinking
Mikawiyanin—I am found by you
Endanakiiyaan—My place of origin
Waasawagamig—A faraway place
Endanakiiyaan—My place of origin

Nindaanisens e—My little daughter
Ningwizisens e—My little son
Izhi-nagadawaad—Oh I leave them
Waasawekamig—In a faraway place

Zhigwa gosha wi—Now
Beshowad e we—It is near
Nazhikeweyaan—I am alone
Izhi-izhayaan—As I go
Endanakiiyaan—My homeland

Endanakiiyaan—My homeland
Nazhikeweyaan—I am alone
Izhi-giiweyaan—I am going home
Nii'aa ningashkendam—Oh I am sad

[Translation by Margaret Noodin]

Ah! When thought reverts to my country so dear,
My heart fills with pleasure, and throbs with a fear:
My country, my country, my own native land,
So lovely in aspect, in features so grand,
Far, far in the West. What are cities to me,
Oh! Land of my mother, compared unto thee?

Fair land of the lakes! Thou are blest to my sight,
With thy beaming bright waters, and landscapes of light;
The breeze and the murmur, the dash and the roar,
That summer and autumn cast over the shore,
They spring to my thoughts, like the lullaby tongue,
That soothed me to slumber when youthful and young.

One feeling more strongly still binds me to thee,
There roved my forefathers, in liberty free—
There shook they the war lance, and sported the plume,
Ere Europe had cast o'er this country a gloom;
Nor thought they that kingdoms more happy could be,
White lords of a land so resplendent and free.

Yet it is not alone that my country is fair,
And my home and my friends are inviting me there;
While they beckon me onward, my heart is still here,
With my sweet lovely daughter, and bonny boy dear;

And oh! What's the joy that a home can impart,
Removed from the dear ones who cling to my heart.

It is learning that calls them; but tell me, can schools
Repay for my love, or give nature new rules?
They may teach them the lore of the wit and the sage,
To be grave in their youth, and be gay in their age;
But ah! My poor heart, what are schools to thy view,
While severed from children thou lovest so true!

I return to my country, I haste on my way,
For duty commands me, and duty must sway;
Yet I leave the bright land where my little ones dwell,
With a sober regret, and a bitter farewell;
For there I must leave the dear jewels I love,
The dearest of gifts from my Master above.

New York, March 18th 1839

 WILLIAM WALKER JR. (HÄH-SHÄH-RÊHS) *(1800–1874),* *Wyandot,* was a Wyandot rights advocate, who served as principal chief of the Wyandot tribe from 1835 to 36 and as the first provisional governor of Nebraska Territory. Educated in Greek, Latin, French, Wyandot, English, Delaware, Shawnee, Miami, and Potawatomi, he was published widely in newspapers throughout the Midwest.

OH, GIVE ME BACK MY BENDED BOW

Oh, give me back my bended bow,
    My cap and feather, give them back,
To chase o'er hill the mountain roe,
    Or follow in the otter's track.

You took me from my native wild,
  Where all was bright, and free and blest;
You said the Indian hunter's child
  In classic halls and bowers should rest.

Long have I dwelt within these walls
  And pored o'er ancient pages long.
I hate these antiquated halls;
  I hate the Grecian poet's song.

EMILY PAULINE JOHNSON (TEKAHIONWAKE) (*1861–1913*), *Mohawk.* As the daughter of a Mohawk chief and his English wife, Emily grew up learning both English and Mohawk language and literature. An author of fiction as well as poetry, she published in journals and anthologies in Canada, the United States, and Great Britain as well as in volumes of her own work such as *The White Wampum* (1895) and *Flint and Feather* (1912). Johnson toured Canada giving dramatic persona performances in which she addressed the dichotomous stereotypes of the Native and European woman.

MARSHLANDS

A thin wet sky, that yellows at the rim,
And meets with sun-lost lip the marsh's brim.

The pools low lying, dank with moss and mold,
Glint through their mildews like large cups of gold.

Among the wild rice in the still lagoon,
In monotone the lizard shrills his tune.

The wild goose, homing, seeks a sheltering,
Where rushes grow, and oozing lichens cling.

Late cranes with heavy wing, and lazy flight,
Sail up the silence with the nearing night.

And like a spirit, swathed in some soft veil,
Steals twilight and its shadows o'er the swale.

Hushed lie the sedges, and the vapours creep,
Thick, grey and humid, while the marshes sleep.

THE SONG MY PADDLE SINGS

West wind, blow from your prairie nest,
Blow from the mountains, blow from the west.
The sail is idle, the sailor too;
O! wind of the west, we wait for you.
Blow, blow!
I have wooed you so,
But never a favour you bestow.
You rock your cradle the hills between,
But scorn to notice my white lateen.

I stow the sail, unship the mast:
I wooed you long but my wooing's past;
My paddle will lull you into rest.
O! drowsy wind of the drowsy west,
Sleep, sleep,
By your mountain steep,
Or down where the prairie grasses sweep!
Now fold in slumber your laggard wings,
For soft is the song my paddle sings.

August is laughing across the sky,
Laughing while paddle, canoe and I,
Drift, drift,
Where the hills uplift
On either side of the current swift.

The river rolls in its rocky bed;
My paddle is plying its way ahead;
Dip, dip,
While the waters flip
In foam as over their breast we slip.

And oh, the river runs swifter now;
The eddies circle about my bow.
Swirl, swirl!
How the ripples curl
In many a dangerous pool awhirl!

And forward far the rapids roar,
Fretting their margin for evermore.
Dash, dash,
With a mighty crash,
They seethe, and boil, and bound, and splash.

Be strong, O paddle! Be brave, canoe!
The reckless waves you must plunge into.
Reel, reel.
On your trembling keel,
But never a fear my craft will feel.

We've raced the rapid, we're far ahead!
The river slips through its silent bed.
Sway, sway,
As the bubbles spray
And fall in tinkling tunes away.

And up on the hills against the sky,
A fir tree rocking its lullaby,
Swings, swings,
Its emerald wings,
Swelling the song that my paddle sings.

OLIVIA WARD BUSH-BANKS *(1869–1944), Montaukett,* was a poet and a historian who had both Native and African ancestry. In addition to publishing two poetry collections, she contributed to journals, such as the *Boston Transcript, Voice of the Negro,* and *Colored American Magazine,* and she served as historian for the Montaukett Nation. She also established a private drama school in her name.

On the Long Island Indian

How relentless, how impartial,
   Is the fleeting hand of Time,
By its stroke, great Empires vanish,
   Nations fall in swift decline.

Once resounding through these forests,
   Rang the war-whoop shrill and clear;
Once here lived a race of Red Men,
   Savage, crude, but knew no fear.

Here they fought their fiercest battles,
   Here they caused their wars to cease,
Sitting round their blazing camp-fires,
   Here they smoked the Pipe of Peace.

Tall and haughty were the warriors,
   Of this fierce and warlike race.
Strong and hearty were their women,
   Full of beauteous, healthy grace.

Up and down these woods they hunted,
   Shot their arrows far and near.
Then in triumph to their wigwams,
   Bore the slain and wounded deer.

Thus they dwelt in perfect freedom,
    Dearly loved their native shores,
Wisely chose their Chiefs or Sachems,
    Made their own peculiar laws.

But there came a paler nation
    Noted for their skill and might,
They aroused the Red Man's hatred,
    Robbed him of his native right.

Now remains a scattered remnant
    On these shores they find no home,
Here and there in weary exile,
    They are forced through their life to roam.

Just as Time with all its changes
    Sinks beneath Oblivion's Wave,
So today a mighty people
    Sleep within the silent grave.

 ANONYMOUS CARLISLE STUDENT ("ANONYMOUS POET FROM ROOM 8"). The military-style Carlisle Indian Industrial School in Carlisle, Pennsylvania, was founded by Lieutenant Colonel Richard Henry Pratt in 1879 as a tool of assimilation. Known for its infamous motto—"Kill the Indian . . . and save the man"—the school recruited more than ten thousand children from 141 tribes. Many suffered and died from poor conditions at the school. One hundred eighty-six graves can be found there, and more are still being located. This anonymous poem is noted as written in 1913.

MY INDUSTRIAL WORK

At half past two in the afternoon
You can find me in the twenty-eight room,
About three of four covers deep;
You turn them back and you'll find me asleep.
And there I lie and patiently wait
For the final exams we have in Room Eight.
When the whistle blows at half past five,
Once more I am up and still alive.
Then I run down and wash my face,
Then comb my hair and I'm ready for grace.
In fifteen minutes there's a bugle call,
The troops fall in and the roll is called.
Then out in front the troops all stand,
Saluting the flag with our hats in our hand.
While standing in the wind our hair gets wavy
But, just the same, we right face, and march to gravy.
Now this may sound like going a fishing,
But this is my only industrial position.

 GERALD VIZENOR *(1934–), Anishinaabe–White Earth Nation,* has published more than thirty books in genres that include poetry, fiction, literary scholarship, and cultural studies. Known for unique depictions of Trickster, his haiku, and his "re-expressions" of Anishinaabe dream songs and stories, Vizenor is also responsible for inciting new critical approaches to Native literary studies and creating terms to better characterize the "postindian" "survivance" of contemporary mixed-bloods. A White Earth tribal member, Vizenor's accolades include a Lifetime Achievement Award from the Native Writers' Circle of the Americas and a Distinguished Achievement Award from the Western Literature Association.

Seven Woodland Crows

seven woodland crows
stayed all winter
this year
among the white earth trees

down around us on the edge of roads
passing in the eyes of strangers
tribal land wire marked
fox runs under rusting plows

stumps for eagles

white winter savages
with brackish blue eyes
snaring their limbs on barbed wire

brackish winter blood

seven woodland crows
stayed all winter
this year
marking the dead
landmen who ran the woodland
out of breath

Family Photograph

among trees
my father was a spruce

corded for tribal pulp
he left the white earth reservation
colonial genealogies
taking up the city at twenty-three

telling stories
sharing dreams from a mason jar
running
low through the stumps at night
was his line

at twenty-three
he waited with the old men
colorless
dressed in their last uniforms
reeling on the nicollet island bridge

arm bands adrift
wooden limbs
men too civilized by war
thrown back to evangelists and charity

no reservation superintendents there
no indian agents
pacing off allotments twenty acres short
only family photographs ashore

no catholics on the wire
tying treaty money to confirmations

in the city
my father was an immigrant
hanging paper flowers
painting ceilings white for a union boss
disguising saint louis park

his weekend women
listened to him measuring my blood at night

downtown rooms were cold
half truths

peeling like blisters of history
two sizes too small

he smiles
holding me in a photograph then
the new spruce
half white
half immigrant
taking up the city and losing at cards

Fat Green Flies

fat green flies
square dance across the grapefruit
honor your partner

PETER BLUE CLOUD (ARONIAWENRATE) *(1935–2011)*, *Mohawk,* was a poet, painter, sculptor, and carpenter who was born on the Caughnawaga Reserve in Kahnawake, Quebec, Canada. Blue Cloud, who won an American Book Award for *Back Then Tomorrow*, was influenced by the Beat culture of California and also worked as a writer and editor for the influential *Akwesasne Notes*. In addition to producing complex and often playful creative work, Blue Cloud clocked time as a steelworker, logger, ironworker, archaeological field worker, and ranch hand.

The Old Man's Lazy

I heard the Indian agent say,
has no pride, no get up
and go. Well, he came out
here and walked around my

place, that agent. Steps
all thru the milkweed and
curing wormwood; tells me
my place is overgrown
and should be made use
of.

The old split cedar
fence stands at many
angles, and much of it
lies on the ground like
a curving sentence of
stick writing. An old
language, too, black with
age, with different
shades of green of moss
and lichen.
        He always
says he understands us
Indians,
        and why don't
I fix the fence at least;
so I took some fine
hawk feathers fixed
to a miniature woven
shield
        and hung this
from an upright post
near the house.
                He
came by last week
and looked all around
again, eyed the feathers
for a long time.
                He didn't
say anything, and he didn't

smile even, or look within
himself for the hawk.

Maybe sometime I'll
tell him that the fence
isn't mine to begin with,
but was put up by
the white guy who used
to live next door.
　　　　　It was
years ago. He built a cabin,
then put up the fence. He
only looked at me once
after his fence was up,
he nodded at me as if
to show that he knew I
was here, I guess.
　　　　　It was
a pretty fence, enclosing
that guy, and I felt lucky
to be on the outside
of it.
　　　　　Well that guy
dug holes all over his
place, looking for gold,
and I guess
　　　　　he never
found any. I watched
him grow old for over
twenty years, and bitter,
I could feel his anger
all over the place.
　　　　　And
that's when I took to
leaving my place to do
a lot of visiting.

Then
one time I came home
and knew he was gone
for good.

My children would
always ask me why I
didn't move to town
and be closer to them.

Now, they
tell me I'm lucky to be
living way out here.
            And
they bring their children
and come out and visit me,
and I can feel that they
want to live out here
too, but can't
for some reason, do it.

Each day
a different story is
told me by the fence,
the rain and wind and snow,
the sun and moon shadows,
this wonderful earth,
        this Creation.
I tell my grandchildren
many of these stories,
        perhaps
this too is one of them.

Rattle

When a new world is born, the old
turns itself inside out, to cleanse
and prepare for a new beginning.
                    It is
told by some that the stars are
small holes piercing the great
intestine
of a sleeping creature. The earth is
a hollow gourd and earthquakes are
gas rumblings and restless dreaming
of the sleeping creature.
                    What
sleeping plant sings the seed
shaken in the globe of a rattle,
the quick breath of the singer warms
and awakens the seed to life.

    The old man rolled fibres of
milkweed across his thigh, softly
speaking to grandchildren, slowly
saying
the thanksgiving to a sacred plant.

His left hand coiled the string as it
grew thin and very strong; as he
explained the strength of a unity
of threads combined.
        He took his
small basket of cocoons and poured
grains of coarse sand, poured from
his hand the coarse sand like a
funnel
of wind, a cone between hand and
cocoon.

Let us shake
the rattle
to call back
a rattlesnake
to dream back
            the dancers.

When the wind
sweeps earth
there is fullness
of sound,
we are given
a beat
to dance by
and drum
now joins us

and flutes
are like gentle
birds and

crickets on
  branches,
swaying trees.
The fan of
winged hawks
brush clouds like
streaks of
white clay upon
a field
of blue sky

water base.
The seeds in

Then, seven by seven, he bound
these nests to a stick with the
string,
and took the sap of white blood
of the plant, and with a finger,
rubbed
the encircling string.
          And waited, holding
the rattle to the sun for drying. And
when
he shook the first sound, the
children
sucked in their breaths and felt
strange
stirrings in their minds and
stomachs.
And when he sang the first song of
many,
the leaves of the cottonwood joined
in,
and desert winds shifted sand.
          And the
children closed their eyes, the better
     to hear tomorrow.
What sleeping plant sings the seed
in the gourd of night within the
hollow moon, the ladder going down,
down into the core of this good earth
leads to stars and wheeling suns
and
planets beyond count.
          What sound
is that in the moist womb of the sea;
the softly swaying motion in a
multitude of sleeping seeds.
          Maybe it

the pod
of a plant

are children
of the sun

of earth
that we sing
we are

a rainfall voice

a plumed

and sacred bird

we are

shadows come back

to protect
the tiny seedlings
we are
a memory in
single dance
which is all
dancing forever.
We are eyes
looking about

for the children
do they
run and play
our echoes
our former joys
in today?

is rattlesnake, the medicine singer.
                  And
it is gourd, cocoon, seed pod, hollow
horn,
shell of snapping turtle, bark of
birch,
hollowed cedar, intestines of
creatures,
     rattle
is an endless element in sound and
vibrations, singing the joys of
awakening
shushing like the dry stalks of corn
in wind, the cradle songs of night.
     Hail-heavy wind bending upon
a roof of elm bark,
          the howling song
of a midwinter blizzard heard by
a people sitting in circle close to
the fire. The fire is the sun, is the
burning core of Creation's seed,
sputtering
and seeking the womb of life.

     When someone asked Coyote, why
is there loneliness, and what is the
reason and meaning of loneliness:
Coyote
took an empty gourd and began
shaking
it, and he shook it for a long time.
                  Then
he took a single pebble and put it
into the gourd, and again began to
shake the gourd for many days, and
the pebble was indeed loneliness.

Let us shake
the rattle
for the ancients

who dwell

upon this land

whose spirits
joined to ours
guide us

          and direct us
that we
may ever walk
a harmony
that our songs
be clear.
Let us shake
the rattle
for the fliers

and swimmers

for the trees
and mushrooms
for tall grasses

blessed by

a snake's passage
for insects
keeping the balance,
and winds
which bring rain
and rivers

Again	going to sea
Coyote paused to put a handful of	and all
pebbles into the gourd.	Things of Creation.
And the sound	Let us
now had a wholeness and a meaning	shake the rattle
beyond questioning.	always, forever.

 JIM NORTHRUP (CHIBINESI) *(1943–2016), Anishinaabe,* of the Fond du Lac Band of Lake Superior, was vocal about his early boarding school experience and advocated for Indigenous language revitalization. A marine who served in the Vietnam War, he drew from that experience in his poetry and prose and often worked with veterans. The author of the frequently humorous syndicated column the *Fond du Lac Follies,* Northrup was also known for his plays and stage performances. His work was gathered in several collections including *Walking the Rez Road* (1993).

SHRINKING AWAY

Survived the war but
was having trouble
surviving the peace
Couldn't sleep more than two hours
was scared to be without a gun
nightmares, daymares
guilt and remorse
wanted to stay drunk all the time
1966 and the VA said
Vietnam wasn't a war
They couldn't help
but did give me a copy
of the yellow pages
picked a shrink off the list

50 bucks an hour
I was making 125 a week
We spent six sessions
establishing rapport
Heard about his military life
his homosexuality
his fights with his mother
and anything else he
wanted to talk about
At this rate, we would have
got to me in 1999
Gave up on that shrink
couldn't afford him
wasn't doing me any good
Six weeks later my shrink
killed himself—great
Not only guilt about the war
but new guilt about my dead shrink
If only I had done a better job
I could have kept on seeing him
I thought we were making real progress
maybe in another six sessions
I could have helped him
That's when I realized that
surviving the peace was up to me

Rez Car

It's 24 years old.
It's been used
a lot more than most.
It's louder than a 747.
It's multicolored and none
of the tires are brothers.
I'm the 7th or 8th owner

I know I'll be the last.
What's wrong with it?
Well, the other day
the steering wheel fell off.
The radio doesn't work
but the heater does.
The seats have seen more
asses than a proctologist.
I turn the key, it starts.
I push the brake, it stops.
What else is a car
supposed to do?

 GAIL TREMBLAY (*1945–*), *Onondaga* and *Mi'Kmaq*, is a poet, mixed-media artist, and educator from Buffalo, New York. She earned her MFA in creative writing from the University of Oregon, and she has taught at Evergreen State College in Olympia, Washington, for twenty-five years. The author of three books of poetry, Tremblay has also had her artwork displayed at museums around the country, including the Smithsonian's National Museum of the American Indian.

INDIAN SINGING IN 20TH CENTURY AMERICA

We wake; we wake the day,
the light rising in us like sun—
our breath a prayer brushing
against the feathers in our hands.
We stumble out into streets;
patterns of wires invented by strangers
are strung between eye and sky,
and we dance in two worlds,
inevitable as seasons in one,

exotic curiosities in the other
which rushes headlong down highways,
watches us from car windows, explains
us to its children in words
that no one could ever make
sense of. The image obscures
the vision, and we wonder
whether anyone will ever hear
our own names for the things
we do. Light dances in the body,
surrounds all living things—
even the stones sing
although their songs are infinitely
slower than the ones we learn
from trees. No human voice lasts
long enough to make such music sound.
Earth breath eddies between factories
and office buildings, caresses the surface
of our skin; we go to jobs, the boss
always watching the clock to see
that we're on time. He tries to shut
out magic and hopes we'll make
mistakes or disappear. We work
fast and steady and remember
each breath alters the composition
of the air. Change moves relentless,
the pattern unfolding despite their planning—
we're always there—singing round dance
songs, remembering what supports
our life—impossible to ignore.

CHRYSTOS (1946–), *Menominee,* is a two-spirit, activist poet born in San Francisco. Her poetry collections, which focus on feminism, social justice, and Native rights, include *Not Vanishing* (1988), *Dream On* (1991), and *Fire Power* (1995). She received the Sappho Award of Distinction from the Astraea Lesbian Foundation for Justice and a Lannan Literary Award for Poetry.

THE REAL INDIAN LEANS AGAINST

the pink neon lit window full of plaster of paris
& resin Indians in beadwork for days with fur trim
turkey feathers dyed to look like eagles
abalone & bones
The fake Indians, if mechanically activated
would look better at the Pow Wow than the real one in plain jeans
For Sale   For Sale
with no price tag
One holds a bunch of Cuban rolled cigars
one has a solid red bonnet & bulging eyes ready for war
Another has a headdress from hell
with painted feathers no bird on earth
would be caught dead in
All around them are plastic inflatable
hot pink palm trees   grinning skulls
shepherd beer steins   chuckling checkbooks
black rhinestone cats
& a blonde blow up fuck me doll for horny men
who want a hole that will never talk back
There are certainly more fake Indians
than real ones but this is the u.s.a.
What else can you expect from the land of sell
your grandma   sell our land   sell your ass
You too could have a fake Indian in your parlor
who never talks back

Fly in the face of it
I want a plastic white man
I can blow up again & again
I want turkeys to keep their feathers
& the non-feathered variety to shut up
I want to bury these Indians dressed like cartoons
of our long dead
I want to live
somewhere
where nobody is sold

CEREMONY FOR COMPLETING A POETRY READING

This is a give away poem
You've come gathering   made a circle with me of the places
I've wandered   I give you   the first daffodil opening
from earth I've sown   I give you warm loaves of bread baked
in soft mounds like breasts   In this circle I pass each of you
a shell from our mother sea   Hold it in your spirit   Hear
the stories she'll tell you   I've wrapped your faces
around me   a warm robe   Let me give you ribbonwork leggings
dresses sewn with elk teeth   moccasins woven with red
& sky blue porcupine quills
I give you blankets woven of flowers & roots   Come closer
I have more to give   this basket is very large
I've stitched it of your kind words
Here is a necklace of feathers & bones
a sacred meal of chokecherries
Take this mask of bark which keeps out the evil ones
This basket is only the beginning
There is something in my arms for all of you
I offer this memory of sunrise seen through ice crystals
Here   an afternoon of looking into the sea from high rocks
Here   a red-tailed hawk circles over our heads
One of her feathers drops for your hair

May I give you this round stone which holds an ancient spirit
This stone will soothe you
Within this basket is something you've been looking for
all of your life   Come take it   Take as much as you need
I give you seeds of a new way
I give you the moon shining on a fire of singing women
I give you the sound of our feet dancing
I give you the sound of our thoughts flying
I give you the sound of peace moving into our faces & sitting down
Come   This is a give away poem
I cannot go home
until you have taken everything & the basket which held it
When my hands are empty
I will be full

ROBERTA HILL (ROBERTA HILL WHITEMAN) *(1947–),* ***Oneida,*** is a poet, fiction writer, essayist, and scholar. Her poetry collections include *Star Quilt* (1984, 2001), *Her Fierce Resistance* (1993), *Philadelphia Flowers* (1996), and *Cicadas: New and Selected Poetry* (2013). She edited an issue of *About Place* (2014); "Reading the Streets" (fiction) appeared in *Narrative Witness: Indigenous People Australia–United States* (2016). She is a professor of English and American Indian Studies at the University of Wisconsin–Madison and is an affiliated faculty member of the Nelson Institute for Environmental Studies.

Dream of Rebirth

We stand on the edge of wounds, hugging canned meat,
waiting for owls to come grind
nightsmell in our ears. Over fields,
darkness has been rumbling. Crows gather.
Our luxuries are hatred. Grief. Worn-out hands

carry the pale remains of forgotten murders.
If I could only lull or change this slow hunger,
this midnight swollen four hundred years.

Groping within us are cries yet unheard.
We are born with cobwebs in our mouths
bleeding with prophecies.
Yet within this interior, a spirit kindles
moonlight glittering deep into the sea.
These seeds take root in the hush
of dusk. Songs, a thin echo, heal the salted marsh,
and yield visions untrembling in our grip.

I dreamed an absolute silence birds had fled.
The sun, a meager hope, again was sacred.
We need to be purified by fury.
Once more eagles will restore our prayers.
We'll forget the strangeness of your pity.
Some will anoint the graves with pollen.
Some of us may wake unashamed.
Some will rise that clear morning like the swallows.

In the Longhouse, Oneida Museum

House of five fires, you never raised me.
Those nights when the throat of the furnace
wheezed and rattled its regular death,
I wanted your wide door,

your mottled air of bark and working sunlight,
wanted your smokehole with its stars,
and your roof curving its singing mouth above me.
Here are the tiers once filled with sleepers,

and their low laughter measured harmony or strife.
Here I could wake amazed at winter,
my breath in the draft a chain of violets.
The house I left as a child now seems

a shell of sobs. Each year I dream it sinister
and dig in my heels to keep out the intruder
banging at the back door. My eyes burn
from cat urine under the basement stairs

and the hall reveals a nameless hunger,
as if without a history, I should always walk
the cluttered streets of this hapless continent.
Thinking it best I be wanderer,

I rode whatever river, ignoring every zigzag,
every spin. I've been a fragment, less than my name,
shaking in a solitary landscape,
like the last burnt leaf on an oak.

What autumn wind told me you'd be waiting?
House of five fires, they take you for a tomb,
but I know better. When desolation comes,
I'll hide your ridgepole in my spine

and melt into crow call, reminding my children
that spiders near your door
joined all the reddening blades of grass
without oil, hasp or uranium.

These Rivers Remember

In these rivers, on these lakes
Bde-wa'-kan-ton-wan saw the sky.
North of here lies *Bdo-te*,
Center of the Earth. Through their songs,
the wind held on to visions.
We still help earth walk
her spiral way, feeling
the flow of rivers
and their memories of turning
and change.

Circle on circle supports us.
Beneath the tarmac and steel in St. Paul,
roots of the great wood are swelling
with an energy no one dare betray.

The white cliffs, *I-mni-za ska*,
know the length of *Kangi Ci'stin-na*'s tears.
He believed that words spoken
held truth and was driven into hunger.
Beneath the cliffs, fireflies flickered
through wide swaths of grass.
Oaks grew on savannahs, pleasant
in the summer winds where deer
remain unseen.

These rivers remember their ancient names,
Ha-ha Wa'-kpa, where people moved
in harmony thousands of years
before trade became more valuable than lives.

In their songs, the wind held
on to visions. Let's drop our burdens
and rest. Let's recognize our need

for awe. South of here, the rivers
meet and mingle. Bridges and roads,
highway signs, traffic ongoing.
Sit where there's a center
and a drum, feel the confluence
of energies enter our hearts
so their burning begins to matter.

This is *Maka co-ka-ya kin,*
The Center of the Earth.

/// **AUTHOR'S NOTE:** *The poem refers to the Dakota villages and way of life before white settlement, along with a reference to the Dakota–U.S. War of 1862. The Science Museum Park Project incorporated lines of poems written by poets from communities of color into the small park on Robert Street in St. Paul, Minnesota. Dr. Chris Mato Nunpa taught me the Dakota words. He graciously corrected my spellings and provided the following translations of the Dakota words. The word Bde-wa'-kan-ton-wan, the name of one of the fires of the Isanti (Santee) Dakota, means "Dwellers by Mystic Lake." The Dakota word I-mni-za ska translates as "white cliffs" and is the Dakota name for St. Paul. Kangi Ci'stin-na' means "Little Raven" and refers to the warrior and chief called "Little Crow," who was the leader of the conflict. Ha-ha Wa-kpa has one possible translation as "River of the Falls" and refers to St. Anthony Falls. The Center of the Earth, Maka co-ka-ya kin or Macoke Cocaya Kin, is the confluence where the Minnesota River meets the Mississippi. Dr. Mato Nunpa explained that it can also be translated to mean "the Center of the Universe," which fits with the notion that the Dakota came from the stars. The confluence is a sacred place which is also called Bdo-te, translated as "Mendota."*

LINDA LEGARDE GROVER (1950–), *Anishinaabe,* is an enrolled member of the Bois Forte Band of Ojibwe. A memoirist, fiction writer, and poet, she has received numerous awards, including the Flannery O'Connor Short Fiction Award and the Northeastern Minnesota Book Award for Poetry. She is a professor of American Indian Studies at the University of Minnesota Duluth, researching the effects of government Indian education policy on children and families.

Everything You Need to Know in Life You'll Learn in Boarding School

Speak English. Forget the language of your
grandparents. It is dead. Forget their teachings.
They are unGodly and ignorant. Cleanliness is
next to Godliness. Indians are not clean. Your
parents did not teach you proper hygiene. Stay
in line. This is a toothbrush. Hang it on the hook
next to the others. Do not allow the bristles to
touch. This spreads the disease that you bring
to school from your families. Make your bed with
mitered corners. A bed not properly made will be
torn apart. Start over. Remember and be grateful
that boarding school feeds and clothes you. Say
grace before meals. In English. Don't cry. Crying
never solved anything. Write home once every
month. In English. Tell your parents that you are
doing very well. You'll never amount to anything.
Make the most of your opportunities. You'll never
amount to anything. Answer when the teacher
addresses you. In English. If your family insists on
and can provide transportation for you to visit home
in the summer, report to the matron's office immediately
upon your return. You will be allowed into the
dormitory after you have been sanitized and de-loused.

Busy hands are happy hands. Keep yourself occupied.
You'll never amount to anything. Books are our friends.
Reading is your key to the world. Forget the language
of your grandparents. It is dead. If you are heard speaking
it you will kneel on a navy bean for one hour. We will ask
if you have learned your lesson. You will answer. In English.
Spare the rod and spoil the child. We will not spare the rod.
We will cut your hair. We will shame you. We will lock you
in the basement. Learn from that. Improve yourself.
You'll never amount to anything. Speak English.

RAY YOUNG BEAR (1950–), *Meskwaki*, was raised on the Meskwaki Tribal Settlement in Iowa, which was established in 1856 by his maternal great-great grandfather, a hereditary chief. Young Bear, who speaks and writes in both Meskwaki and English, began publishing poetry just after graduating from high school in 1969. Since then, he has published five collections of poetry including a collected works, *Manifestation Wolverine* (2015), and two works of fiction, most notably *Black Eagle Child* (1992). His awards include the 2016 American Book Award for Poetry and a National Endowment for the Arts Creative Writing Fellowship. He has taught creative writing at numerous schools, including the Institute of American Indian Arts in Santa Fe.

JOHN WHIRLWIND'S DOUBLEBEAT SONGS, 1956

1.

Menwi—yakwatoni—beskonewiani.
Kyebakewina—maneniaki
ketekattiki
ebemanemateki
ebemanemateki

//

Good-smelling are these flowers.
As it turned out, they were milkweeds
dance-standing
as the wind passes by,
as the wind passes by.

2.

Inike—ekatai—waseyaki
netena—wasesi.
Memettine
beskattenetisono.
Memettine.

//

It is now almost daylight,
I said to the firefly.
For the last time
illuminate yourself.
For the last time.

Our Bird Aegis

An immature black eagle walks assuredly
across a prairie meadow. He pauses in mid-step
with one talon over the wet snow to turn
around and see.

Imprinted in the tall grass behind him
are the shadows of his tracks,
claws instead of talons, the kind
that belongs to a massive bear.
And he goes by that name:
Ma kwi so ta.

And so this aegis looms against the last
spring blizzard. We discover he's concerned
and the white feathers of his spotted hat
flicker, signaling this.

With outstretched wings he tests the sutures.
Even he is subject to physical wounds and human
tragedy, he tells us.

The eyes of the Bear-King radiate through
the thick, falling snow. He meditates on the loss
of my younger brother—and by custom
suppresses his emotions.

One Chip of Human Bone

one chip of human bone

it is almost fitting
to die on the railroad tracks.

i can easily understand
how they felt on their long staggered walks back

grinning to the stars.

there is something about
trains, drinking, and
being an indian with nothing to lose.

MARCIE RENDON *(1952–), Anishinaabe,* an enrolled member of the White Earth Nation, is a poet, playwright, and community activist. Rendon's work includes two novels, most recently *Girl Gone Missing* (2019), as well as four children's nonfiction books. She received the Loft Literary Center's 2017 Spoken Word Immersion Fellowship. She is a producer and creative director at the Raving Native Theater in Minnesota.

WHAT'S AN INDIAN WOMAN TO DO?

what's an indian woman to do
when the white girls act more indian
than the indian women do?

my tongue trips over takonsala
mumbles around the word mitakuye oyasin
my ojibwe's been corrected
by a blond U of M undergraduate

what's an indian woman to do?

much to my ex-husband's dismay
i never learned the humble,
spiritual,
Native woman stance
legs tight, arms close, head bowed
three paces behind

my mother worked and fought with men
strode across fields
100-pound potato sacks on shoulders broad as any man
the most traditional thing
my grandfather taught me
was to put jeebik on the cue stick
to win a game of pool

so i never learned the finer
indian arts
so many white women have become adept at
sometimes I go to pow-wows
see them selling wares
somehow the little crystals
tied on leather pouches
never pull my indian heart

huh, what's an indian woman to do?

i remember Kathy She Who Sees the Spirit Lights
when she was still
Katrina Olson from Mankato, Minnesota
and Raven Woman?
damn, i swear i knew her
when she was a jewish girl
over in st. paul

as my hair grays
theirs gets darker
month by month
their reservation accents
thicker
year by year

used to be
reincarnation happened
only to the dead

hmmm?!?!?

what's an indian woman to do
when the white girls act more indian
than the indians do???

ALEX JACOBS (KARONIAKTAHKE) *(1953–), Akwesasne Mohawk,* studied at the Institute of American Indian Arts in Santa Fe and earned a BFA in sculpture and creative writing from the Kansas City Art Institute, where he discovered his interest in collage and mixed-media work. In addition to being a writer, Jacobs is a spoken-word artist, radio deejay, and musician. He has worked at *Akwesasne Notes* and as an ironworker, and he has taught poetry and art in various settings including at the Santa Fe Indian School.

Indian Machismo or Skin to Skin

this is the Blue Jean Nation speakin', bro
and these are the Red Man's Blues, sista
hey ya hey ya hey, what can I say
you could say, cuz, we missed the boat
yeah, the Mayflower, or was it the Nonie, Pinto & Santo Domingo,
i dunno, i wasn't in school that day
but, yo! We ain't no alcatraz, no aim, no wounded knee
we don't vote, but who votes anyway
you kick out the blood-sucking scum
they just come back wiser, richer, hard-core thieves
you can't kick out what you come to depend on?!
They need us weak and weak we get
so what? So what?! So what!
You do your part, you get diddly squat
how many meetings, how many cops, how many knocks
in the dark, leave me alone, just do your thang!

Hey, hey, hey, we missed:
Floyd Westerman, Buffy Ste. Marie, Russell Means
Dennis Banks, we even missed Iron Eyes Cody and
this tear's for you, we missed national indian day
we missed the Trail of Broken Treaties, Plymouth Rock,
the Longest Walk, the fish-ins, the sit-ins, the marches

NO, we don't know tom petty, the allmans, the grateful dead,
we don't know jackson browne, bruce cockburn, neil young,
NO, we don't know fritz scholder or jamake highwater
& MAN, WE DON'T WANT TO
we missed: FORT LAWTON, PIT RIVER, FRANKS LANDING,
we missed: SCOTTSDALE, CUSTER, PINE RIDGE, ROSEBUD
we missed: CROW DOG'S PARADISE, THE FBI RAIDS,
we missed: GANIENKEH & AKWESASNE & MORE FBI RAIDS
THE MOHAWKS DREW A LINE IN THE DIRT & SAID TO THE NY
STATE TROOPERS: "CROSS THIS LINE AND WE WILL ATTICA YOU!"
TROOPERS BEATING BATONS ON THEIR RIOT SHIELDS
THEY WOULD NOT TAKE THAT LAST STEP
TO COLLECT THAT LAST EARTHLY PAYCHECK . . .
we missed them outlawing the Native American Church
we missed them tearing up 4 Corners, fencing Big Mountain
we missed the Vatican wanting to put up a telescope
called Columbus on an Apache Sacred Mountain . . .
we missed: RED & BARRIER & LUBICON LAKES, PARLIAMENT HILL,
we missed: JAMES BAY & OKA & THE TV NEWS
we missed all the new Redman movies
NO, we don't know, brando, dylan, fonda, costner
but, bro, i say, not proud, not wise, just reality
& human-size, from the beat of the street & not a drum

We are the Skins that drink in the ditch
We are the Skins that fill the tanks, cells, jails, wards
We are the Skins that need that spare change, bottle, baggie
We are the Lou Reed Skins, the Funky Skins, the Cowboy Skins
We are the ghosts of Seattle, homeless walking urban spirits
We are the frozen dead of Bigfoot's Band
WE ARE BURNING CORNFIELDS!
We are burned down boarding schools, trashed BIA toilets
government trailer trash, broken glass, broken treaties!
You mean you still believe in treaties?
You be bad, bad judges of character, like the faith of clowns
you trust too much, you believe in people's smiles,

you mean you never seen 'em smile when they stab you in the
back, jack, Billy Jack, what show you been watchin'?
this ain't no rerun! It's reality! It's goin' on right now!

IT'S HAPPENED EVERY DAY FOR 500 YEARS!
But i bet you be there in your buckskins when politicos
celebrate Cristofo Mofo Colombo in 1992 & make him an
honorary Cherosiouxapapanavajibhawk too! Aaaaiiiieeee-yahhhh!

But don't forget to invite us to your par-tee, boyz
we are the skins that fill the bingos, the bootleggers,
the afterhours clubs, we are the skins that speak the language
of currency: toyota, cadillac, colombian, sinsemillian, jim beam,
jack daniels, cuervo, honda, sushi, gilley's hard rock cafe,
santa mantra fe, coors, bud, it's miller time, zenith, motorola,
sony, phony feathers, patent leather, kragers, headers, spoilers
VCR, VHS, CD, DAT, BFA, MFA, PHD, BIA, BMW, LSMFT
machined decks and state of the art funky crapola,
it's all payola, make you feel like the Marlboro-man, aaay! S.A.!

Where we put this stuff, i don't know, but it makes the rounds
thas fer shur, we can't help what we ain't got,
what we ain't got, izzit what we lookin' for?
I think we lookin' for help, that a flash or what?
U can call me bad, bro, but you did it, too, pretty slick of you
to forget to add it to you res-u-may, compadre
we can pass the buck all night long, asking
"How much did you get for your soul?"
but this soul's been punctured, splintered, folded & mutilated
sewn back together into a crazy quilt that catches the wind
it's the only way this soul knows how to pray. I'm sending
signals, bro!, using my genuine, authentic, rubber slicker, neon
patch, imitation yellow tanned bodybag, the same bodybag that
will carry me home when the last round-up happens in some
bloody border bar. Say, bro, say, sista, can you help me read the
signs, i musta missed survival school that day . . .

BUT, WHEN THEY KILL, YOU, ACTIVE,
DO WE, PASSIVE, BECOME VICTIMS OR GHOSTS . . . OR
SURVIVALISTS
DO WE EVEN KNOW HOW TO SURVIVE OUTSIDE OF A CITY
& WHY DOES IT ALWAYS COME DOWN TO
SURVIVAL & SURVIVORS . . . EXTINCTION OR SUBMISSION

but i tell you what, Indians makin' babies will take over
this country, this continent, from the inside out . . .
& i'm not gonna be another sad indian story
passed around the table after midnight

 DENISE SWEET (1953–), *Anishinaabe–White Earth Nation,*
served as Wisconsin Poet Laureate for 2005–8. Her poetry collec-
tions include *Palominos Near Tuba City* (2018) and *Songs for Dis-
charming,* which won both the 1998 Wisconsin Posner Award for Poetry and
the Diane Decorah Memorial Poetry Award from the Native Writers' Circle
of the Americas. She is a professor emerita at the University of Wisconsin–
Green Bay and has performed her work across Europe, Central America,
and North America.

Song for Discharming

Hear the voice of my song—it is my voice
I speak to your naked heart.
  —Chippewa Charming Song

Before this, I would not do or say what impulse
rushes in to say or do
what instinct burns within
I had learned to temper in my clever sick
while stars unlock at dawn, anonymous as the speed of light
my gray mornings began as nothing, freed of geography
and stripped of any source or consequence.

I was, as you may expect, a human parenthesis.
There is no simple way to say this,
but drift closer, Invisible One, swim within this stream
of catastrophic history. Yours? Mine?
No, you decide. And then

come here one more time so that I may numb like dark
and desperate, so that I may speak your name this final round
you might think an infinite black fog waits to envelope me
you might dream an endless flat of light
you might think I drink
at the very edge of you, cowering like passerine while
hawks hunt the open field of my tiny wars,

but, little by little, like centipedes that whirl and spin
and sink into scorching sands of Sonora
or like gulls at Moningwanekaning that rise and stir
and vanish into the heat lightning of August
I will call you down and bring you into that deathly coil
I will show you each step and stair
I will do nothing and yet it will come to you in this way
that sorcery that swallowed me will swallow you too
at your desired stanza and in a manner of your own making

While I shake the rattle of ferocity moments before sunrise
while I burn sage and sweetgrass, and you, my darling,
while I burn you like some ruined fetish and sing over you
over and over like an almighty voice from the skies
it is in that fragile light
that I will love you
it is in that awakening
I will love myself too
in this dry white drought about to end
in this ghostly city of remember.

You will know this, too
and never be able to say.

MAPPING THE LAND

(for James Pipe Moustache)

Like the back of your hand, he said to me,
with one eye a glaucoma gray marble
the brim of his hat shading the good one
*you'll learn the land by feel, each place
a name from memory, each stone
a fingerprint, and the winds:
they have their houses of cedar*

At our feet a five-pound coffee can
of spit and chew; the old man leans towards it
and with remarkable aim, deposits the
thin brown liquid without missing a
step *I never thought much of the running,
the miles between home and
Tomah boarding school* he has since
teased me about the relays
the long-distance marathons, the logic of
treadmills. Who could explain that to this old man?

The sport of running with no destination
no purpose, slogging like wild-eyed sundancers
foolish in the heat, snapping at gnats
and no-seeums, signifying sovereignty
step by step on two-lane highways
raising the dust in unincorporated redneck towns
fluorescent Nikes kicking up blacktop
ogitchiidaa carrying the eagle staff
like an Olympian torch.

SALLI M. KAWENNOTAKIE BENEDICT *(1954–2011)*, *Awkwesasne Mohawk,* was a poet and an author and illustrator of children's books. An early editor of *Akwesasne Notes,* she was an activist and the cultural historian for the St. Regis Tribe, involved in research and land claims, and publishing articles on Native culture. She worked in pottery, sculpture, and quilting. Benedict spent much of her time teaching children, and she headed the Aboriginal Rights and Research Office for the Mohawk Council of Awkwesasne.

Sweetgrass Is Around Her

A woman was sitting
on a rock.
I could see her
clearly,
even though
she was far away.
She was Teiohontasen,
my mother's aunt.
She was a
basket maker.
When I was young,
my mother told me
that her name meant,
"Sweetgrass is all around her."
I thought that it was a good name
for a basket maker.
She was in her eighties
then.
She was short like me,
and a bit stout.
She knew the land well;
and the plants,
and the medicines,

and the seasons.
She knew how to talk
to the Creator too;
and the thunderers,
and the rainmakers.
She had a big bundle of sweetgrass
at her side.
It was long, and green,
and shiny.

Her big straw hat
shaded
her round face.
It was very hot.
She pulled her mid-calf-length dress
down to her ankles,
over her rubber boots.
She brought her lunch
in a paper bag;
a canning jar of cold tea,
fried bread,
sliced meat,
and some butter,
wrapped in tin foil.
She placed them carefully
on the rock.
She reached
into the bag,
and pulled out a
can of soft drink.
I thought it strange.
She didn't drink
soft drinks.
Then,
she reached for her
pocket knife.
Basket makers always

have a good knife.
It was in the pocket of
the full-length
canvas apron,
that was always
safety-pinned to her dress.
She made two sandwiches,
. . . looked around.
Saw me looking at her.
Her eyes sparkled,
she smiled.
She lifted up the soft drink,
and signaled me to come.

After we ate,
she stood up
on the rock
and looked out.
She smelled the air.
I knew that she
could smell the sweetgrass.
I never could.
She pointed to
very swampy land.
Mosquitos, I thought.
I was dressed poorly.
We didn't talk much
but we could hear,
and listen to each other.
She never forced me
to speak Mohawk.
Mohawk with an
English accent
made her laugh.
She didn't
want to hear
English though.

We would spend
all day
picking sweetgrass.
Sometimes
we would look for
medicines.
One time,
my mother asked her
what she thought
Heaven would be like.
She said
that there was sweetgrass everywhere
and people made
the most beautiful
baskets.

 KIMBERLY M. BLAESER (1955–), *Anishinaabe,* poet, pho-
tographer, fiction writer, and scholar, is an enrolled member of the
White Earth Nation and grew up on the White Earth reserva-
tion. She earned her MA and PhD at the University of Notre Dame. The
author of four poetry collections, most recently *Copper Yearning,* Blaeser
served as Wisconsin Poet Laureate for 2015–16. She is the editor of *Traces
in Blood, Bone, and Stone: Contemporary Ojibwe Poetry* and her monograph
Gerald Vizenor: Writing in the Oral Tradition was the first Native-authored
book-length study of an Indigenous author. She is a professor at University
of Wisconsin-Milwaukee and an MFA faculty member at the Institute of
American Indian Arts in Santa Fe.

Dreams of Water Bodies Nibii-Wiiyawan Bawaadanan

Wazhashk, Wazhashk
small whiskered swimmer, agaashiinyi memiishanowed bagizod
you, a fluid arrow crossing waterways biwak-dakamaadagaayin
with the simple determination mashkawendaman
of one who has dived googiigwaashkwaniyamban
purple deep into mythic quest. dimii-miinaandeg gagwedweyamban.

Belittled or despised Gigoopazomigoog
as water rat on land; ninii-chiwaawaabiganoojinh akin
hero of our Anishinaabeg people ogichidaa Anishinaabe
in animal tales, creation stories awesiinaajimowinong, aadizookaanag
whose tellers open slowly, dash debaajimojig onisaakonanaanaawaa
magically like within a dream, nengaaj enji-mamaanjiding
your tiny clenched fist gdobikwaakoninjiins
so all water tribes miidash gakina Nibiishinaabeg
might believe. debwewendamowaad.

See the small grains of sand— Waabandan negawan
Ah, only those poor few— aah sa ongow eta
but they become our turtle island maaaji-mishiikenh-minis
this good and well-dreamed land minwaabandaan aakiing maampii
where we stand in this moment niigaanigaabawiying
on the edge of so many bodies of water agamigong
and watch *Wazhashk*, our brother, Wazhashk waabamang, niikaaninaanig
slip through pools and streams and lakes zhiibaasige zaaga'iganan gaye ziibiinsan
this marshland earth hallowed by mashkiig zhawendang
the memory mikwendang
the telling waawiindang
the hope ezhi-bagosendamowaad
the dive ezhi-googiiwaad
of sleek-whiskered-swimmers agaashiinyag memiishanowewaad begizojig
who mark a dark path. dibiki-miikanong.

And sometimes in our water dreams Nangodinong enji-nibii-bawaajiganan
we pitiful land-dwellers gidimagozijig aakiing endaaying
in longing bakadenodang
recall, and singing dash nagamoying
make spirits ready jiibenaakeying
to follow: noosone'igeying
bakobii.** bakobiiying.

**Go down into the water.

[Translation by Margaret Noodin]

Apprenticed to Justice

The weight of ashes
from burned-out camps.
Lodges smoulder in fire,
animal hides wither
their mythic images shrinking
pulling in on themselves,
all incinerated
fragments
of breath bone and basket
rest heavy
sink deep
like wintering frogs.
And no dustbowl wind
can lift
this history
of loss.

Now fertilized by generations—
ashes upon ashes,
this old earth erupts.
Medicine voices rise like mists
white buffalo memories
teeth marks on birch bark
forgotten forms
tremble into wholeness.

And the grey weathered stumps,
trees and treaties
cut down
trampled for wealth.
Flat Potlatch plateaus
of ghost forests
raked by bears
soften rot inward

until tiny arrows of green
sprout
rise erect
rootfed
from each crumbling center.

Some will never laugh
as easily.
Will hide knives
silver as fish in their boots,
hoard names
as if they could be stolen
as easily as land,
will paper their walls
with maps and broken promises,
scar their flesh
with this badge
heavy as ashes.

And this is a poem
for those
apprenticed
from birth.
In the womb
of your mother nation
heartbeats
sound like drums
drums like thunder
thunder like twelve thousand
walking
then ten thousand
then eight
walking away
from stolen homes
from burned out camps
from relatives fallen

as they walked
then crawled
then fell.

This is the woodpecker sound
of an old retreat.
It becomes an echo,
an accounting
to be reconciled.
This is the sound
of trees falling in the woods
when they are heard,
or red nations falling
when they are remembered.
This is the sound
we hear
when fist meets flesh
when bullets pop against chests
when memories rattle hollow in stomachs.

And we turn this sound
over and over again
until it becomes
fertile ground
from which we will build
new nations
upon the ashes of our ancestors.
Until it becomes
the rattle of a new revolution
these fingers
drumming on keys.

CAPTIVITY

I.

A mark across the body. The morning I watched my beloved uncle
disappear down the alley. His car left sitting in our yard for thirty days.
This tattoo we cover with shame. The stories my mother whispered as if
gitchi-manidoo was a child who should not be told of the troubles of humans.
All those taken. Visits made on dusty trains. Letters adorned like birch
bark art with lines and tiny holes. My shriveled grandma "an accessory"
hiding my cousin from the interchangeable uniforms of civil pursuit. Her
white hair another flag of truce.

II.

This is how we look over our shoulders. This is how we smile carefully in
public places. This is how we carry our cards, our identities. This is how we
forget—and how you remind us.

III.

Mary Rowlandson made it big in the colonial tabloids. Indian captivity
narrative a seeming misnomer. But ink makes strong cultural bars of bias.
This is how we remain captured in print.

IV.

Now I harbor fugitive names. ▉c▉sin came to my reading in ankle tether.
Qu▉i chained herself before the R▉▉C building in protest. M▉cus who
cannot receive email. The Ar▉tc▉at manager from Thi▉f▉ive▉ls. His
whiskey-inspired stories tell of cicada existence—a cyclical shedding of
"dangerous" identities.

V.

We molt. The shell of our past a transparent *chanhua*. Yes, we will eat it like
medicine.

GORDON HENRY JR. *(1955–)*, *Anishinaabe,* poet, fiction writer, and essayist, is an enrolled member of the White Earth Nation. He is the author of the poetry collection *The Failure of Certain Charms* (2008) and the novel *The Light People* (1994), which was the recipient of an American Book Award. Henry has held a Fulbright lectureship in Spain and is currently a professor of literature and creative writing at Michigan State University, where he also serves as editor of its American Indian Studies Series.

November Becomes the Sky with Suppers for the Dead

I am standing outside
in Minnesota
ghost wind recalling
names in winter mist

The road smells
of dogs two days dead

White photographers talk in
the house of mainstream
media

I can't articulate
the agony of Eagle Singer's
children to them.

We celebrate the old
man while another
generation shoots
crushed and heated
prescriptions,
sells baskets,
machinery,

the fixtures yet to be
installed in the house,
yet to be heated
by the tribal government,
for another night
stolen by the stupors
and the wondrous
pleasure of forget
everything medicines.

Back inside
Uncle Two Dogs rolls me
a smoke out of
organic American Spirit

I look to a last cup
of coffee.

The way home
fills with snow
our tracks
human and machine.

WHEN NAMES ESCAPED US

The boy painted himself white and ran into the darkness.

We let the words "he may be dead, bury him,"
bury him.

We took his clothes to the rummage sale
in the basement of the mission.
We put his photographs and drawings
in a birdcage and covered it with a starquilt.

For four nights voices carried clear to the river.

After winter so many storms moved in
strangers came among us.
They danced.
They shoveled in the shadows of trees.

Then, somehow we all felt
all of us were of this one boy.

SLEEPING IN THE RAIN

I.

Wake chants circle, overhead, like black crows watching her will stumble
through weak moments. Like when she heard the carriage outside and went
to the window with his name on her lips. Or when she looked over in the
corner and saw him sleeping, with his mouth open, in the blue chair, next
to the woodstove. She saw them, dissembled reflections, on the insides of
her black glasses. Moments passed, etched, like the lines of age in the deep
brown skin of her face. She's somewhere past ninety now; bent over, hollow
boned, eyes almost filled. She lives in a room. A taken care of world. Clean
sheets, clean blankets, wall-to-wall carpeting, a nightstand, and a roommate
who, between good morning and good night, wanders away to card games
in other rooms. Most of her day is spent in the chair, at the foot of the bed.
Every now and then, she leaves and takes a walk down one of the many
hallways of the complex. Every now and then, she goes to the window and
looks out, as if something will be there.

II.

Motion falls apart in silence, tumbling, as wind turns choreographed snow
through tangents of streetlights. I am alone; to be picked up at the Saint
Paul bus terminal. I fucked up. Dropped out. Good, it's not what I wanted.
What is a quasar? The tissue of dreams. Fuck no, there are no secrets. There
is nothing hard about astronomy, sociology, calculus, or Minnesota winters.

Those are just reasons I used to leave. To go where? To go watch my hands become shadows over assembly lines?

A voice clicks on in the darkness. "We are now in Saint Paul and will be arriving at the Saint Paul terminal." Let me guess. In five minutes. "In ten minutes," the driver says. It figures.

III.

My uncle's eyes have long since fallen from the grasp of stars. Now, they are like the backends of factories; vague indications of what goes on beneath the tracks of comb in his thick black hair. He was waiting when I arrived. Waiting, entranced in existence. A series of hypnotic silences, between words, that had to be spoken. Silences leading me to a beat-up car in a dark parking lot. I am too far away from him; too far away to be leaving for something further. I don't believe he doesn't like me. No, that's not quite what I'm getting at. It's something I saw when his shadow exploded into a face as he bent down, over the steering wheel, to light his cigarette.

IV.

The cold white moon over houses too close together. Front windows, where shadows pass in front of blue lights of televisions. I am one of them now; a sound on wood stairs. There is a sanctuary of dreams waiting for my footsteps to fade.

V.

The old woman dreams she is up north, on the reservation. It is autumn. Pine smoke hanging over the tops of houses, leaves sleepwalking in gray wind, skeletal trees scratching ghost gray sky. She is in the old black shack. At home. Stirring stew in the kitchen. The woodstove snaps in the next room. Out the window, he lifts the axe. He is young. She watches as it splits a log on the tree stump. He turns away and starts toward the house. He is old. He takes out his pipe and presses down tobacco. She goes to the door to meet him. She opens the door. She tries to touch him. He passes through her, like a cold shiver, and walks into a photograph on the wall.

VI.

The mind bends over, in the light through a window, down and across the body of Jesus Christ as he stumbles through the sixth station of the cross. It comes to me sometimes, when I close my eyes. September sun in the old church. Smoke of sweet grass in stained glass light. Red, blue and yellow light. Prisms of thought behind every eye. Chippewa prayers stumbling through my ears. Old Ojibwa chants fading away in the walk to the cemetery. I look at the hole in the ground. I look at the casket beside it. I look at the hole, I look at the casket. At the hole, at the casket, at the hole, at the casket, at the hole.

   The clock glows red across the room; a digital 2:37. My cousin lies in darkness. Another figure covered up in sleep.

VII.

Dust swims in sunlight of an open door as dreams evaporate in the face of a clock.

VIII.

"Get up, I said. It's raining. It's raining and you, lying there. Get up, old man, I said." It is my uncle talking. He found the old man where he lay in the rain. He had fallen asleep and fallen down from his seat on an old bench I tried to set on fire when I was ten or eleven. The next week they buried him in the coolness of the Autumn coming. Weeks after, the old woman thought she heard his carriage outside the window of her new room in the city.

IX.

Cities of snow melt, blurred in liquid between wiper blades. We are waiting for the light to change. My uncle is driving. The old woman is waiting. Not really for us. Not for us, but waiting. I will see her this morning. This afternoon I will be gone. Another bus. Home. The light changes in the corner of my eye turning away.

X.

The room never moves for her. It is not like snow falling, like leaves falling, like stones through water. It is a window, a bed, and a chair.

XI.

As the old woman touches me it is like air holding smoke. I am something else. Vestiges of prayer, gathered in a hollow church. Another kind of reflection. A reflection on the outsides of her black glasses. A reflection that cries when eyes leave it.

As the old woman touches me it is like air holding smoke. I am something else. Fleet anguish, like flying shadows. A moment vanishing. A moment taken, as I am being.

As the old woman touches me it is like air holding smoke. It spins it. It grasps it. It shapes it in a wish. After that there is a mist too fine to see.

DIANE BURNS (1957–2006), *Anishinaabe-Lac Courte Oreilles and Chemehuevi,* was raised near various Native boarding schools where her parents worked as teachers. After graduating from Barnard College, she became an established member of New York's Lower East Side poetry scene in the 1980s and published *Riding the One-Eyed Ford* in 1981. In 1988, she was invited by the Sandinista government to Nicaragua with other American poets to participate in the Rubén Darío poetry festival.

SURE YOU CAN ASK ME A PERSONAL QUESTION

How do you do?
No, I am not Chinese.
No, not Spanish.
No, I am American Indian, Native American.

No, not from India.
No, not Apache.

No, not Navajo.
No, not Sioux.
No, we are not extinct.
Yes, Indian.

Oh?
So that's where you got those high cheekbones.
Your great grandmother, huh?
An Indian Princess, huh?
Hair down to there?
Let me guess. Cherokee?

Oh, so you've had an Indian friend?
That close?

Oh, so you've had an Indian lover?
That tight?

Oh, so you've had an Indian servant?
That much?

Yeah, it was awful what you guys did to us.
It's real decent of you to apologize.
No, I don't know where you can get peyote.
No, I don't know where you can get Navajo rugs real cheap.
No, I didn't make this. I bought it at Bloomingdales.

Thank you. I like your hair too.
I don't know if anyone knows whether or not Cher
is really Indian.
No, I didn't make it rain tonight.

Yeah. Uh-huh. Spirituality.
Uh-huh. Yeah. Spirituality. Uh-huh. Mother
Earth. Yeah. Uh-huh. Uh-huh. Spirituality.

No, I didn't major in archery.
Yeah, a lot of us drink too much.
Some of us can't drink enough.

This ain't no stoic look.
This is my face.

Big Fun

I don't care if you're married I still love you
I don't care if you're married
After the party's over
I will take you home in my One-Eyed Ford
Way yah hi yo, Way yah hi yo!

    Modene!
    The roller derby queen!
    She's Anishinabe,
       that means Human Being!
That's H for hungry!
And B for frijoles!
      Frybread!
      Tortillas!
      Watermelon!
      Pomona!
Take a sip of this
and a drag of that!
At the rancheria fiesta
it's tit for tat!
Low riders and Levis
go fist in glove!
Give it a little pat
a push or a shove
Move it or lose it!
Take straight or bruise it!

Everyone
has her fun
when the sun
is all done
We're all one
make a run
hide your gun
Hey!
I'm no nun!
'49 in the hills above
    Ventura
Them Okies gotta drum

I'm from Oklahoma
I got no one to call my own
if you will be my honey
I will be your sugar pie, Way hi yah,
Way yah hey way yah hi yah!

We're gonna sing all night
bring your blanket
or
be that way then!

AL HUNTER (*1958–*), *Anishinaabe,* is a member and former chief of the Rainy River First Nations. He is an experienced land claims negotiator and activist for Indigenous and environmental rights. In 2000, he led a 1,200-mile "Walk to Remember" around Lake Superior to spur future conservation efforts. Hunter has published three books of poetry through Kegedonce Press including *Beautiful Razor: Love Poems and Other Lies,* and his work has been widely anthologized.

PRAYER BOWL

When the moon is turned upwards like a bowl waiting to be filled
We must fill it. We must fill it by honoring the spirits of creation
With songs of our joy and thanks, with foods created with our own hands,
Water for the thirsty, prayers for the people, prayers for the spirits,
Prayers for the Creator, prayers for ourselves, and the sacred instruments
That join us to the glory of this world, that join us to the glory of this world
And to the world beyond our sleep.

 KARENNE WOOD *(1960–2019), Monacan,* was a poet and a linguistic anthropologist. She earned an MFA at George Mason University and a PhD in anthropology at the University of Virginia. Wood received a Diane Decorah Memorial Poetry Award from the Native Writers' Circle of the Americas for her first collection, *Markings on Earth* (2001), which was followed by *Weaving the Boundary* in 2016. She served on the Monacan Tribal Council and directed the Virginia Indian Programs at Virginia Humanities in Charlottesville, Virginia.

CHIEF TOTOPOTAMOI, 1654
after Miller Williams

This is to say we continued. As though continuing changed us.
As though continuing brought happiness as we had known.

On a dry field without cover, his skin blistered raw in the sun.
Not one among us came, as though he had no relations.

What did we say to our brother? How could we leave him alone
while soldiers guarded his corpse as though precious to them?

One of the women, in darkness, crept to the field where he died,
prayed for him, covered him up. Dust over what was not dust.

We would have ventured out with her if we had loved ourselves less.
We had to think of our children, and he was not coming back.

How could we live with the silence, live with our grief and our shame?
Death did not heal what he suffered. He was making demands.

We did not want him to be there, asking the question he asked us,
changing the sound of his name. He had embarrassed us.

This is the memory we carried, avoiding the thought that he remained
face down among the charred grasses, holding the earth with his hands.

Hard Times

A woman sits on a porch of weathered boards,
her skin the color and texture of the dried-apple dolls
that grandmothers gave to children years ago.
When asked about the past, she will not speak.
They were hard times.

Maybe she sits on the parched earth instead,
looks toward fields of rice, cotton, sugarcane, tobacco.
Maybe she wears a printed housedress or sarong
with hair covered or plaited, her face etched
in memories of joy snatched from her
in daylight and auctioned to strangers.

Her hands have scrubbed cities of floors, washed
the nameless dead, cooked food for armies, so little of it
hers; hands that failed to protect her or any of her children.
She believes that if she speaks, she might break apart,
the dust of her flying across stooped men

chained by their debt to the fields. She presses both lips
together, an effort to hold her own grief in her skin.

Maybe evening wears into night. The stars that connect us
gather like sisters around her. We hear, *They were hard times,*
across the continuous land of our women, until as sun
rises above the droning flies and the garrulous chickens,
a voice speaks in our old language, which we do not know.
We sift through a history with dust on our hands,
the empty rocker creaking in the breeze.

ERIC GANSWORTH *(1965–), Onondaga,* is a poet, playwright, novelist, and visual artist who was born and raised at the Tuscarora Nation. The author of five poetry collections, most recently a YA memoir-in-verse, *Apple: Skin to the Core* (2020), Gansworth has also received recognition for his nonfiction, visual art, and fiction, which has won both a PEN Oakland Award and an American Book Award. Gansworth is a Lowery Writer-in-Residence and a professor of English at Canisius College in Buffalo, New York.

Eel

1

I don't understand this kindergarten
assignment: "Draw Your Clan."
The three letters live in abstraction.
A friend suggests mine looks like his, minus
legs, and that day I believe my clan is
a species of amputee Snipes, birds
forced to fly the skies forever, and I
wonder if we are meant to symbolize
endurance or something beyond
my five-year-old comprehension.

2

My mother explains we are not legless
birds and if she had a more worldly
vocabulary she would have suggested
we were ambiguous, not quite a fish,
more than a water snake, but she says
we are among the few. The last Tuscarora Eel
died out a generation ago, so we are left
Onondaga Eels among the Tuscarora,
voiceless as well as legless.

3

I find an encyclopedia photo,
see jagged rows of razor teeth
in a mouth perpetually grinning
and when I show it to her, she says
clans are a system to keep track
of families, so we don't inadvertently
marry our relatives, and that we have no
more affinity with eels than anyone else
on the reservation has with their animals.

4

"If I threw you in the dike," she says
"you'd drown as fast as anyone else," done
with this lesson. I remember older cousins,
swimming between my legs, and suddenly I am rising,
their hands grabbing my knees as my balls collide
with the backs of their necks, and they break
the surface, toss me into deeper water, probably
watching to make sure I surface, after they've had
some amusement at my struggle.

5

In wet darkness, I imagine opening
my eyes and mouth, taking water in,
filling my lungs, discovering gills
like Aquaman or Namor, the Sub-mariner.
Knowing I had better odds of dying, face down,
no voice to call out for help, I am
never quite brave enough to try it, not daring
enough, even, to open my eyes when my face breaks
the stillness of river water contained.

6

But I flip on my back, ears below the surface, listen
to mysteries, breathe shallowly at that level, and float,
wondering what it would be like to glide the depths
on fins, knowing if I were there, I would desire
legs and lungs, and then I fill my chest to capacity,
and dive, loving and begrudging the ache I find there,
the throbbing of my chest begging for release,
and I swim back up, eyes still closed, wondering how
long it will take to find the surface again.

JAMES THOMAS STEVENS (ARONHIÓTAS) (1966–), *Akwesasne Mohawk,* is the author of seven books of poetry as well as a collaborative poetry and translation project with Caroline Sinavaiana-Gabbard. His work has received many awards, including a Whiting Writers Award, and he was a finalist for the 2005 National Poetry Series. Stevens has taught at the State University of New York at Fredonia and at Haskell Indian Nations University and is currently an associate professor at the Institute of American Indian Arts in Santa Fe.

TONAWANDA SWAMPS

As it would for a prow, the basin parts with your foot.
Never a marsh, of heron blue
                                        but the single red feather
from the wing of some black bird, somewhere
a planked path winds above water,
the line of sky above this aching space.

Movement against the surface
is the page that accepts no ink.
A line running even
over alternating depths, organisms, algae,
a rotting leaf.

Walk naked before me
carrying a sheaf of sticks.
It's the most honest thing a man can do.

As water would to accept you,
I part
a mouth, a marsh, or margin
is of containment,
the inside circuitous edge.

No line to follow out to ocean,
no river against an envelope
                              of trembling white ships.
Here I am landlock.
Give me your hand.

St. James Lake

On a footbridge
crossing
          the lake toward
                    Horse Guards Road,

I stop to listen
as dim twitterings grow to a deafening roar.

This is how the body is,
suddenly aware of its own dull thud.

Knowing, how our own song
completes the chorus. How each preened park-goer
carries a specific yet woefully similar call,
                              Sanctuary.

You, singing beautifully in churches and town squares.
Us, humming in harmony once
beneath arched vaults above the *Isère*.

I can never think far from the heart.

Nearing Birdcage Walk,
I envision the intricate cage of your ribs at night.

Imagine the frightened flocks we carry:

Grey Wagtail
Swan
Shoveler
Pelican
Raven
Golden Eye

Oh plucking Zeus. Oh Ganymede. Oh frightened furies flying breakneck
in our chests.

How it all becomes fantastical, here.

All elephants and castles, chalk farms and canaries. All mile ends and
mudchutes. All circus.

Birdkeep of a brain,
there must be someone
watching out
            for the heart.

Between that Charybdian eye and Buckingham,
we near Duck Island, and of a sudden

                      it appears.

The birdkeeper's cottage.
Its thatched roof hanging

                impossibly heavy.

How idyllic, how monstrous
that responsibility for these many birds.

I could live here, I say.
I could live here too.

I hear, *with*, take flight. Its gently upturned wings lifting from water.

Turning to go to sleep at night, you offer your sore shoulder,
and in the strain of muscle beneath my thumbs, I note its avian blade.

KIMBERLY WENSAUT *(1971–)*, *Potawatomi,* is a member of
the PaperBirch Poets in Wisconsin and is a linguist with a focus on
her tribe's Bodwéwadmimwen language. She has been published in
Sister Nations: Native American Women Writers on Community (Minnesota
Historical Society Press) and in 1995 established the first tribal newspaper
for her nation, the *Potawatomi Traveling Times.*

PRODIGAL DAUGHTER

Once, when I came home
after sixty days on the road,
my mother said, *Oh–*
the prodigal daughter has returned.

Prodigal, prodigious, prodigy.

In my blood is a way of life.
Migration and distance bridge the gap
in our seasonal souls.
Winter camp, summer camp
kept those villages on the move.

Or maybe it is because
no one remembered
to save my cord at birth.
That sturdy life line
which delivered me whole
into this world, anchored me
to the generations.

They used to do this. Kept it
in a finely beaded pouch
as one would keep a thing
of immense worth. If this was not done,

they said the child would be foolish
or would always be searching.

Maybe it is the thunders
who breathed life into my body.
They are forever wanting
to lift me high and carry me away.

Once, I thought I could settle
into the arms of pine, hemlock,
spruce and icy river.
But this has not happened yet.

Home is elusive.
It shapeshifts with the currents
of my heart and its will.
Home is a trickster changing
according to the medicine
of the season and its lesson.

I was weary, this last ride home.
Every fiber ready to surrender.
Sage and a small courage
begged my continuance.

There is frost on my doorway,
and leaves unswept.
There are miles to dream
before I meet the morning again.

STEVE PACHECO *(1975–), **Mdewakanton Dakota.*** From the Lower Sioux Indian Community in southwestern Minnesota, Pacheco is a coauthor of *Shedding Skins: Four Sioux Poets* (2008) and a past guest editor for the literary journal *Yellow Medicine Review*. He has worked as a guidance counselor and advocate and is currently an asssistant professor at Southwest Minnesota State University.

HISTORY

Cousin, how useless now
are the dirt road days
when we whirled roundhouse
kicks at one another with our bare feet,

and how we listened to our fathers
kindle the fire water in the kitchen
gives us January memories

of times we spent in the gravel pit
playing war with plastic Army men
only tells half the history
of the little lives we razed.

Your first winter home
snowfall arrived early.
The multihued hills of the rez
turned the same color brown
as your camouflage fatigues.
I thought it was coincidence.
Maybe the snow flourished
to welcome you like a kindred spirit.
Maybe, *tahansi*, it was our time
for history to surround us.

LAURA DA' *(1979–), Eastern Shawnee,* is a lifetime resident of the Pacific Northwest, where she teaches and writes. She studied creative writing at the University of Washington and at the Institute of American Indian Arts in Santa Fe. In 2015, she was named both a Made at Hugo House fellow and a Jack Straw fellow. She is the author of *Instruments of the True Measure* (2018) and *Tributaries* (2016), which won an American Book Award.

NATIONHOOD

I am a citizen of two nations: Shawnee and American. I have one son who is a citizen of three. Before he was born, I learned that, like all infants, he would need to experience a change of heart at birth in order to survive. When a baby successfully breathes in through the lungs, the heart changes from parallel flow to serial flow and the shunt between the right and left atriums closes. Our new bodies obliterate old frontiers.

North America is mistakenly called nascent. The Shawnee nation is mistakenly called moribund. America established a mathematical beginning point in 1785 in what was then called the Northwest Territory. Before that, it was known in many languages as the eastern range of the Shawnee, Miami, and Huron homelands. I do not have the Shawnee words to describe this place; the notation that is available to me is 40°38′32.61′ N 80°31′9.76′ W.

Measuring the Distance to Oklahoma

Shell shaking in the state of the coin toss and sorrowful walk.

Weaving through the powwow grounds
grass stomped low and buzzing with flies
     your son walks two quick steps ahead of me
     to point out a tiny bow and arrow at a vendor's booth.

Rats scuttle in the grain silo.
The gentle clamor of the casino washes through the parking lot.
A table is piled with half a dozen corn cakes,
each one embossed with the maker's thumbprint.
Your grandfather recounts
catching water moccasins as a boy
and spitting wads of tobacco down their throats
just to watch them squirm.

You sink onto a dusty quilt
gently pull the empty Coke can from your boy's sleeping fist
shake your head impatiently when your daughter whines for you to
untie an intricately beaded belt from her regalia.
Child's arrow, capped with a pencil eraser twirling in your fingers.

Ottawa County moon as seen from a distance:
pale vodka swirling in an open mouth.
Driving home on the frontage road,
green and riveted as a turtle's back.
Highway sketched into place by the broken black lines
of oil rigs at midnight.

B: WILLIAM BEARHART *(1979–), Anishinaabe–St. Croix,* earned an MFA from the Institute of American Indian Arts in Santa Fe. In addition to writing and editing, bearhart works as a poker dealer at a small casino in Wisconsin. His poetry has been published in *The Boston Review, Prairie Schooner, North American Review, Tupelo Quarterly,* and *PANK Magazine.*

WHEN I WAS IN LAS VEGAS AND SAW A WARHOL PAINTING OF GERONIMO

I thought *We could be related,* Andy and I. We're both
blue walls and yellow cows in a gallery of pristine white. We're both
screen prints, off-set and layered. Under exposed. We're both
silver clouds filled with helium and polluted rain. We're both
white and blonde and scared of hospitals. Only I'm not really any of those
    things.

And then I thought *We could be related,* Geronimo and I. We're both
code names for assassinations. We're both first
names you yell when you jump from a plane. We're both
gamblers and dead and neon acrylic brush strokes on a screen printed
    image. Only I'm more
like a neon beer sign sputtering in a tavern window: burned out, broke,
a heart with arrhythmic beats.

PLAINS AND
MOUNTAINS

PLACED WITH OUR POWER

Heid E. Erdrich

T HIS REGION is represented by powerful poems that sing, narrate, and argue, that are lyrical, and often witty, all the while bearing witness to generations of Indigenous people living in enormous, often harsh, and beloved lands. Here some of the last and most brutal repression of our people took place, battles by the U.S. military against men, women, and children, including the shame of the Wounded Knee massacre in 1890. Poets of the Plains and Mountains do not forget such injustice but lend their voices to a resistance active across three centuries.

This section asserts an historicism while offering re-visioning, resistance, and survivance based in culture, tribal stories or tribalography, and tribal languages. To begin, two poets born in the 1870s, Zitkála-Šá (also known as Gertrude Simmons Bonnin) and Elsie Fuller, call out politicians by name and fault Congress with scathing sarcasm. Political content is one characteristic of Native poets of the Plains and Mountains. Other poems make historical reference to conflict with (un)settlers and perform resistance to colonization. Many of the poems in this section concern themselves with events and figures familiar to the general public such as Sitting Bull, Crazy Horse, the Ghost Dance, Custer's defeat, and the Dakota "Uprising." Lois Red Elk's "Our Blood Remembers," an elegy to Tȟatȟáŋka Íyotake/Sitting Bull, suggests that our ancestral blood contains the tribal past. The vital perspectives in these poems differ from the vague, romantic notions people might have about warriors and conflicts: these poets are directly related to well-known chiefs, to unknown survivors of massacres (Indian wars) that displaced their Plains relatives, often in forced marches and migrations, to the harsh climates near the more mountainous regions.

Several poems reveal deep and personal consideration of lesser-known conflicts as well: the Sand Creek massacre (Lance Henson), the oil-driven greed of the Osage Murders (Elise Paschen), and the mass hanging of thirty-eight Dakota warriors (Layli Long Soldier) whose execution, the largest in U.S. history, was commanded by Abraham Lincoln the same week he signed the Emancipation Proclamation. Such poems recognize, as Lois Red Elk says, our "guardian relatives" and "ancestor of our blood." These are not historical accounts, not reenactments, but personal poems from survivors whose understanding of the U.S. Cavalry, Custer, and disappearances of Native women are not imagined, but inherited, embodied memories.

A clash of imaginations informs these poems. The world's image of the Plains and Mountains, the "Wild West," remains populated by cowboys, outlaws, and Indian chiefs on war horses. Poems in this section do present Native figures on horseback (Elizabeth Cook-Lynn and James Welch) but these riders long for peace and place. "The West," the land rush, the last Indian wars, all took place in the Plains and Mountains, but the West these poets depict is not a place to be tamed, settled, or claim-staked. Instead these lands claim us. They are our origin places and the sites of our power, as the poets Richard Littlebear, Sy Hoahwah, and John Trudell remind us. In pulp fiction and old movies, the reason "Indians" were "on the war path" goes unexplained. These poems are explanation offered: Our warriors were and are preoccupied with ongoing defense of our sacred spaces and places of power—the prairies, rivers, canyons, and mountains that birthed us remain our relatives.

These poems point out crucial differences between Native and (un)settler understanding of history. For Natives, these poems say, history is active and ongoing, rather than residing in distant memory. In her poem on the annual commemorative horseback ride by Dakota people, Long Soldier writes: "The memorial for the Dakota 38 is not an object inscribed with words, but an *act*." The memorial is not a static memory, but an active resistance. Action as a cultural distinction concerns Hoahwah as well. His notion of memorial is an act continued at a linguistic level:

> The other sister Tsi-yee, named after a war deed
> (her father charged a cavalry officer
> knocked him off his horse then lanced him to the prairie)

Hoahwah's relative, Tsi-yee, carries in her name a memorial to "a war deed," an act against a U.S. soldier. In Comanche, Hoahwah illustrates, one's name can participate in an ongoing and active resistance. For many women poets in this region, resistance can take the shape of creatures or women imbued with supernatural powers: In Louise Erdrich's "Jacklight," for example, an uncanny doe fights back at male hunters. Tiffany Midge's "Teeth in The Wrong Places" writes a monstrous feminine strength that's bawdy, funny, and fierce. Such protections are warranted today when statistics for sexual assault in the United States show that Native women make up the highest number of victims. What happens to the land, happens to us, is a lesson learned across centuries of desecration.

What's become an American standard, the wilderness pastoral or eco-poetic lyric, might work as metaphor for a non-Native poet, but these poems are from place and related to place. These poems become acts of power and profound connection. N. Scott Momaday notes a season that "centers on this place" in the "deep ancestral air," stating he stands "in good relation to the earth"; and Victor Charlo describes "mountains so close we are relative."

Power from the land goes beyond romanticizing Native relationships with nature, in part by revealing the power of words in silent places. The iconic figure, a man named Earthboy, in James Welch's poem, "farmed the sky with words." Welch's line reveals a complex relationship to place as it transposes earth and sky; we understand the "Earthboy 40" of the poem's title to be a storied place, a place where words form their power. In response to Robert Frost's depiction of the American landscape as an "unstoried" place, in my poem "The Theft Outright" I write back in time to our first stories of how we came from the earth itself: "We were the land before we were a people."

Our relationship to language *within* land arises from the silence, the vastness of our homelands, as expressed by Suzan Shown Harjo:

> The Song that sang itself
>   had no language
>   it was a heartbeat that thundered
>   through the canyons of time

It is the place itself that gives power, and that power carries across time and distance. It is not an uncommon notion in the nations represented here that all of our power comes from the earth, which we need, but which does not need us. When John Trudell recalls being under police control and told to squat, he points out the mistake his captors made: "They placed me with my power"—the earth. Such power allows the speaker to move across time, even while restrained:

> I was their captive
> But my heart was racing
> Through the generations

The ability to hold and express a distinct sense of time is how these poets remain, in Momaday's words, "in good relation" to those who came before and those still to come.

Ultimately what bridges the generations of the diverse poets of Plains and Mountains is the resurgence of Indigenous languages that began in the late twentieth century and continues to grow. Ute language is at the heart of Tanaya Winder's moving and elegiac poem "learning to say i love you." Richard Littlebear's "We Are the Spirits of these Bones," told alternately in Cheyenne and English, alludes to repatriation and ancestral spirits troubled by and unfamiliar with their new place of rest. In the face of generations of government attempts to teach only English to Native children, the existence of poems in Indigenous languages represents a hard-won resurgence.

The grassy plains and powerful mountains that many consider the middle of the country are, these poets assert, their own places with their own histories and boundaries. They speak their own poems daily. Plains and mountains formed the lives within them. Rocks and waters came first, then plants, creatures, and then we humans. Indigenous ways of being arose in relation to land. So too our poetry comes from place and from acts of resistance—from Little Big Horn to Standing Rock—our historic and ongoing battles to protect our homelands.

ELSIE FULLER (*1870-unknown*), *Omaha,* was a poet who attended the Hampton Institute in Hampton, Virginia, from 1885 to 1888. The institute took students from sixty-five northern and western tribes. As at other American Indian boarding schools, students were taught in English and punished for speaking in their native languages, given religious instruction, and enrolled in programs that emphasized trade, agriculture, and teacher training. The school created one of the earliest "outing" programs, which sent students to work for families in New England when the school was closed in the summer months. More than 1,300 students attended Hampton Institute between 1878 and 1923. This poem was published in *Talks and Thoughts of the Hampton Indian Students.* It refers to U.S. Senator Henry Laurens Dawes of Massachusetts, the author of the Dawes Severalty Act of 1887.

A New Citizen

Now I am a citizen!
    They've given us new laws,
Just as were made
    By Senator Dawes.

We need not live on rations,
    Why? There is no cause,
For "Indians are citizens,"
    Said Senator Dawes.

Just give us a chance,
    We never will pause.
Till we are good citizens
    Like Senator Dawes.

Now we are citizens,
    We all give him applause—
So three cheers, my friends,
    For Senator Dawes!

ZITKÁLA-ŠÁ (GERTRUDE SIMMONS BONNIN) (1876–
1938), *Dakota,* was a writer, editor, musician, teacher, political
activist, and cofounder and president of the National Council of
American Indians in 1926. Born on the Yankton Sioux Reservation, she was
sent to a Quaker missionary school in Wabash, Indiana, and later studied
at Earlham College and the Boston Conservatory of Music. Along with her
English translation of Native American oral stories, her autobiographical
essays, and her political writing, she co-wrote one of the first operas to deal
extensively with Indigenous themes and subjects.

THE RED MAN'S AMERICA

My country! 'tis to thee,
Sweet land of Liberty,
My pleas I bring.
  Land where OUR fathers died,
  Whose offspring are denied
  The Franchise given wide,
  Hark, while I sing.

My native country, thee,
Thy Red man is not free,
Knows not thy love.
  Political bred ills,
  Peyote in temple hills,
  His heart with sorrow fills,
  Knows not thy love.

Let Lane's Bill swell the breeze,
And ring from all the trees,
Sweet freedom's song.
  Let Gandy's Bill awake
  All people, till they quake,
  Let Congress, silence break,
  The sound prolong.

Great Mystery, to thee,
Life of humanity,
To thee, we cling.
    Grant our home land be bright,
    Grant us just human right,
    Protect us by Thy might,
    Great God, our king.

D'ARCY McNICKLE *(1904–1977), Métis* and *Confederated Salish and Kootenai Tribes,* was an author, activist, academic, and community organizer. He was born and raised in St. Ignatius, Montana. Following the Riel Rebellion (or North-West Rebellion) in what is now Saskatchewan and Alberta in 1885, his Cree Métis mother had fled with her family to Montana, where they were formally adopted into the Confederated Salish and Kootenai Tribes of the Flathead Reservation. McNickle attended the University of Montana from 1921 to 1925 and sold his allotment to raise money to study at Oxford and the University of Grenoble. He worked as an administrator at the Bureau of Indian Affairs, served as director of American Indian Development at the University of Colorado, and was the primary author of the "Declaration of Indian Purpose" for the American Indian Chicago Conference in 1961. He helped to establish the D'Arcy McNickle Center for American Indian and Indigenous Studies at Chicago's Newberry Library in 1972. His best-known literary work is the novel *The Surrounded.*

Man Hesitates but Life Urges

There is this shifting, endless film
And I have followed it down the valleys
And over the hills,–
Pointing with wavering finger
When it disappeared in purple forest-patches
With its ruffle and wave to the slightest-breathing wind-God.

There is this film
Seen suddenly, far off,
When the sun, walking to his setting,
Turns back for a last look,
And out there on the far, far prairie
A lonely drowsing cabin catches and holds a glint,
For one how endless moment,
In a staring window the fire and song of the martyrs!

There is this film
That has passed to my fingers
And I have trembled,
Afraid to touch.

And in the eyes of one
Who had wanted to give what I had asked
But hesitated—tried—and then
Came with a weary, aged, "Not quite,"
I could but see that single realmless point of time,
All that is sad, and tired, and old—
And endless, shifting film.

And I went again
Down the valleys and over the hills,
Pointing with wavering finger;
Ever reaching to touch, trembling,
Ever fearful to touch.

 ELIZABETH COOK-LYNN (*1930–*), *Crow Creek Sioux,* is from Fort Thompson, South Dakota, and was raised in a Sisseton Santee Dakota family. She is an editor, essayist, and novelist and co-founded *Wičazo Ša Review*. She has written several books of prose and poetry. She received the 2007 Lifetime Achievement Award from the Native Writers' Circle of the Americas.

At Dawn, Sitting at My Father's House

I.

              I sit quietly
in the dawn; a small house in the Missouri breaks.
A coyote pads toward the timber, sleepless as I,
guilty and watchful. The birds are commenting on his
passing. Young Indian riders are here to take the old
man's gelding to be used as a pick-up horse at the
community rodeo. I feel fine. The sun rises.

II.

              I see him
from the window; almost blind, he is on his hands and
knees gardening in the pale glow. A hawk, an early riser,
hoping for a careless rodent or blow snake, hangs in the wind-
current just behind the house; a signal the world is
right with itself.
              I see him
from the days no longer new chopping at the hard-packed
earth, mindless of the dismal rain. I hold the seeds
cupped in my hands.

III.

              The sunrise nearly finished
the old man's dog stays here waiting, waiting, whines
at the door, lonesome for the gentle man who lived here. I
get up and go outside and we take the small footpath to the
flat prairie above. We may pretend.

N. SCOTT MOMADAY *(1934–)*, **Kiowa,** is a poet and novelist who is best known for his 1969 Pulitzer Prizewinning novel *House Made of Dawn*. Born in Lawton, Oklahoma, he lived most of his young life in Arizona, eventually moving to Jemez Pueblo in New Mexico at the age of twelve. He attended the University of New Mexico, graduating in 1958 with a BA in English, went to Stanford on a poetry fellowship, and earned his PhD in English literature in 1963. He has taught in numerous universities, including University of California at Berkeley and Santa Barbara. In 2007 he was named Oklahoma's sixteenth poet laureate and was awarded the National Medal of Arts.

Angle of Geese

How shall we adorn
Recognition with our speech?—
        Now the dead firstborn
Will lag in the wake of words.

        Custom intervenes;
We are civil, something more:
        More than language means,
The mute presence mulls and marks.

        Almost of a mind,
We take measure of the loss;
        I am slow to find
The mere margin of repose.

        And one November
It was longer in the watch,
        As if forever,
Of the huge ancestral goose.

        So much symmetry!
Like the pale angle of time

And eternity.
The great shape labored and fell.
　　Quit of hope and hurt,
It held a motionless gaze,
　　Wide of time, alert,
On the dark distant flurry.

THE GOURD DANCER

Mammedaty, 1880–1932

1. THE OMEN

Another season centers on this place.
Like memory the blood congeals in it;
Like memory the sun recedes in time
Into the hazy, southern distances.

A vagrant heat hangs on the dark river,
And shadows turn like smoke. An owl ascends
Among the branches, clattering, remote
Within its motion, intricate with age.

2. THE DREAM

Mammedaty saw to the building of this house. Just
there, by the arbor, he made a camp in the old way,
and in the evening when the hammers had fallen silent
and there were frogs and crickets in the black grass—
and a low hectic wind upon the pale, slanting plane
of the moon's light—he settled deep down in his
mind dream. He dreamed of dreaming, and of the
summer breaking upon his spirit, as drums break upon
the intervals of the dance, and of the gleaming gourds.

3. THE DANCE

Dancing,
He dreams, he dreams—
The long wind glances, moves
Forever as a music to the mind;
The gourds are flashes of the sun.
He takes the inward, mincing steps
That conjure old processions and returns.
Dancing,
His moccasins,
His sash and bandolier
Contain him in insignia;
His fan is powerful, concise
According to his agile hand,
And holds upon the deep, ancestral air.

4. THE GIVEAWAY

Someone spoke his name, Mammedaty, in which
his essence was and is. It was a serious matter that his
name should be spoken there in the circle, among the
many people, and he was thoughtful, full of wonder,
and aware of himself and of his name. He walked
slowly to the summons, looking into the eyes of the man
who summoned him. For a moment they held each
other in close regard and all about them there was
excitement and suspense.

Then a boy came suddenly into the circle, leading
a black horse. The boy ran, and the horse after him.
He brought the horse up short in front of Mammedaty,
and the horse wheeled and threw its head and cut
its eyes in the wild way. And it blew hard and quivered
in its hide so that light ran, rippling, upon its shoulders
and its flanks—and then it stood still and was calm.
Its mane and tail were fixed in braids and feathers, and

a bright red chief's blanket was draped in a roll over
its withers. The boy placed the reins in Mammedaty's
hands. And all of this was for Mammedaty, in his honor,
as even now it is in the telling, and will be, as long as
there are those who imagine him in his name.

THE DELIGHT SONG OF TSOAI-TALEE

I am a feather on the bright sky.
I am the blue horse that runs in the plain.
I am the fish that rolls, shining, in the water.
I am the shadow that follows a child.
I am the evening light, the luster of meadows.
I am an eagle playing with the wind.
I am a cluster of bright beads.
I am the farthest star.
I am the cold of dawn.
I am the roaring of the rain.
I am the glitter on the crust of the snow.
I am the long track of the moon in a lake.
I am a flame of four colors.
I am a deer standing away in the dusk.
I am a field of sumac and the pomme blanche.
I am an angle of geese in the winter sky.
I am the hunger of a young wolf.
I am the whole dream of these things.
You see, I am alive, I am alive
I stand in good relation to the earth.
I stand in good relation to the gods.
I stand in good relation to all that is beautiful.
I stand in good relation to the daughter of Tsen-tainte.
You see, I am alive, I am alive.

VICTOR CHARLO (1937–), *Bitterroot Salish* **and an elder of the** *Confederated Salish and Kootenai Tribes,* is a direct descendant of Chief Victor (Many Horses), who refused to sign the historic Hellgate Treaty of 1855. Born on the Flathead Reservation in western Montana, Charlo's first calling was the priesthood. He left the seminary to pursue a career as an English teacher. He studied at Gonzaga University and the University of Montana, earning degrees in English and Latin, and a master's in curriculum. He is an activist for Indigenous issues. He lives in Old Agency, Dixon, Montana.

Frog Creek Circle

Mountains so close we are relative.
Creek so cold it brings winter rain.

We return to warm August home,
Frog Creek, where I've lived so long
that smells are stored, opened only
here. This land never changes, always
whole, always the way we want it to be.
We always come back
to check our senses or to remember
dreams. We are remembered today in circles
of family, of red pine, of old time chiefs,
of forgotten horses that thunder dark stars.

There are songs that we come to this day,
soft as Indian mint, strange as this sky.

LOIS RED ELK *(1940–)*, *Isanti, Hunkpapa,* and *Ihanktonwa,* was born on the Fort Peck Reservation in Montana. She lived in Los Angeles, where she worked as a TV talk show host, an actor, and a technical advisor for many Hollywood productions. Her first book, *Our Blood Remembers* (2011), was awarded the Best Non-Fiction award from Wordcraft Circle of Native Writers and Storytellers. She lives in Montana, where she is adjunct faculty at Fort Peck Community College.

Our Blood Remembers

The day the earth wept, a quiet wind covered the
lands weeping softly like an elderly woman, shawl
over bowed head. We all heard, remember? We were
all there. Our ancestral blood remembers the day
Sitting Bull, the chief of chiefs, was murdered. His
white horse quivered as grief shot up through the
crust of hard packed snow. Guardian relatives mourned
on our behalf. They knew our loss, took the pain from
our dreams, left us with our blood. We were asked to
remember the sweeter days, when leaves and animals
reached to touch him as he passed by. You know those
times, to reach for a truth only the pure of heart
reflect. Remember the holy man—peace loving. He
was a sun dancer—prayed for the people, water, land and
animals. Blessed among the blessed, chosen to lead the
people, he showed us the good red road, the one that
passes to our veins from earth through pipestone. Our
blood remembers. In vision he foresaw the demise of
that man, the one with yellow hair. "Soldiers falling
upside down into camp," he saw. Champion of the people,
a visionary, he taught us how to dream, this ancestor
of our blood. He instructed, "Let us put our minds
together to see what life we will make for our children"—
those pure from God. Remember? Pure from God, the

absolute gift, from our blood and blessed by heaven's
stars. And, we too, pure from God, our spirit, our blood,
our minds and our tongues. The sun dancer knew this,
showed us how to speak the words and walk the paths
our children would follow. Remember?

 JAMES WELCH (*1940–2003*), *Gros Ventre* and *Blackfeet,* was a
poet and a novelist born in Browning, Montana. He earned a degree
in literature and an MFA at the University of Montana, where he
studied with Richard Hugo. His book of poetry, *Riding the Earthboy 40,* was
published in 1971. He is known for his novels *Winter in the Blood, The Death
of Jim Loney,* and *The Indian Lawyer,* among others. He taught at the University
of Washington and Cornell University, and he served on the Montana
State Board of Pardons.

HARLEM, MONTANA: JUST OFF THE RESERVATION

We need no runners here. Booze is law
and all the Indians drink in the best tavern.
Money is free if you're poor enough.
Disgusted, busted whites are running
for office in this town. The constable,
a local farmer, plants the jail with wild
raven-haired stiffs who beg just one more drink.
One drunk, a former Methodist, becomes a saint
in the Indian church, bugs the plaster man
on the cross with snakes. If his knuckles broke,
he'd see those women wail the graves goodbye.

Goodbye, goodbye, Harlem on the rocks,
so bigoted you'd forget the latest joke,

so lonely, you'd welcome a battalion of Turks
to rule your women. What you don't know,
what you will never know or want to learn—
Turks aren't white. Turks are olive, unwelcome
alive in any town. Turks would use
your one dingy park to declare a need for loot.
Turks say bring it, step quickly, lay down and dead.

Here we are when men were nice. This photo, hung
in the New England Hotel lobby, shows them nicer
than pie, agreeable to the warring bands of redskins
who demanded protection money for the price of food.
Now, only Hutterites out North are nice. We hate
them. They are tough and their crops are always good.
We accuse them of idiocy and believe their belief all wrong.

Harlem, your hotel is overnamed, your children
are raggedy-assed but go on, survive
the bad food from the two cafes and peddle
your hate for the wild who bring you money.
When you die, if you die, will you remember
the three young bucks who shot the grocery up,
locked themselves in and cried for days, we're rich,
help us, oh God, we're rich.

THE MAN FROM WASHINGTON

The end came easy for most of us.
Packed away in our crude beginnings
in some far corner of a flat world,
we didn't expect much more than firewood and buffalo robes
to keep us warm. The man came down,
a slouching dwarf with rainwater eyes,
and spoke to us. He promised
that life would go on as usual,

that treaties would be signed, and everyone—
man, woman and child—would be inoculated
against a world in which we had no part,
a world of money, promise and disease.

RIDING THE EARTHBOY 40

Earthboy: so simple his name
should ring a bell for sinners.
Beneath the clowny hat, his eyes
so shot the children called him
dirt, Earthboy farmed this land
and farmed the sky with words.

The dirt is dead. Gone to seed
his rows become marker to a grave
vast as anything but dirt.
Bones should never tell a story
to a bad beginner. I ride
romantic to those words,

those foolish claims that he
was better than dirt, or rain
that bleached this cabin
white as bone. Scattered in the wind
Earthboy calls me from my dream:
Dirt is where the dreams must end.

RICHARD LITTLEBEAR (*1941–*), *Northern Cheyenne,* is a poet and an advocate for bilingualism and bilingual education, who considers his greatest achievement having learned to read and write in the Cheyenne language. He was born on the Northern Cheyenne Reservation and grew up in Busby, Montana. He received his BA from Bethel College in Kansas and his MA from Montana State University. In 1994, he received his Ph.D. in education from Boston University. He is the president and interim dean of culture affairs at the Chief Dull Knife College on the Northern Cheyenne Reservation.

NAMÁHTA'SOOMÁHEVEME

We Are the Spirits of these Bones

He'tohe he'konòtse nataosee'ešèhae'eševe'òhtsemo'tanonèstse.
    We have been with these bones for a long time.
Naa ovahe nataešeasèhetotaetanome hetsèstseha
    And we are beginning to feel a whole lot better
he'tohe he'konòtse tse'ešeevàho'èhoo'òhtseto hetseohe
    now that these bones are now back here
Tsetsèhestàhese tsestaomepo'anomevòhtsevòse he'tohe ho'e.
    among the Northern Cheyenne people on their Reservation.
Naa ovahe mato nahotoanavetanome.
    But we are troubled for another reason.
Nao'omeaseohtsetanome
    We want to travel on
he'tohe he'konòtse etaešeevaovana'xaeno'oma'enenèstse.
    now that these bones are safely buried.
Ooxesta etaeševàhešeovèšemanenèstse.
    They have now been properly put to rest.
Hene netao'o etaešenèšepèheva'e.
    All that has happened is all very good.
Naa ovahe naso'hotoanavetanome:
    But we are still troubled:
He'tohe he'konòtse etaešekanomeevapèhevo'tanèstse.

These bones are now in a good place.
Naa taamahe tsemȧhta'soomȧhevetse,
    But we, as the spirits,
tsexho'eohtsėhanetse hetseohe nasaahene'enahenone.
    do not know this place.
Hetseohe na'ȯhkeva'neamėsohpeohtseme heva
    We just used to travel through this place
ho've'otsetse naa mato heva ho'eemȯhonetse.
    when we were hunting the enemy or hunting for food.
Hetseohe nasaahestȧheheme, nėhešėhene'enome.
    We are not from here, we want you to know that.
Hetsėstseha naeveamemano'eeme.
    We have been meeting and singing.
Emȧhemoheevameo'o tse'tohe mȧhta'soomaho.
    All the spirits who have been with these bones for a long time were
    called to a meeting to sing songs.
Nanȯhtsenanonėstse ho'nehenoonȯtse tsetao'seevane'evaotsêhaaetse
    ma'tao'omeaseohtsetse.
    We are looking for the right wolf songs that will guide us.
Hetsėstseha naohkenemeneme.
    So now we are singing.
Naohkeonesėhahtsenonėstse nemeotȯtse.
    We are trying different songs.
Ma'tame'enomatse, nėstseo'omeaseohtseme,
    Whenever we find the right wolf songs,
hapo'e tosa'e nėtseovėšename, tosa'e tsehpêhevėhene'enomatse.
    we will travel on to a place we know, to a familiar place where we can
    sleep peacefully.
Tsestao'sėsaa'evave'šėhavėsevetanohetse.
    Where we will no longer feel bad.
Tsestao'sėsaa'evave'šėhoonȯsetanohetse.
    Where we will no longer feel homesick.
"Taaxa'e netaoneseme'enanonėstse ho'nehenoonȯtse," naheme.
    "Let us find some wolf songs," we said.
Naevemaemamȯhevananonėstse onehavo'ėstse.
    We put together some drums.
Hene koomaa'ėse naevepo'ponȯhanonėstse.

Once we were finished we sadly pounded on the drums.
Naa hetsėstseha naeveno'nȯhtse'anonėstse nemenestotȯtse
  And now we are looking for songs that will
tsetao'seve'šeo'omėhoxovestavatse
    help us as we travel on or maybe we can now be here and sleep restfully.
Naa mato heva hetseohe nȧhtanėšeeveovana'xaenaootseme. He'tohe
  naonėsaanėšekanomepėhevėhene'enahenone.
    Even though we do not know this place so well.

LANCE HENSON (*1944–*), *Southern Cheyenne,* was born in Washington, DC in 1944, and raised by his great aunt and uncle on a farm in Oklahoma. He served in the U.S. Marine Corps in Vietnam, and he is a member of the Cheyenne Dog Soldier Society. He is an activist, having worked with the American Indian Movement, and has served eighteen years as an NGO member at the United Nations Working Group of Indigenous Populations. He has published several volumes of poetry and two plays.

SITTING ALONE IN TULSA AT 3 A.M.

round dance of day has gone

a siren's scream splashes the blinds like ice
a fly sits frozen on a yellow plastic cup
the end tables huddle in pairs

sale at renbergs on ladies shoes
    felt squares and soft knits at the mill outlet

whatever I have done today has done without me

the edges of the city and the pale moon reflect
    in the same river

how easily we forget

Anniversary Poem for Cheyennes Who Died at Sand Creek

when we have come this long way
past cold grey fields
past the stone markers etched with the
names they left us

we will speak for the first time to the season
to the ponds

touching the dead grass

our voices the color of watching

 SUZAN SHOWN HARJO *(1945–), Southern Cheyenne* **and** *Hodulgee Muscogee,* served as Congressional liaison for Indian affairs in the administration of President Jimmy Carter and later served as executive director of the National Congress of American Indians. She is president of the Morning Star Institute and in 2014 received the Presidential Medal of Freedom, the United States' highest civilian honor.

The Song Called "White Antelope's Chant"

White Antelope had a song
    it was a Tsistsistas song
    it was his song
    because he sang it

Clouding Woman had a song
    it was a Tsistsistas song
    it was her song
    because she sang it

Buffalo Walla had a song
  it was a Tsistsistas song
  it was her song
  because she sang it

Bull Bear had a song
  it was a Tsistsistas song
  it was his song
  because he sang it

The Song that sang itself
  had a Tsistsistas sound
  and a truth for all who heard it
  at the hour of the end

The Song that sang itself
  had no language
  it was a heartbeat that thundered
  through the canyons of time

The Song that sang itself
  had no chorus
  its voice was the Morning Star
  and the rain at the edge of time

The Song that sang itself
  had no time
  knew no season
  it sounded with the power of the end

The Song sang a Tsistsistas Man
  in the prayers in the sun
  in the sighs on the wind
  in the power of the end

The Song sang a Tsistsistas Woman
      in the offerings at dawn
      in the sighs of the wind
      in the power of the end

The Song sang a Tsistsistas Child
      in the cries in the night
      in the sighs in the wind
      in the power of the end

The Song sang a Tsistsistas sound
      in the peace before dark
      in the sighs on the wind
      in the power of the end

Only Mother Earth endures
      sang the man

Only Mother Earth endures
      sang the woman

Only Mother Earth endures
      sang the child

Only Mother Earth endures
      sang the song

Only Mother Earth endures

JOHN TRUDELL *(1946–2015), Santee Dakota.* In 1969, Trudell became the spokesperson for the United Indians of All Tribes' nineteen-month takeover of Alcatraz, using his training in radio broadcasting to run Radio Free Alcatraz. After the occupation, Trudell joined the 1972 American Indian Movement (AIM) occupation of the Bureau of Indian Affairs office building in Washington, D.C.; he served as chairman of AIM from 1973 to 1979. In 1979, his pregnant wife, three children, and mother-in-law were all killed in a house fire on the Duck Valley Indian Reservation in Nevada. Only twelve hours earlier, he had been a part of a protest in Washington, D.C. Following the deaths of his family, Trudell stepped back from the front lines, turning to his writing and music. In 1986, Trudell released the album *A.K.A. Grafitti Man* with Kiowa guitarist Jesse Ed Davis. On its release, Bob Dylan called it "the album of the year."

DIABLO CANYON

Today I challenged the nukes
The soldiers of the state
Placed me in captivity
Or so they thought
They bound my wrists in their
Plastic handcuffs
Surrounding me with their
Plastic minds and faces
They ridiculed me
But I could see through
To the ridicule they brought
On themselves
They told me squat over there
By the trash
They left a soldier to guard me
I was the Vietcong
I was Crazy Horse

Little did they understand
Squatting down in the earth
They placed me with my power
My power to laugh
Laugh at their righteous wrong
Their sneers and their taunts
Gave me clarity
To see their powerlessness

It was in the way they dressed
And in the way they acted
They viewed me as an enemy
A threat to their rationalizations
I felt pity for them
Knowing they will never be free

I was their captive
But my heart was racing
Through the generations
The memories of eternity

It was beyond their reach
I would be brought to the
Internment camp
To share my time with allies

This time I almost wanted to believe you
When you spoke of peace and love and
Caring and duty and god and destiny
But somehow the death in your eyes and
Your bombs and your taxes and your
Greed and your face-life told me

This time I cannot afford to believe you

HENRY REAL BIRD (*1948–*), *Crow*, began writing in 1969 after an extended stay in a hospital. He raises bucking horses on Yellow Leggins Creek in Montana and still speaks Crow as his primary language. His collection *Horse Tracks* (2011) was named Poetry Book of the Year by the High Plains Book Awards. He was named Montana's poet laureate in 2009.

THOUGHT

"Thought is like a cloud
You can see through shadow to see nothing
But you can see shadow
When it touches something you know,
Like that cloud's shadow
Touching the Wolf Teeth Mountains.
When the clouds touch the mountain's top
Or where it is high
The wind is good
When you're among the clouds
Blurred ground among fog,
You are close to He Who First Did Everything,"
Said my Grandfather Owns Painted Horse.
We are but nomads asking for nothing
But the blessing upon our Mother Earth.
We are born as someone new
So then
We have to be taught
The good from the bad.
What is good, we want you to know.
What is good, we want you to use,
In the way that you are a person.

NILA NORTHSUN (1951–), *Shoshone* and *Anishinaabe,* was born in Shurz, Nevada. Her father, Adam Fortunate Eagle, was a Native activist and a prominent figure in the occupation of Alcatraz. She was raised in the Bay Area and attended California State University in Hayward and Humboldt, where she met her first husband, Kirk Robertson. Together, they collaborated on the literary magazine *Scree.* She completed her BA in art at the University of Montana-Missoula. She was awarded the Silver Pen Award from the University of Nevada Friends of the Library in 2000, and in 2004 she received ATAYAL's Indigenous Heritage Award for Literature. In addition to her writing, she works as a grant writer for the Reno-Sparks Indian Colony.

99 THINGS TO DO BEFORE YOU DIE

cosmo mag came out with a list
of 99 things to do before you die
        i had done 47 of them
or at least my version of them
like make love on the forest floor
spend a day in bed reading a good book
sleep under the stars
learn not to say yes when you mean no
but the other things
were things only rich people could do
and we certainly know
you don't have to be rich before you die
things like
dive off a yacht in the aegean
buy a round-the-world air ticket
go to monaco for the grand prix
go to rio during carnival
sure would love to but
no maza-ska
money honey

so what's a poor indian to do?
come up with a list that's more
culturally relevant
so my list includes
go 49ing at crow fair
learn of 20 ways to prepare
         commodity canned pork
fall in love with a white person
fall in love with an indian
eat ta-nee-ga with a sioux
learn to make good fry bread
be an extra in an indian movie
learn to speak your language
give your gramma a rose and a bundle
         of sweet grass
watch a miwok deer dance
attend a hopi kachina dance
owl dance with a yakama
curl up in bed with a good indian novel
better yet
curl up in bed with a good indian novelist
ride bareback and leap over a small creek
make love in a tipi
count coup on an enemy
bathe not swim in a lake or river
wash your hair too and don't forget your pits
stop drinking alcohol
tell skinwalker stories by campfire
almost die then appreciate your life
help somebody who has it worse than you
donate canned goods to a local food bank
sponsor a child for christmas
bet on a stick game
participate in a protest
learn a song to sing in a sweat
recycle
grow a garden

say something nice everyday to
        your mate
say something nice everyday to
        your children
chop wood for your grandpa
so there
a more attainable list
at this rate
i'm ready to die anytime
not much left undone
though cosmo's
have an affair in paris while
discoing in red leather and sipping champagne
could find a place on my list.

COOKING CLASS

when you've starved most of your life
when commodities
the metallic instant potatoes
the hold your nose canned pork
the pineapple juice that never dies
the i didn't soak them long enough pinto beans
the even the dog won't eat this potted meat
potted as in should have been buried
in a potter's field
when the wonderful commodity cheese
or terrible commodity cheese
that winos tuck 'neath their pits
and knock on your door
trying to sell it for $5
but taking $3
is all stored in the basement
or in closets

or left in the original boxes
lining hallways
of your hud house
cause there's just no more room
you wonder
how can anyone starve
with so much food
but there are other starvations
like developing the taste for
lard sandwiches
or mustard and commodity cheese sandwiches
just cut the mold off the crusts of bread
and boil the tomato juice until it's useable as
a spaghetti sauce
certainly don't use the tomato sauce for
your Sunday morning bloody mary
to accompany your blueberry blintzes
or smoked salmon quiche
unless
you have a major change in attitude
cause the dried egg product can quiche
with the flour
and powdered milk
and if you're a northwest coast tribe
salmon or sockeye or whatever fish
thing is possible
if not
some rich people pay good money
for the antelope or elk you can knock off
in your back yard
why bother with just goose liver pate
when you can have the whole damn canadian honker
blasted from its migratory path?
pheasants and quail are roadkill all the time
it's just tenderized
it's all in the attitude

and the presentation
parsley does wonders
for aesthetic contrast to
macaroni and cheese
again
and again
and again

 JOE DALE TATE NEVAQUAYA (1954–), *Yuchi* and *Comanche*, is a poet and a visual artist. His poetry collection, *Leaving Holes*, had won the first Native Writers' Circle of the Americas First Book Award for Poetry and was set to be published when the book's small press shut down. Nearly twenty years later, the book was finally published as *Leaving Holes and Selected New Writings* and won the 2012 Oklahoma Book Award for Poetry. Nevaquaya spent his childhood years in Bristow and Oklahoma City. He lives now in Norman, Oklahoma, where he is a resource teacher at the alternative school.

Poem for Sonya Thunder Bull

The imprint of birds' feet
scatter,
leaving the flecks
with which we muse the darkness.

It is only the wind
forgetting himself.

We remember.

LOUISE ERDRICH *(1954–), Anishinaabe–Turtle Mountain Band,* was born in Little Falls, Minnesota. She was the oldest of seven children, and two of her sisters are writers as well, including the poet Heid Erdrich. She earned her AB from Dartmouth College in 1976, a part of the first class of women admitted to the college. She earned her MA from Johns Hopkins University. Her first collection of poetry, *Jacklight,* was published in 1984, the same year that her novel *Love Medicine* won the National Book Critics Circle Award. The author of fifteen novels, she was a finalist for the Pulitzer Prize and winner of the Anisfield-Wolf Book Award and a National Book Award for Fiction, among numerous other awards. In addition to her novels, children's books, and short-story collections, she has published three critically acclaimed collections of poetry. She lives in Minnesota, where she owns Birchbark Books, an independent bookstore.

JACKLIGHT

> *The same Chippewa word is used both for flirting and hunting games, while another Chippewa word connotates both force in intercourse and also killing a bear with one's bare hands.*
> —R. W. DUNNING

We have come to the edge of the woods,
out of brown grass where we slept, unseen,
out of knotted twigs, out of leaves creaked shut,
out of hiding.

At first the light wavered, glancing over us.
Then it clenched to a fist of light that pointed,
searched out, divided us.
Each took the beams like direct blows the heart answers.
Each of us moved forward alone.

We have come to the edge of the woods,
drawn out of ourselves by this night sun,
this battery of polarized acid
that outshines the moon.

We smell them behind it,
but they are faceless, invisible.
We smell the raw steel of their gun barrels,
mink oil on leather, their tongues of sour barley.
We smell their mothers buried chin-deep in wet dirt.
We smell their fathers with scoured knuckles,
teeth cracked from hot marrow.
We smell their sisters of crushed dogwood, bruised apples,
of fractured cups and concussions of burnt hooks.

We smell their breath steaming lightly behind
the jacklight. We smell the itch underneath the caked guts
on their clothes. We smell their minds like
silver hammers cocked back, held in readiness
for the first of us to step into the open.

We have come to the edge of the woods,
out of brown grass where we slept, unseen,
out of leaves creaked shut, out of hiding.
We have come here too long.

It is their turn now,
their turn to follow us. Listen,
they put down their equipment.
It is useless in the tall brush,
and now they take their first steps, not knowing
how deep the woods are and lightless.
How deep the woods are.

I Was Sleeping Where the Black Oaks Move

We watched from the house
as the river grew, helpless
and terrible in its unfamiliar body.
Wrestling everything into it,
the water wrapped around trees
until their life-hold was broken.
They went down, one by one,
and the river dragged off their covering.

Nests of the herons, roots washed to bones,
snags of soaked bark on the shoreline:
a whole forest pulled through the teeth
of the spillway. Trees surfacing
singly, where the river poured off
into arteries for fields below the reservation.

When at last it was over, the long removal,
they had all become the same dry wood.
We walked among them, the branches
whitening in the raw sun.
Above us drifted herons,
alone, hoarse-voiced, broken,
settling their beaks among the hollows.
Grandpa said, *These are the ghosts of the tree people
moving among us, unable to take their rest.*

Sometimes now, we dream our way back to the heron dance.
Their long wings are bending the air
into circles through which they fall.
They rise again in shifting wheels.
How long must we live in the broken figures
their necks make, narrowing the sky.

Advice to Myself

Leave the dishes.
Let the celery rot in the bottom drawer of the refrigerator
and an earthen scum harden on the kitchen floor.
Leave the black crumbs in the bottom of the toaster.
Throw the cracked bowl out and don't patch the cup.
Don't patch anything. Don't mend. Buy safety pins.
Don't even sew on a button.
Let the wind have its way, then the earth
that invades as dust and then the dead
foaming up in gray rolls underneath the couch.
Talk to them. Tell them they are welcome.
Don't keep all the pieces of the puzzles
or the doll's tiny shoes in pairs, don't worry
who uses whose toothbrush or if anything
matches, at all.
Except one word to another. Or a thought.
Pursue the authentic—decide first
what is authentic,
then go after it with all your heart.
Your heart, that place
you don't even think of cleaning out.
That closet stuffed with savage mementos.
Don't sort the paper clips from screws from saved baby teeth
or worry if we're all eating cereal for dinner
again. Don't answer the telephone, ever,
or weep over anything at all that breaks.
Pink molds will grow within those sealed cartons
in the refrigerator. Accept new forms of life
and talk to the dead
who drift in through the screened windows, who collect
patiently on the tops of food jars and books.
Recycle the mail, don't read it, don't read anything

except what destroys
the insulation between yourself and your experience
or what pulls down or what strikes at or what shatters
this ruse you call necessity.

 GWEN NELL WESTERMAN *(1957–), Dakota and Cherokee,* received her BA and MA at Oklahoma State University and her PhD in English from the University of Kansas. She teaches American Literature and American Indian Literature at Minnesota State University, Mankato. She is the director of the Native American Literature Symposium, a Native American Studies conference founded in 2001. She has won awards for her research on Dakota history and language. Her collection of poems, *Follow the Blackbirds*, written in Dakota and English, was published in 2013.

Wicaṅĥpi Heciya Taṅhaṇ Uṅhipi

(We Come from the Stars)

Stellar nucleosynthesis.
That explains
where everything

in our universe

came from according to astrophysicists who
only recently discovered the cosmological constant causing
the expansion

of our universe.

Our creation story tells us we came from the stars to this place Bdote
where the Minnesota and Mississippi rivers converge,
our journey along the Wanaġi Caṇku,

in our universe,

that stargazers later called the Milky Way now disappearing
in the excessive glow of a million million urban uplights.
The original inhabitants of this place,

of our universe,

we are Wicaŋȟpi Oyate, *Star* People
and will remain here as long as
we can see ourselves

in the stars.

 MARK TURCOTTE (1958–), *Anishinaabe–Turtle Mountain
Band,* grew up in North Dakota on the Turtle Mountain Reserva-
tion and later in Lansing, Michigan. Turcotte won the first Gwen-
dolyn Brooks Open Mic Award, and the Wisconsin Arts Board named him a
literary fellow in 1999 and 2003. He has published four books of poetry, and
his work has appeared in several anthologies. He lives and works in Chicago.

BURN

Back when I used to be Indian
I am crushing the dance floor,
jump-boots thumping Johnny Rotten,
Johnny Rotten. Red lights blue bang
at my eyes. The white girl watching
does not know why and it doesn't matter.
I spin spin, eat I don't care for breakfast,
so what for lunch. She moves to me,
dark gaze, tongue hot to lips. The music
is hard, lights louder. She slides low

against my hip to hiss, *go go Geronimo.*
I stop.
All silence he sits beside the fire
at the center of the floor, hands stirring
through the ashes, mouth moving in the shape
of my name. I turn to reach toward him,
take one step, feel my skin begin
to flame away.

BATTLEFIELD

Back when I used to be Indian
I am standing outside the
pool hall with my sister.
She strawberry blonde. Stale sweat
and beer through the
open door. A warrior leans on his stick,
fingers blue with chalk.
Another bends to shoot.
His braids brush the green
felt, swinging to the beat
of the jukebox. We move away.
Hank Williams falls again
in the backseat of a Cadillac.
I look back.
A wind off the distant hills lifts my shirt,
brings the scent
of wounded horses.

ELISE PASCHEN (*1959–*), *Osage,* was born and raised in Chicago. While an undergraduate at Harvard University, she won the Garrison Medal for poetry. She earned her M.Phil and D.Phil from Oxford University, studying twentieth-century British and American literature. While at Oxford, she cofounded the journal *Oxford Poetry.* Her 1996 collection *Infidelities* won the Nicholas Roerich Poetry Prize. She is also the author of *Houses; Coasts; Bestiary*; and most recently, *The Nightlife*. The daughter of the Osage prima ballerina Maria Tallchief, she lives in Chicago, where she teaches in the MFA writing program at the School of the Art Institute of Chicago.

WI'-GI-E

Anna Kyle Brown. Osage.
1896–1921. Fairfax, Oklahoma.

Because she died where the ravine falls into water.

Because they dragged her down to the creek.

In death, she wore her blue broadcloth skirt.

Though frost blanketed the grass she cooled her feet in the spring.

Because I turned the log with my foot.

Her slippers floated downstream into the dam.

Because, after the thaw, the hunters discovered her body.

Because she lived without our mother.

Because she had inherited head rights for oil beneath the land.

She was carrying his offspring.

The sheriff disguised her death as whiskey poisoning.

Because, when he carved her body up, he saw the bullet hole in her skull.

Because, when she was murdered, the *leg clutchers* bloomed.

But then froze under the weight of frost.

During *Xtha-cka Zhi-ga Tze-the, the Killer of the Flowers Moon.*

I will wade across the river of the blackfish, the otter, the beaver.

I will climb the bank where the willow never dies.

HIGH GROUND

Across the meadow flecks
of elk congregate into the dark.

Their hooves mark the soaked hillock
rimming the pond. A garter

snake zags, silvery as lightning.
Through scrub brush a shade ripples,

crosses ancient earth mounds
where, during the *Bear Dance,* sage sprigs

once topped every stone altar.
A meteor plunges fast

as Great Horned Owl swerves
across rooftop at sun-fall.

Along the ridge a coyote yowls,
echoes by others from all corners.

The song chills the dead, wakes the living.

HEID E. ERDRICH *(1963–), Anishinaabe–Turtle Mountain Band,* earned degrees at Dartmouth College and Johns Hopkins University, and she holds an interdisciplinary doctorate. Her sister, Louise Erdrich, is also a writer. Heid is the author of seven collections of poetry. Her writing has won fellowships and awards from the National Poetry Series, Native Arts and Cultures Foundation, and Loft Literary Center, and she has twice won a Minnesota Book Award for poetry. She edited the 2018 anthology *New Poets of Native Nations* from Graywolf Press. Her poetry collection *Little Big Bully* is forthcoming from Penguin in fall of 2020. Heid grew up in Wahpeton, North Dakota.

Pre-Occupied

River   river   river
I never never never
etched your spiral icon in limestone
or   for that matter   pitched a tent on cement
near your banks

Banks of marble   stock still   all movement in the plaza
river walking its message on an avenue
rallied in bitter wind

Excuse my digression my mind tends . . .

In reality   my screen is lit with invitations
bake a casserole—send pizza—make soup for the 99%

Sorry   somehow I haven't time

Flow   flow   flow both ways in time
There's a river to consider after all

No time   no hours   no decades   no millennia.
No   I cannot dump cans of creamed corn
and turkey on noodles and offer forth
sustenance again

A bit pre-occupied, we original 100%
who are also 1%, more or less
Simply distracted by sulfide emissions   tar sands   pipelines   foster
care   polar bears   hydro-fracking   and the playlist deeply intoning
Superman never made any money . . .

River   river   river   Our river
Map of the Milky Way
reflection of stars
whence all life commenced

100% of all life on our planet

River in the middle   Mississippi
not the East Coast Hudson where this all started
waterway Max Fleischer's team lushly rendered
via the wonder of Technicolor

Emerging from an underwater lair
a Mad Scientist we comprehend as indigenous
has lost his signifiers (no braids, no blanket)
but we recognize him
A snappy dresser who flashes a maniac grin
he is not   *not*   your TV Indian

Ignoble Savage " . . . and I still say Manhattan
rightfully belongs to my people"
Superman "Possibly   but just what
do you expect us to do about it?"

Occupy   Occupy   Worked for the 99
Occupy   Re-occupy   Alcatraz and Wounded Knee

Sorry   somehow now I've too much time
Flow   flow   flow both ways   story-history-story
There's a river that considers us after all

All time   all hours   all decades   all millennia

River   river   river
I never   never   never—but that is not to say that I won't ever

/// **NOTES OF PRE-OCCUPIED DIGRESSION:** *Descendants of the indigenous population of the US remain just a tad less than 1% of the population according to the 2010 census. If you add Native Hawaiians to the total we are 1.1% of the population. So, we are, more or less, the original 1% as well as the original 100%. As the Occupy Movement took hold, indigenous groups continued struggles to protect our homelands from imminent threats such as the tar sands in Canada and its Keystone pipeline, copper mining in Minnesota and Wisconsin, and hydro-fracking elsewhere—everywhere, it seems. This era of alternative energy has become the new land grab, the new water grab. Indigenous activists are thoroughly pre-occupied with the social and environmental issues I mention and more. Activists can't be everywhere at once—not like Superman. I refer here, of course, to the Crash Test Dummies' 1991 "Superman's Song," that despairs the world will never see altruism like that of the unpaid hero. In the 1942 cartoon* Electric Earthquake, *an indigenous (but not stereotypically "Indian") Mad Scientist is thwarted, of course, by Superman. At one point Clark Kent admits indigenous land claim as "possibly" valid, but says there's nothing the* Daily Planet *can do about it. A shrewd Tesla wanna-be, our villain attempts to publish his demands first, then occupies Lois Lane while toppling Manhattan skyscrapers. You can see this beauty all over the Internets.*

Offering: First Rice

for Jim Northrup

The grains should be green as river rocks,
long as hayseed, with the scent of duckweed
and sweetgrass that grows along the lake's banks.
First *manoomin*, feast plate laid for the spirits—
berries and tobacco offered with song.
What it must have meant to give
what little the people had to give:
herbs left in thanks for the food that will sustain us,
for the water that gives up that food,
for the world working the way it should
—living and full of living god.

The Theft Outright

after Frost

We were the land's before we were.

Or the land was ours before you were a land.
Or this land was our land, it was not your land.

We were the land before we were people,
loamy roamers rising, so the stories go,
or formed of clay, spit into with breath reeking soul—

What's America, but the legend of Rock 'n' Roll?

Red rocks, blood clots bearing boys, blood sands
swimming being from women's hands, we originate,
originally, spontaneous as hemorrhage.

Un-possessing of what we still are possessed by,
possessed by what we now no more possess.

We were the land before we were people,
dreamy sunbeams where sun don't shine, so the stories go,
or pulled up a hole, clawing past ants and roots—

Dineh in documentaries scoff DNA evidence off.
They landed late, but canyons spoke them home.
Nomadic Turkish horse tribes they don't know.

What's America, but the legend of Stop 'n' Go?

Could be cousins, left on the land bridge,
contrary to popular belief, that was a two-way toll.
In any case we'd claim them, give them someplace to stay.

Such as we were we gave most things outright
(the deed of the theft was many deeds and leases and claim stakes
and tenure disputes and moved plat markers stolen still today . . .)

We were the land before we were a people,
earthdivers, her darling mudpuppies, so the stories go,
or emerging, fully forming from flesh of earth—

The land, not the least vaguely, realizing in all four directions,
still storied, art-filled, fully enhanced.
Such as she is, such as she wills us to become.

TIFFANY MIDGE (1965–), *Standing Rock Sioux,* grew up in the Pacific Northwest and lives in Idaho. She received her MFA from the University of Idaho. Her poetry collection *Outlaws, Renegades and Saints: Diary of a Mixed-Up Halfbreed* won the Diane Decorah Memorial Poetry Award from the Native Writers' Circle of the Americas, and her collection *The Woman Who Married a Bear* won the Kenyon Review Earthworks Prize for Indigenous Poetry. Her most recent book is a collection of comic essays, *Bury My Heart at Chuck E. Cheese's.*

TEETH IN THE WRONG PLACES

Coyote was ripe for adventure and wanted to visit the evil old woman he'd been warned about; she lived with her two wicked daughters and those who had slept with the handsome girls were never seen again.

—Ponca story

Sister—

Coyote's just like any man,
hungry for the dark loaves
of a woman's thighs.

You peel the skin of the tongue;
they complain it's burnt, add Tabasco.
You boil the last of the turnips;
they whine, it goes down like gall stones.

Beauty's just a bite
away from want.
I've seen fox chew
off her own limb
for just one more taste
of freedom. Mother set
the trap lines near beavers'

dens—hauled in more
than she could skin.
They moved farther
upriver next spring.

What west wind blew
those men into our house?
Who ransacked the curio
shelf, the burlap quilt and button jar?
Whose boots are these tracking
swamp rot through the kitchen?
Where's yesterday's bread
and which dolt didn't cover the butter?

Tomorrow, I'm fixing to kill
the angel of this house.

These men that come through here—
shooting lead slugs through my green
bottles; water logging a season of straw;
taking liberties with my good hen.

Remember that one, those moons back,
who stepped out of the beets like a jackrabbit,
and ornery as a circle saw; that other, eyes
a sweet blue, but disposition salty as piss
and vinegar in the noon-day sun.

I say, Coyote's same as any man.

Sister—
desire's fixed to cut a tooth.
Sister—
I'm set to start grinding.

If he's still here come morning,
lay out the linen and splash

on the toilet water; put the beans
on to soak, and bring up the choke-
cherries. Lend your voice

to some pretty hymn, occupy his ears
so he's not to hear that clackety-clack
racket; that awful gnashing of teeth
going on *down there*; should he ask,
say how bitter an autumn we've had,
wouldn't he like to keep you warm?
Then fasten your eye to his fly,
give his nether-regions a good scratch,
fall open to the place where the moon rides up—
north of the trap line, in a thicket of hairy frost.

Sister—
desire's fixed to cut a tooth.
Sister—
get set to start grinding.

Night Caller

The mollusk inching toward my door,
        its body a broad wet muscle of rain and ascent,
reminds me how all things are possible,
        just as the rain foretells certainty

in a language of unquestionable voice.
        I hear the night break, the moon
toss back her hair. I hear the hum
        of contentment shuddering in the grass.

The mollusk seeks direction, drinks
        in the door's pool of light, charts
a course for warmth, its horns
        pivots of radar, exclamation points,

exquisite attachments puzzling out the smell
      of water and storms. In the last twenty-four hours
there've been slews of visitors to this porch:
      half-drowned spiders, stinkbugs, furious horseflies.

We've discarded them tenderly, others
      mercifully tended and killed, unnamed shadows,
unmarked graves, wings and songs put to rest,
      lunacies of want laid down. You turn in sleep,

then wake and tell me about tropical weddings
      and masked brides, guests who speak only
the warbled tongue of sparrows, and fall back again
      dreaming your night stories, hosting the night visits—

each with its own small creature,
      each with its own grand light.

 LAYLI LONG SOLDIER (1973–), *Oglala Lakota,* received her BFA from the Institute of American Indian Arts in Santa Fe and her MFA with honors from Bard College. She published her chapbook, *Chromosomory,* in 2010, and her 2017 collection, *Whereas,* won the National Book Critics Circle Award and the PEN/Jean Stein Book Award and was a finalist for the National Book Award. In 2015, she was awarded a National Artist Fellowship from the Native Arts and Cultures Foundation, and a Lannan Literary Fellowship for Poetry. Long Soldier is also an installation artist.

38

Here, the sentence will be respected.

I will compose each sentence with care by minding what the rules of writing dictate.

For example, all sentences will begin with capital letters.

Likewise, the history of the sentence will be honored by ending each one with appropriate punctuation such as a period or question mark, thus bringing the idea to (momentary) completion.

You may like to know, I do not consider this a "creative piece."

I do not regard this as a poem of great imagination or a work of fiction.

Also, historical events will not be dramatized for an interesting read.

Therefore, I feel most responsible to the orderly sentence; conveyor of thought.

That said, I will begin.

You may or may not have heard about the Dakota 38.

If this is the first time you've heard of it, you might wonder, "What is the Dakota 38?"

The Dakota 38 refers to thirty-eight Dakota men who were executed by hanging, under orders from President Abraham Lincoln.

To date, this is the largest "legal" mass execution in U.S. history.

The hanging took place on December 26th, 1862—the day after Christmas.

This was the *same week* that President Lincoln signed The Emancipation Proclamation.

In the preceding sentence, I italicize "same week" for emphasis.

There was a movie titled *Lincoln* about the presidency of Abraham Lincoln.

The signing of The Emancipation Proclamation was included in the film *Lincoln*; the hanging of the Dakota 38 was not.

In any case, you might be asking, "Why were thirty-eight Dakota men hung?"

As a side note, the past tense of hang is *hung*, but when referring to the capital punishment of hanging, the correct tense is *hanged*.

So it's possible that you're asking, "Why were thirty-eight Dakota men hanged?"

They were hanged for *The Sioux Uprising*.

I want to tell you about The Sioux Uprising, but I don't know where to begin.

I may jump around and details will not unfold in chronological order.

Keep in mind, I am not a historian.

So I will recount facts as best as I can, given limited resources and understanding.

Before Minnesota was a state, the Minnesota region, generally speaking, was the traditional homeland for Dakota, Anishinaabeg and Ho-Chunk people.

During the 1800s, when the U.S. expanded territory, they "purchased" land from the Dakota people as well as the other tribes.

But another way to understand that sort of "purchase" is: Dakota leaders ceded land to the U.S. Government in exchange for money and goods, but most importantly, the safety of their people.

Some say that Dakota leaders did not understand the terms they were entering, or they never would have agreed.

Even others call the entire negotiation, "trickery."

But to make whatever-it-was official and binding, the U.S. Government drew up an initial treaty.

This treaty was later replaced by another (more convenient) treaty, and then another.

I've had difficulty unraveling the terms of these treaties, given the legal speak and congressional language.

As treaties were abrogated (broken) and new treaties were drafted, one after another, the new treaties often referenced old defunct treaties and it is a muddy, switchback trail to follow.

Although I often feel lost on this trail, I know I am not alone.

However, as best as I can put the facts together, in 1851, Dakota territory was contained to a twelve-mile by one-hundred-fifty-mile-long strip along the Minnesota river.

But just seven years later, in 1858, the northern portion was ceded (taken) and the southern portion was (conveniently) allotted, which reduced Dakota land to a stark ten-mile tract.

These amended and broken treaties are often referred to as The Minnesota Treaties.

The word *Minnesota* comes from *mni* which means water; *sota* which means turbid.

Synonyms for turbid include muddy, unclear, cloudy, confused and smoky.

Everything is in the language we use.

For example, a treaty is, essentially, a contract between two sovereign nations.

The U.S. treaties with the Dakota Nation were legal contracts that promised money.

It could be said, this money was payment for the land the Dakota ceded; for living within assigned boundaries (a reservation); and for relinquishing rights to their vast hunting territory which, in turn, made Dakota people dependent on other means to survive: money.

The previous sentence is circular, which is akin to so many aspects of history.

As you may have guessed by now, the money promised in the turbid treaties did not make it into the hands of Dakota people.

In addition, local government traders would not offer credit to "Indians" to purchase food or goods.

Without money, store credit or rights to hunt beyond their ten-mile tract of land, Dakota people began to starve.

The Dakota people were starving.

The Dakota people starved.

In the preceding sentence, the word "starved" does not need italics for emphasis.

One should read, "The Dakota people starved," as a straightforward and plainly stated fact.

As a result—and without other options but to continue to starve—Dakota people retaliated.

Dakota warriors organized, struck out and killed settlers and traders.

This revolt is called *The Sioux Uprising*.

Eventually, the U.S. Cavalry came to Mnisota to confront the Uprising.

More than one thousand Dakota people were sent to prison.

As already mentioned, thirty-eight Dakota men were subsequently hanged.

After the hanging, those one thousand Dakota prisoners were released.

However, as further consequence, what remained of Dakota territory in Mnisota was dissolved (stolen).

The Dakota people had no land to return to.

This means they were exiled.

Homeless, the Dakota people of Mnisota were relocated (forced) onto reservations in South Dakota and Nebraska.

Now, every year, a group called The Dakota 38 + 2 Riders conduct a memorial horse ride from Lower Brule, South Dakota to Mankato, Mnisota.

The Memorial Riders travel 325 miles on horseback for eighteen days, sometimes through sub-zero blizzards.

They conclude their journey on December 26th, the day of the hanging.

Memorials help focus our memory on particular people or events.

Often, memorials come in the forms of plaques, statues or gravestones.

The memorial for the Dakota 38 is not an object inscribed with words, but an *act*.

Yet, I started this piece because I was interested in writing about grasses.

So, there is one other event to include, although it's not in chronological order and we must backtrack a little.

When the Dakota people were starving, as you may remember, government traders would not extend store credit to "Indians."

One trader named Andrew Myrick is famous for his refusal to provide credit to Dakotas by saying, "If they are hungry, let them eat grass."

There are variations of Myrick's words, but they are all something to that effect.

When settlers and traders were killed during the Sioux Uprising, one of the first to be executed by the Dakota was Andrew Myrick.

When Myrick's body was found,

his mouth was stuffed with grass.

I am inclined to call this act by the Dakota warriors a poem.

There's irony in their poem.

There was no text.

"Real" poems do not "really" require words.

I have italicized the previous sentence to indicate inner dialogue, a revealing moment.

But, on second thought, the particular words "Let them eat grass" click the gears of the poem into place.

So, we could also say, language and word choice are crucial to the poem's work.

Things are circling back again.

Sometimes, when in a circle, if I wish to exit, I must leap.

And let the body   swing.

From the platform.

                                        Out

                                                    to the grasses.

DILATE

                                I.

            Placed

on my chest   warm fragile

as the skin of nightfall she was   heavier than imagined   her eyes

untied from northern poles from   hard unseen   winter months

she arrived safely   mid-spring she   scrunched her brow an up-look   to her father. There's a turning   as pupils dilate

as black vernal suns slip   into equinox. This was

we never forget her

first act.

II.

All is experienced

throu

g

h

the

body

somebody told me.

III.

Though I did not feel it

when the midwife invited   when he cut   the tie

the clean   umbilical sever when   I smiled I did   not feel it

as they took her   to wash and weigh   when I said   *you should go with her.*

Both of them gone   father and baby

in a supple empty   orange light   I listened from behind   a clock on
    the wall

  my own face   heavy plate glass   though all experience

is ~~through~~ the body   I did not feel

  my hands pull   white sheets my legs shake when   two nurses cooed

    lean back   *honey you are*   *bleeding more than expected.*

SY HOAHWAH (1973–), *Yapaituka Comanche* and *Southern Arapaho,* received an NEA Literature Fellowship in 2013. He received his MFA from the University of Arkansas. He published the poetry collection *Velroy and the Madischie Mafia* in 2009 and the chapbook *Night Cradle* in 2011.

FAMILY TREE OR COMANCHES AND CARS DON'T MIX

Spanish captive, Hoahwah, married twin sisters.
The one wife called Double
turned into a snake
after eating a nest of glossy eggs.
Snake Woman still lives on Mt. Scott,
sleeps facing west.
The sun a white skull itself
bathes her on the cedar breaks.
In rectangular dreams
she calls the young men *grandson.*

The other sister Tsi-yee, named after a war deed
(her father charged a cavalry officer
knocked him off his horse then lanced him to the prairie)
bore three children: Tabe titah, Namnetse, and Sam Hoahwah.

Lena, Sam Hoahwah's favorite daughter
ran off with an Arapaho from Canton.
Sam sent his men after her
on horseback, their ranch-hand-shadows
overcast the Cheyenne and Arapaho Rez.
Lena said: I ain't comin back.
She bled to death on a mattress after a miscarriage.

Mother couldn't remember Lena
just the car ride to Post Oak Cemetery
and watching wind in the pinwheels.
Mother died the same age, fish-tailing
into Comanche history
in a Chevy Z-28 without car insurance.

Great grandfather Sam Hoahwah
first Indian in southwest Oklahoma to own a car
got run over with his own Model-T.
His Mexican cowboy-chauffeur
forgot to take it out of gear
when Sam crank-started the car.

Not far from his own car, Uncle Fredrick
was found dead in the weeds of Cache Road,
keys missing.
He sang gospels in Comanche,
and backup on Robbie Robertson's
Contact from the Underworld of RedBoy.
(Uncle liked Levon Helm better.)

Frederick Jr. caught ghost sickness
bicycling across Post Oak Cemetery at night.

He looked past his shoulder
it twisted his face.
The moon mocks him now.

After the incident, his girlfriend fell
in love with his cousin Rusty
nicknamed Rabbit
who loves fried baloney
and calls it Indian Steak.

Rabbit's younger brother
paints abstract horse murals
in empty swimming pools,

and images of a 20 foot long red talking snake
who calls him grandson in his dreams.

TYPHONI

This is the deepest part of the world.

Bird don't fly here,
but there is the sound of wings.

The smell, just a struggle in the earth
underneath the musty floorboards.

Monsters hatch fully-grown from their eggs.
Snaky legs indicate chaos.

I carry sad omens,

slobber down the psychic's legs
to her feet pointed backwards.

I roll off the back of a skull strapped on top
of a fox who shape-shifts into the irresistible.

A Christian, Oklahoma-shaped and melancholic,
caught at the entrance of a ditch

as the best breath of me tornadoes into the next county.

M. L. SMOKER (1975–), *Assiniboine and Sioux,* received her BA
from Pepperdine University and her MFA from the University of
Montana, where she received the Richard Hugo Memorial Schol-
arship. She also attended UCLA and was a Battrick Fellow at the Univer-
sity of Colorado. Hanging Loose Press published her first collection, *Another
Attempt at Rescue,* in 2005. In 2009, she coedited a collection of human rights
poetry, *I Go to the Ruined Place,* with Melissa Kwasny. She lives in Helena,
Montana, where she works in the Indian Education division of the Office of
Public Instruction. Her family home is on Tabexa Wakpa (Frog Creek).

CROSSCURRENT

For James Welch

The first harvest of wheat in flatlands
along the Milk startled me into thoughts of you
and this place we both remember and also forget as home.
Maybe it was the familiarity or maybe it was my own
need to ask if you have ever regretted leaving.
What bends, what gives?
And have you ever missed this wind?—it has now
grown warm with late summer, but soon
it will be as dangerous as the bobcat stalking calves
and pets just south of the river.

Men take out their dogs, a case of beer and wait
in their pickups for dawn, for a chance with their rifles.
They don't understand that she isn't going to make
any mistakes. With winter my need for an answer
grows more desperate and there are only four roads out.
One is the same cat hunters drive with mannish glory
and return along, gun still oil-shined and unshot.
Another goes deeper into Assiniboine territory:
This is the one I should talk myself into taking next.
I haven't much traveled the third except to visit
a hospital where, after the first time,
my mother had refused chemotherapy.
And the last road you know as well as I do—
past the coral-painted Catholic church, its doors
long ago sealed shut to the mouth of Mission Canyon,
then south just a ways, to where the Rockies cut open
and forgive. There you and I are on the ascent.
After that, the arrival is what matters most.

CASUALTIES

> *. . . linguistic diversity also forms a system necessary to our survival as human beings.*
>
> —MICHAEL KRAUSS

The sun has broken through.
Breaking through,
this sun—but still
today my words   are dying out.

Still as I tell of   stillness
of a very word
as (   )   as it leaves this world.

*My grandmother was told that the only way to survive was
     to forget.*

Where   were you?
        Where were
you? Speaking of myself
for   my own neglect: too often
I was nowhere to be found.
            I will not lie.
                I heard the ruin in each Assiniboine voice.
I ignored them
all. On

        the vanishing, I have been
mute. I have risked
a great deal.
Hold   me   accountable
because I have not done my part
        to stay alive.

As a child I did not hear the words often enough to recognize
what I was losing.
        There are a great many parts of my own
body that are gone:

where hands
belong there is   one lost syllable.
And how a tooth might sound—
its absence
        a falling.

Sound   is so frail a thing.
(   )   hold me responsible,
in light   of failure
        I have let go   of one too many.

I have never known where or how
        to begin.

TREVINO L. BRINGS PLENTY *(1976–)*, *Minneconjou Lakota,* was born and raised on the Cheyenne River Sioux Reservation in South Dakota and now lives and works in Portland, Oregon. His books include *Wakpá Wanáǧi, Ghost River* (2015) and *Real Indian Junk Jewelry* (2012), and his poetry is included in *Shedding Skins: Four Sioux Poets* (2008), edited by Adrian C. Louis.

GHOST RIVER

I'm mostly water.
There has been family swept under by raw currents.

I'm from planters from the river.
We dredged riverbed bones.

Water is faces lined blue.
Red horses bay bodies hooked from fish line.

And what was sown, brown hands dug free.
I'm mostly other people.

Family is pulled pail full from source.
I'm from river people.

We prep the light from matted hair.
Water catches flame.

The black horses hoof rock, halving them like thin, infant skulls.
And what was sown, brown hands dug free.

Blizzard, South Dakota

Months afterwards, I see the electrical poles
piled along the road.

When the blizzard smothered the land,
my tribe was displaced.
Like shot gun blasts heard in the distance,
those poles snapped,
weighted by ice.

A month in motels,
we ate fast food,
while the winter deer meat
expired in the basement.

Movie stars flocked to Haiti.
We watched the news,
wondered about us,
about our reservation,
about our home.

Those dialysis machines failed
without electricity,
pushed people farther away,
closer to the spirit world.

I still hear those poles
ricochet at these wakes.

HEATHER CAHOON (1976–), *Confederated Salish and Koo-
tenai Tribes,* received her MFA from the University of Montana
in 2001, where she was a Richard Hugo Scholar. She went on to
earn an interdisciplinary PhD in history, anthropology, and Native Amer-
ican studies. Her chapbook *Elk Thirst* received a Merriam-Frontier Award

from the University of Montana's College of Humanities and Sciences in 2005, and in 2015, she received a Montana Arts Council Artist's Innovation Award. She is the author of the poetry collection *Horsefly Dress* and works as a state-tribal policy analyst for the Montana Budget and Policy Center and lives in Missoula.

BLONDE

It is November and the sun has gone south almost
as far as it can. Cold air flies wildly through the sky,
the bare and frantic reaches of trees, and through
the dying grasses on Camas Prairie. This wind
knows me by the color of my hair, a light in darkness.

It is November and I can see my soul
slowly leaving my body every time I exhale.

Dad and I take the shortcut across Camas Prairie
to Dog Lake. He is telling me stories
of children with black hair and brown eyes.
My reflection in the side mirror tells me
what I already know. He talks
of these children until I am left standing
in the icy wind watching as he drives away.

It is November and the dying grasses on the prairie
are the same color as my hair. If I wanted I could
lie down in them and disappear, I could escape
the angry wind. But I don't, I know the land and I
would blend together into one and then no one
would ever know I had existed. So I stand.

TANAYA WINDER (1985–), *Duckwater Shoshone, Southern
Ute,* and *Pyramid Lake Paiute,* grew up in Ignacio, Colorado, on
the Southern Ute Reservation. She received her BA in English from
Stanford University and her MFA from the University of New Mexico. Her
debut poetry collection, *Words Like Love,* was published in 2015, followed by
Why Storms Are Named After People and Bullets Remain Nameless in 2017.
She cofounded *As/Us: A Space for Women of the World,* a magazine focused
on publishing works by underrepresented writers, and she founded Dream
Warriors, an Indigenous artist management company. She has taught at the
University of Colorado Boulder, Stanford University, and the University of
New Mexico, and is the director of the University of Colorado Boulder's
Upward Bound program.

LEARNING TO SAY *I LOVE YOU*

my favorite conversations are with my grandmother while she
teaches me words in "Indian" as she says. I ask,

how do you say, *where did you go?* and *where are you going?*
Questions that layer my tongue in ash, reminding me of fire,

the taste. Each time I speak, the slow burn of every loss I have
witnessed cracks my lips. Go and going—acts singed

into my bones so I ask. Teach me *I'm coming with you* so it sits
rock heavy in my mouth because my tongue is at war

with history, boarding school "Kill the Indian, Save the Man"
acts of colonization. Strain pronunciation. When I want to say,

take me with you   it **dis**   so   l   v   e   s

before I can stomach the sweetness of language. Ours,
I am losing. I am lost lodged somewhere in my throat

between decades of **bro ken syl la bles.** Teach me
how to reach the ones who are born already running.

Teach me how to talk to the ones who need it most.
Dear Universe, gift me words

that   l   i   n   g   e   r

softly like dusk. There must be a phrase
to contain wherever you go

whether or not you know where you've been
or where you are going.

THE MILKY WAY ESCAPES MY MOUTH

whenever two lips begin to form your name
I cough stars lodged deep within my lungs. They rush
       from tongue weighted in dust, words
               I didn't ask

where are you going? or notice the blank spaces
in your breathing as you slept. They say
       the more massive the star, the shorter
              the lifespan.

They have greater pressure on their cores. Yours burned
so brightly I should have known you'd collapse, disappear
       into image, a black hole dissolving
             trace amounts.

I am left stargazing five times a day for years. Catalogue
phrases. Chart each word. Label every facial expression.
       Telescope until eyes bleed constellations
            even then

I can't navigate my way into understanding light years—
how we let darkness slip in. Is it madness to wonder
          if it ever really happened? You, a shadow never
                    leaving until I

inserted continents between us. *I lost you* in the crevice
between night and day. You died while I was sleeping
          dreaming of a galaxy far far away where
                    love eclipses.

A rising tide of longing fills my body, bones, the ribs
sheltering the cave within me echoing. Each night,
          I open mouth sky-wide to swallow stars
                    and sing

to the moon a story about the light of two people
who continue to cross and uncross in their falling
          no matter how unstable
                    in orbit.

PACIFIC NORTHWEST, ALASKA, AND PACIFIC ISLANDS

Poetry of the Pacific Northwest: The Arc of the Edifice

Cedar Sigo

Native people of the Northwest had no choice but to live in relation to poetry from the very outset of creation. We had to learn to identify and convert the individual elements of earth into forms of protection and sustenance, a so-called lifestyle. This would involve courtship, and gathering of every necessary berry, moss, bark, and wood. I remember stories of Suquamish women leaving for several days on summer journeys over the Cascade Mountains into eastern Washington to gather luminous bear grass, those pieces that would sometimes tell stories along the outer surface of our baskets.

This draping of my history within the landscape has become an available arc that we tap into at will. Michael Wasson's "Poem for the háawtnin' & héwlekipx" [*The Holy Ghost of You, the Space & Thin Air*] is driven by a similar recognition as well as a willingness to reveal aspects of composition within the poem itself:

> I imagine
> smudging my tongue along a wall
> > > like the chest

> I dare to plunge in-
> > to, the Braille of every node

> blooming out
> > as if the first day-

> light of wintered
> > snowfall.

The surfaces gained in Wasson's poem are intensely reflective, throwing light at every break in the line. The poem forms an enclosure around its reader; nothing so simple as a hall of mirrors, this feels more like an alchemical bath. The poet is being reborn and seemingly splintered back into the natural world.

Gloria Bird is another master of the lyric, often leaving a secret door (or mirror) in the turn of her lines, hinting at another arc the poem might have taken. She dissolves the needless walls between syllables through an ingrained, behind-the-beat feel for phrasing, and this hypnotic rhythm often takes the lead in unlocking her expansive imagery:

> appointed places set in motion like seasons. We are like salmon
> swimming against the mutation of current to find
> our heartbroken way home again, weight of red eggs and need

Duane Niatum's lines are as deeply graven as those of any bent-wood box or totem carving. His work reminds us that poetry can incur the weight and grandeur of a ceremonial object. I seem to remember his poems as a series of interconnected, colorful weavings intent on charting a poet's journey in and out of the realm of magic. He seems to soar above the poem as it is being uncovered and to light each of his images individually:

> I camp in the light of the fox
> Within the singing mirror of night,
> Hunt for courage to return to the voice
> Whirling my failures through the meadow

Elizabeth Woody's work uses elements of traditional art-making to recast her tribal narrative as one of continued survival. Her poems feel like power deconstructed, as only a sculptor might attempt, language arranged into objects we cannot turn away from. We witness her incredible agency and all-enveloping tone throughout "Translation of Blood Quantum":

> *THIRTY-SECOND PARTS OF A HUMAN BEING*
> SUN   MOON   EVENING STAR   AT DAWN CLOUDS
>   RAINBOW   CEDAR
> LANGUAGE   COLORS AND SACRIFICE   LOVE

THE GREAT FLOOD

THE TORTOISE   CARRIES   THE PARROT   HUMMINGBIRD   TRILLIUM

After breaking into this imaginative and itemized list (this is only an excerpt), she goes on to detail her sense of what a politics of self-determination looks like and how to actualize this energy within our work:

Our *Sovereignty* is permeated, in its possession
of our individual rights, by acknowledgment of good
for the whole
and this includes the freedom of the *Creator* in these teachings
given to and practiced by *The People*.

Poetry can contain so many types of voices within one instance of writing; its restlessness and need for flexibility are two of its greatest strengths. This sensation can border upon utopia as syllabic, concrete-sounding sections of a poem may lie next to restorative political strategies and then begin to break into rhythms of incantation and chant. I tend to cast Elizabeth Woody's work in a heroic light because of her unwavering willingness to write the world she wants to live in as well as for her willingness to speak for more than just herself. She defines our struggle as ongoing, as an eternal and aspirational state, a substance from which we are meant to form poetry as well as to speak out in protest. Her poem is reminiscent of Chief Seattle's speech during the treaty negotiations of 1854 addressing then-governor of Washington State, Isaac Stevens:

And when the last red man shall have perished from the earth and his memory among the white men shall have become a myth these shores will swarm with the invisible dead of my tribe; and when your children's children shall think themselves alone in the fields, the store, the shop, upon the highway, or in the silence of the pathless woods, they will not be alone. In all the earth there is no place dedicated to solitude.

Just as we first formed a poetry out of our literal surroundings, we then had to move on to preserving these traditions as they were quickly becoming outlawed by the U.S. government. When elements of trauma begin to surface within our histories, the action begins to be told in reverse. To this day we are still fighting to be seen as living, breathing, contemporary artists.

I have come to think of Native Poets as warrior/prophets that can move (almost routinely) beyond our own bodies. We are hovering, scribing entities, free to drop back into our trenches as needed. It is the poems themselves that provide the bedrock for further resistance and redefinition. Becoming a better listener is also such a huge part of becoming a more complete poet, to always leave ourselves open to new frequencies. This collection will no doubt spark new changes and touchstones for artists of every discipline.

POETRY OF ALASKA

Diane L'xeis' Benson

A LASKA—A RUGGED LAND of gold; the great land; the last frontier—
these are the descriptions of newcomers, but for Alaska Native peo-
ple it is life, and the home of ancestors. In contrast, the seven Iñupiaq, five
Tlingit, one Yup'ik, two Athabascan, and one Aleut (Tangirnaq) writers
reflect an eternal connection to place that runs through their veins cycling
through the generations.

Beginning with the singing words shared by Lincoln Blassi appealing to
the "Whale of distant ocean," the intimate knowledge of land and sea offer-
ings of the treeless and windswept St. Lawrence Island is evident. In this
most remote northwestern environment and Siberian Yup'ik culture, time
is polychronic, cyclical, as it is with all Alaska's indigenous peoples and is
clear in this reverence of the whale harvest season. Respect of the landscape
and what it holds is an important thread for continuance—the people are
not separate from the landscape but a part of it. *They belong to it.* It is this
that is shared from one indigenous group to the next in this vast and diverse
land called Alaska.

There are loosely seven different regions of Alaska that by their size and
geographic differences could be countries within their own right: South-
east, Northeast, Aleutians, Northwest, North, South Central, and the
Interior. Unlike many other tribes in the United States, Alaskan tribes still
exist on the very land of their ancestors. The Alaskan poets represented
here have all had the benefit of either living in their community of origin,
or returning to it.

Alaskan tribes speak twenty distinct languages and numerous dialects.
Each distinct language is representative of a distinct culture intrinsically
woven into time and space of place. Language represents not only the values
and social systems but the relationship to land and to its subsequent spiritual
realities. Interestingly, we see this even in English—in the poems of the poets
across the generations from "Spirit Moves," by Fred Bigjim, to "Anatomy of a
Wave" by Abigail Chabitnoy. The voices of the old ones, the dark secrets held

by the landscape, are present in the poetry. And all the while life, indigenous life, insists on finding a way.

The regions of Alaska that are the origins of these poets are the terrain of their poetic souls.

Contained by glacial fields, Southeast Alaska's spruce-covered mountains dive into the sea, facing islands and rugged coasts, where rain can be relentless. It is a place of abundance—rich with berries, mammals, deer, sea greens, and fish. Tlingit story, friendship, and life all revolve through the sharing of this wealth no matter the location, as in "How to make good baked salmon from the river" by Nora Marks Dauenhauer. Although having to adapt, ancestral relatives are still present and remembered and all are nourished.

Family is always central, and for the Interior Athabascans life along the many rivers and birch-wooded forests through harsh winters and hot, dry summers is reliant on their unity and reciprocity. Although Dian Million was removed from Alaska at the age of twelve, she illustrates this timeless principle in "The Housing Poem." Mary TallMountain, also of the same region and similar circumstance, alliterates the sharing of grease from caribou, and gently brings home to the reader the deeply held bonds that go beyond time and distance in her two poems, "Good Grease" and "There is No Word for Goodbye."

The voice of Alaska Native poets began to challenge the status quo and twist the canon around the end of World War Two, when Alaska Native people became the minority demographic: many were forced off to boarding schools, and traditions and languages were banned. Conflicting worldviews and painful ironies emerge as acculturation meets cultural studies in "At the Door of the Native Studies Director," by Robert Davis Hoffman. Andrew Hope III, in one of his less minimalist poems, "Spirit of Brotherhood," creates a cross-rhythmic theme of religion and cultural adaptation as he situates the cultural placement of the oldest Native American organization, the Alaska Native Brotherhood.

Dominant in much of the Alaskan poetry is the reality of loss, cultural disruption, and the effort to reconcile cultural existence in a continually colonizing and commodifying world. What is notable is that voice is given to these themes primarily by more recent poets. This is evident in a number of poems by Iñupiaq writers Joan Kane, Cathy Tagnak Rexford, Carrie Ayaġaduk Ojanen, and Ishmael Hope—all of whom were born long after the Alaska Native Claims Settlement Act of 1971. Internal and external struggles are laid bare in the poetry and are seemingly interwoven into historical trauma and circumpolar politics by this generation now coping with the undeniable urgency of global threats to subsistence and humanity, climate change, and war. Inupiat are on the front line of the north, and these poets, perhaps influenced by the activists before them, speak to current issues and their own fragility juxtaposed with Alaskan Native life that often appears to be teetering on the edge. Even in the darkness, there remains a glowing undercurrent of perseverance.

POETRY OF THE PACIFIC

Brandy Nālani McDougall

T HROUGH INCORPORATED and unincorporated territories, free asso-
ciated states, and ocean monuments, the United States currently con-
trols one-third of the Pacific Ocean, which itself comprises one-third of the
earth's surface. Continuing manifest destiny beyond the continental borders,
the United States formally annexed Hawai'i and Guåhan (Guam) in 1898
and Amerika Sāmoa in 1900 to bolster militarization and trade in the Asia-
Pacific region. Though dominant historical narratives are vague and imply
that American colonialism has been benevolent and beneficial for us, they
conveniently omit the violence behind the establishment and ongoing main-
tenance of American empire in (and because of the location of) our islands
in the Pacific. These colonial stories also enable tourism, another leading
economic industry in our region, to profit from exploitative images of us as
happy, simple natives living in a paradise that is open and ready to serve.

If you ask for *our* stories, however, you will likely hear our poetry, the genre
we tend to prefer, which stands as testament to the superficiality and brevity
of the United States in the Pacific; to the resilience, ingenuity, and strength of
our communities; and to our fierce love for our islands and ocean, our cultures,
and our ancestors. It would not be an overstatement to share that there is a
poet, an orator with a love and healthy reverence for the power of language, in
every Pacific family. Therefore, this section showcases only a few of the poets
from Hawai'i, Amerika Sāmoa, and Guåhan and should definitely not be con-
sidered exhaustive. There are many others whose powerful, wise, inspiring,
and talented voices fill other books and anthologies, lift our peoples through
movements and rallies, heal our hearts, and nourish our imaginations.

Given the diversity of our cultures, languages, histories, and political issues
in the Pacific, I will treat each Pacific archipelago separately and begin with
Hawai'i, as the Pacific selections start with the first *wā* (epoch) in the *Kumulipo*,
a genealogical chant tracing more than eight hundred human generations—as
well as plant and animal ancestors—that emerge after the universe comes into
being. The first *wā* details cosmogenesis as spontaneous and generative, end-

ing with the birth of night. Though the *Kumulipo* was first recorded in writing under the direction of King David Kalākaua, who reigned from 1874 to 1891, Queen Liliʻuokalani began the translation in 1895 while imprisoned in ʻIolani Palace in Honolulu and completed it in 1897 in Washington, D.C., as she lobbied against Hawaiʻi's annexation to the United States. The *Kumulipo* has since become one of the most important poems of our people.

Literary scholar and poet kuʻualoha hoʻomanawanui uses the metaphor of the *haku* (braided) lei to describe how Hawaiian poems use overlapping meanings, interweave traditions, and yet adhere to craft and structure. Though applied to Hawaiian poetry, the metaphor holds true for all of the contemporary Pacific selections that follow. We begin with John Dominis Holt's "Ka ʻIli Pau," a poem reflecting on how we are continuations of our ancestors, and Leialoha Perkins' "Plantation Non-Song," a strong indictment of Hawaiʻi's sugar plantations for fostering "ghettos of mind, slums of the heart." Holt first published in 1965 and Perkins in 1979, following the near extinction of the Hawaiian language and other forms of colonial silencing since annexation in 1898. The next generation of poets began writing in the 1980s and '90s—Imaikalani Kalahele, Michael McPherson, Mahealani Perez-Wendt, Dana Naone Hall, Joe Balaz, Wayne Kaumualii Westlake, and Haunani-Kay Trask. Their poems are emblematic of their political activism and ancestrally rooted commitment to social and environmental justice. Kalahele's "Make Rope," McPherson's "Clouds, Trees, & Ocean: North Kauaʻi," Balaz's "Charlene," Westlake's "Hawaiians Eat Fish," and Trask's "Night is a Sharkskin Drum" and "Koʻolauloa" emphasize continuance and ongoing connections to ʻāina (land) and suggest we are able to move between ancestral time and our own. In these poems, the poet's duty is to "become the memory of our people" (Kalahele). Perez-Wendt's "Uluhaimalama," Hall's "Hawaiʻi '89," and Trask's "Agony of Place" lay bare and fight the ravages of American colonialism "grinding vision/ from the eye, thought/ from the hand/ until a tight silence/ descends" (Trask), while also taking spiritual sustenance in ancestral connection and the land's enduring beauty, "feast[ing] well/ On the stones" (Perez-Wendt) and "blooming [like kokiʻo] on the long branch" (Hall). Notably, much of the poetry of this period is lyrical and elegaic, yet insistent on how healing is rooted in our return to culture and ʻāina.

Poets who began writing in the 2000s and 2010s, including Christy Passion, Donovan Kūhiō Colleps, Noʻu Revilla, Jamaica Heolimeleikalani Osorio, and myself, share intimate portraits of ʻohana (family) and continue the work of truth-telling and memory-keeping alongside political activism and community engagement. As it was for the poets before us, ancestral connection, which includes human, plant, and animal ancestors, is a significant thematic thread, one that informs a predilection for decoloniality. My sonnet series "Ka 'Ōlelo" allays the trauma of the English-only law through a love song for my grandfather and 'ōlelo Hawai'i (the Hawaiian language); and "He Mele Aloha no ka Niu" honors the generosity of the *niu*, or coconut. Passion's "Hear the Dogs Crying" and Colleps's "Kiss the Opelu" lovingly invoke sonicality in rendering their grandmothers' stories. Similarly, the moving "Smoke Screen" by Revilla imagines her father's days working at the sugar mill where he "marr[ied] metal in his heavy/ gloves . . . He was always burning into something." The last of the Pacific selections, Osorio's "Kumulipo," is a spoken-word poem referencing Lili'uokalani's *Kumulipo* and voicing her own genealogy to stave off colonial forgetting. Perhaps diverging from their predecessors, these poets openly reflect on issues of cultural and political identity, including language, gender, and sexual identity, and use the lyric and other forms to show the trauma of colonial loss and violence experienced by the *'ohana*, while also affirming a strong commitment to justice and sovereignty.

The work of American empire and militarism has also meant Indigenous displacement and a growing Pacific Islander diaspora—to the point that some off-island populations outnumber their on-island kin. In their poetry collections Dan Taulapapa McMullin (from Amerika Sāmoa), Craig Santos Perez (who is CHamoru from Guåhan), and Lehua M. Taitano (who is also CHamoru from Guåhan) all write from the diaspora, sharing their individual stories of having to leave their home islands. Here, McMullin's "Doors of the Sea" lyrically follows an overseas journey that separates brothers and plays with gendered language, a signature of McMullin's *fa'afafine* (non-binary) perspective. Perez's "*ginen* the micronesian kingfisher [*i sihek*]" mourns the loss of birdsong after U.S. military ships brought brown tree snakes to the island and details colonial efforts to save the Micronesian kingfisher. Finally, Taitano's "Letters from an Island" offers us a glimpse into a family's correspondence between Guåhan and the continental United States. Both Perez and Taitano are avant-garde poets who incorporate CHamoru language and culture, visuality, history, and politics into their poetics. Collectively, these writers, like others in the Pacific, are creating new literatures in order to honor our ancestors, remember our histories, revitalize our cultures, decolonize our islands and ocean, and imagine sovereign futures.

KUMULIPO WĀ ʻEKAHI

The *Kumulipo* is a Hawaiian creation chant. Below is the version recorded in writing under the direction of King David Kalākaua. The accompanying translation into English was completed by Queen Liliʻuokalani in 1897. King Kalākaua reigned over the Hawaiian Kingdom from 1874 until his death in 1891. His sister, Queen Liliʻuokalani, succeeded him on the throne. They were the last two monarchs of the Hawaiian Kingdom before the U.S. military–backed overthrow in 1895.

O ke au i kahuli wela ka honua
O ke au i kahuli lole ka lani
O ke au i kukaiaka ka la.
E hoomalamalama i ka malama
O ke au o Makali'i ka po
O ka walewale hookumu honua ia
O ke kumu o ka lipo, i lipo ai
O ke kumu o ka Po, i po ai
O ka lipolipo, o ka lipolipo
O ka lipo o ka la, o ka lipo o ka po
           Po wale hoi
           Hanau ka po

[*Translation into English*]
At the time that turned the heat of the earth,
At the time when the heavens turned and changed,
At the time when the light of the sun was subdued
To cause light to break forth,
At the time of the night of Makalii (winter)
Then began the slime which established the earth,
The source of deepest darkness.
Of the depth of darkness, of the depth of darkness,
Of the darkness of the sun, in the depth of night,
           It is night,
           So was night born

CHIEF SEATTLE *(1786–1866), Suquamish* **and** *Duwamish.* The city of Seattle, Washington, is named after Chief Seattle, who ruled over both the Suquamish and the Duwamish though the two tribes were separated by the Puget Sound. In addition to his leadership skills and his ability to understand the intentions of the white settlers, he was also a noted orator in the Northern Lushootseed language. During the treaty proposals of 1854, Chief Seattle delivered a speech that is still remembered today. At the time of his death, protests over treaty rights and resettlement were still ongoing.

Excerpts from a Speech by Chief Seattle, 1854

The speech was originally transcribed by Dr. Henry Smith into a trade language known as Chinook Jargon before he attempted his own translation into English. The speech was transcribed into Northern Lushootseed by Vi Hilbert, July 27, 1985, then subsequently into English.

Your religion was written on tablets of stone by the iron finger of an angry God, lest you forget.

The red man could never comprehend nor remember it. Our religion is the tradition of our ancestors, the dreams of our old men, given to them in the solemn hours of the night by the great spirit and the visions of our leaders, and it is written in the hearts of our people.

Your dead cease to love you and the land of their nativity as soon as they pass the portals of the tomb; they wander far away beyond the stars and are soon forgotten and never return. Our dead never forget this beautiful world that gave them being. They always love its winding rivers, its sacred mountains, and its sequestered vales, and they ever yearn in tenderest affection over the lonely hearted living and often return to visit, guide and comfort them.

We will ponder your proposition, and when we decide we will tell you. But should we accept it, I here and now make this the first condition that we will not be denied the privilege, without molestation, of visiting at will the graves where we have buried our ancestors, and our friends and our children. Every part of this country is sacred to my people. Every hillside, every valley, every plain and grove has been hallowed by some fond memory or some sad experience of my tribe.

Even the rocks which seem to lie dumb as they swelter in the sun along the silent seashore in solemn grandeur thrill with memories of past events connected with the lives of my people.

And when the last red man shall have perished from the earth and his memory among the white men shall have become a myth, these shores will swarm with the invisible dead of my tribe; and when your children's children shall think themselves alone in the fields, the store, the shop, upon the highway, or in the silence of the pathless woods, they will not be alone. In all the earth there is no place dedicated to solitude.

At night when the streets of your cities and villages will be silent and you think them deserted, they will throng with returning hosts that once filled and still love this beautiful land. The white man will never be alone. Let him be just and deal kindly with my people, for the dead are not powerless.

Dead—did I say? There is no death, only a change of worlds.

[*Translated by Vi Hilbert*]

 LINCOLN BLASSI (*1892–1980*), *St. Lawrence Island Yup´ik*, was born in Gambell, Alaska, where he worked as a whaling harpooner. The story of his childhood appeared in the July and August 1978 issues of *Alaska Magazine*. As the number of the region's whales decreased, Blassi sold his ceremonial whaling gear, which the ethnographer Otto Geist acquired for the University of Alaska Museum of the North.

Prayer Song Asking for a Whale

(told in St. Lawrence Island Yup´ik)

IVAGHULLUK ILAGAATA

Ighivganghani, eghqwaaghem elagaatangi taakut atughaqiit. Ilagaghaqut angyalget taakut. Ivaghullugmeng atelget.

　　Elngaatall, repall tusaqnapangunatengllu. Nangllegsim angtalanganeng, wata eghqwaalleghmi tawani nangllegnaghsaapigllluteng ilaganeghmeggni iglateng qughaghteghllaglukii piiqegkangit. Nangllegsim angtalanganeng Kiyaghneghmun.

> Uuknaa-aa-aanguu-uuq.
> Saamnaa-aa-aanguu-uuq,
> Taglalghii-ii-ii saa-aamnaa.
> Ketangaa-aan aghveghaa-aa saa-aamnaa-aa
> Aghvelegglaguu-uu-lii.
> Ellngalluu-uu-uu.
> Qagimaa iluganii-ii-ii.

> Uuknaa-aa-aanguu-uuq.
> Saamnaa-aa-aanguuq,
> Taglalghii-ii-ii saa-aamnaa.
> Ketangaa-aa-aan ayveghaa-aa saa-aamna.
> Aghveleglllaaguluu-uu-lii
> Elngaa-aa-aalluu-uungu-uuq
> Qagimaa iluganii-ii-ii.

> Uuknaa-aa-aanguu-uuq.
> Saamnaa-aa-aanguu-uuq
> Taglalghii-ii-ii saa-aamnaa.
> Ketangaa-aan maklagaa-aa-aanguuq.
> Aghveleglllaguulii-ii-iingii.
> Ellngalluu-uu-uu.
> Qagimaa iluganii-ii-ii-ngiy.

Before the whaling season, the boat captain would sing ceremonial songs in the evening. The ceremony of singing was called *ivaghulluk*.

The boat captain would sing these songs in such a low reverent voice that you could hardly make out the words. Especially before the whaling season began, the songs of petition were sung to God in a prayerful pleading voice.

> The time is almost here.
> The season of the deep blue sea . . .
> Bringing good things from the deep blue sea.
> Whale of distant ocean . . .
> May there be a whale.
> May it indeed come . . .
> Within the waves.

> The time is almost here.
> The season of the deep blue sea . . .
> Bringing good things from the deep blue sea.
> Walrus of distant ocean . . .
> May there be a whale.
> May it indeed come . . .
> Within the waves.

> The time is almost here.
> The season of the deep blue sea . . .
> Bringing good things from the deep blue sea.
> Bearded seal of distant ocean . . .
> May there be a whale.
> May it indeed come . . .
> Within the waves.

MARY TALLMOUNTAIN *(1918–1994), Koyukon,* was a poet, stenographer, and educator. Born in Nulato, Alaska, along the Yukon River, she was adopted and relocated to Oregon. In her later years she moved to San Francisco, started her own stenography business, and began to write poetry. She is the author of *The Light on the Tent Wall* (1990), *A Quick Brush of Wings* (1991), and the posthumous collection *Listen to the Night* (1995). While living in San Francisco she founded the Tenderloin Women Writers Workshop, which supported women's literary expression.

GOOD GREASE

The hunters went out with guns
at dawn.
We had no meat in the village,
no food for the tribe and the dogs.
No caribou in the caches.

All day we waited.
At last!
As darkness hung at the river
we children saw them far away.
Yes, they were carrying caribou!
We jumped and shouted!

By the fires that night
we feasted.
The Old Ones chuckled,
sucking and smacking,
sopping the juices with sourdough bread.
The grease would warm us
when hungry winter howled.

Grease was beautiful—
oozing,
dripping and running down our chins,

brown hands shining with grease.
We talk of it
when we see each other
far from home.

Remember the marrow
sweet in the bones?
We grabbed for them like candy.
Good.
Gooooood.

Good grease.

There Is No Word for Goodbye

Sokoya, I said, looking through
        the net of wrinkles into
        wise black pools
        of her eyes.

What do you say in Athabascan
        when you leave each other?
        What is the word
        for goodbye?

A shade of feeling rippled
        the wind-tanned skin.
        Ah, nothing, she said,
        watching the river flash.

She looked at me close.
        We just say, *Tłaa*. That means,
        See you.
        We never leave each other.
        When does your mouth
        say goodbye to your heart?

She touched me light
    as a bluebell.
    You forget when you leave us;
    you're so small then.
    We don't use that word.

We always think you're coming back,
    but if you don't,
    we'll see you some place else.
    You understand.
    There is no word for goodbye.

 JOHN DOMINIS HOLT (*1919–1993*), *Kanaka Maoli,* was a poet, short-fiction writer, novelist, publisher, and cultural historian whose collective works contributed to the rise of the second Hawaiian renaissance movement in the 1960s and '70s. He received several honors and accolades, including recognition as a Living Treasure of Hawai'i in 1979 and the Hawai'i Award for Literature in 1985. Additionally, Holt started Topgallant Press (Ku Pa'a Press), which published numerous books by authors in Hawai'i.

Ka 'Ili Pau

Give me something from
The towering heights
Of blackened magma
Not a token thing
Something of spirit, mind or flesh, something of bone
The undulating form of
Mauna Loa
Even lacking cold and mists
Or the dark of night, it
Is always forbidding: there is a love

That grows between us.
Ka ʻili pau, you are a crazed *ʻanā-ʻanā*
With a shaman's tangled hair,
Reddened eyes, and his
Laho—maloʻo.
He falls in love with his *ʻumeke* and its
Death giving objects.
These gifts form the times of confusion
Come from the mountain heights
Wild skies, deep valley cliffs and
Darkened caves
Where soft air creeps into darkness
Gently touching bones and
The old canoe's prow
Inside the stunning skeletal remains
Of *moe puʻu*
My companions in death
My own skeleton stretches long
Across a ledge
Above the ancient remains
Of boat and bones
Give me your secrets locked
In lava crust
Give me your muscled power
Melted now to air and dust
Give me your whitened bones
Left to sleep
These many decades now as
The *pua* of your semen have multiplied down through
The centuries.
Sleep *aliʻi nui* and your
Companions
Sleep in your magic silence in
Your love wrapped in the total
Embrace of death
You have given us our place
Your seed proliferates

We are here
And we sing and laugh and love
And give your island home
A touch (here and there) of
Love and magic, these
Live in you *makua aliʻi* sleep on.
In your silence there is strength
Accruing for the *kamaliʻi.*

◇ **NORA MARKS DAUENHAUER** *(1927–2017), Tlingit,* was a
poet, fiction writer, and Tlingit language scholar. Born in Juneau,
Alaska, to a fisherman and a beader, Dauenhauer researched
Tlingit language and translated works of Tlingit culture at the Alaska
Native Language Center. She received numerous honors and awards, includ-
ing a National Endowment for the Humanities grant, a Humanist of the
Year award, and an American Book Award. She also served as Alaska's Poet
Laureate from 2012 to 2014.

In Memory of Jeff David

(Regional Basketball "All-American Hall of Famer")

Even your name
proclaims it.
In Tlingit: Sʼukḵées,
"Wolf Rib, Like a Bracelet,
Like a Hoop."
Scoring hook shots,
as center,
shooting from the key,
your body motion
forming a hoop
wolfing up the points.

Letter to Nanao Sakaki

I dance with
dancing cranes
(lilies of the valley),
transplanting them
under a tree until
next summer
when there will be
more dancers.

How to make good baked
salmon from the river

> *for Simon Ortiz*
> *and for all our friends and relatives*
> *who love it*

It's best made in dry-fish camp on a beach by a
fish stream on sticks over an open fire, or during
fishing or during cannery season.

In this case, we'll make it in the city, baked in
an electric oven on a black fry pan.

INGREDIENTS
Barbecue sticks of alder wood.
In this case the oven will do.
Salmon: River salmon, current super market cost
$4.99 a pound.
In this case, salmon poached from river.
Seal oil or olachen oil.
In this case, butter or Wesson oil, if available.

DIRECTIONS
To butcher, split head up the jaw. Cut through,
remove gills. Split from throat down the belly.
Gut, but make sure you toss all to the seagulls and
the ravens, because they're your kin, and make sure
you speak to them while you're feeding them.
Then split down along the back bone and through
the skin. Enjoy how nice it looks when it's split.

Push stake through flesh and skin like pushing
a needle through cloth, so that it hangs on stakes
while cooking over fire made from alder wood.

Then sit around and watch the slime on the salmon
begin to dry out. Notice how red the flesh is,
and how silvery the skin looks. Watch and listen
to the grease crackle, and smell its delicious
aroma drifting around on a breeze.

Mash some fresh berries to go along for dessert.
Pour seal oil in with a little water. Set aside.

In this case, put the poached salmon in a fry pan.
Smell how good it smells while it's cooking,
because it's soooooooo important.

Cut up an onion. Put in a small dish. Notice how
nice this smells too, and how good it will taste.
Cook a pot of rice to go along with salmon. Find
some soy sauce to put on rice, maybe borrow some.

In this case, think about how nice the berries would
have been after the salmon, but open a can of fruit
cocktail instead.

Then go out by the cool stream and get some skunk
cabbage, because it's biodegradable, to serve the

salmon from. Before you take back the skunk cabbage,
you can make a cup out of one to drink from the
cool stream.

In this case, plastic forks, paper plates and cups will do, and
drink cool water from the faucet.

TO SERVE
After smelling smoke and fish and watching the
cooking, smelling the skunk cabbage and the berries
mixed with seal oil, when the salmon is done, put
salmon on stakes on the skunk cabbage and pour
some seal oil over it and watch the oil run into
the nice cooked flakey flesh which has now turned
pink.

Shoo mosquitoes off the salmon, and shoo the ravens
away, but don't insult them, because mosquitoes
are known to be the ashes of the cannibal giant,
and Raven is known to take off with just about
anything.

In this case, dish out on paper plates from fry pan.
Serve to all relatives and friends you have invited
to the barbecue and those who love it.

And think how good it is that we have good spirits
that still bring salmon and oil.

TO EAT
Everyone knows that you can eat just about every
part of the salmon, so I don't have to tell you
that you start from the head, because it's everyone's
favorite. You take it apart, bone by bone, but make
sure you don't miss the eyes, the cheeks, the nose,
and the very best part—the jawbone.

You start on the mandible with a glottalized
alveolar fricative action as expressed in the Tlingit
verb als'oss'.

Chew on the tasty, crispy skins before you start
on the bones. Eeeeeeeeeeeee!!!! How delicious.

Then you start on the body by sucking on the fins
with the same action. Include the crispy skins, then
the meat with grease dripping all over it.

Have some cool water from the stream with the salmon.

In this case, water from the faucet will do.
Enjoy how the water tastes sweeter with salmon.

When done, toss the bones to the ravens and
seagulls and mosquitoes, but don't throw them in
the salmon stream because the salmon have spirits
and don't like to see the remains of their kin
among them in the stream.

In this case, put bones in plastic bag to put
in dumpster.

Now settle back to a story telling session, while
someone feeds the fire.

In this case, small talk and jokes with friends
will do while you drink beer. If you shouldn't
drink beer, tea or coffee will do nicely.

Gunalchéesh for coming to my barbecue.

LEIALOHA PERKINS *(1930–2018), Kanaka Maoli,* was a poet, publisher, fiction writer, and educator. She earned her PhD in folklore and folklife from the University of Pennsylvania. In 1998 she received the Hawai'i Award for Literature. In addition to writing poetry, Perkins founded Kamalu'uluolele Publishers, which specialized in Pacific Islands subjects as they relate to both East and West, and taught at universities in Hawai'i and Tonga.

PLANTATION NON-SONG

Those years of lung-filling dust in Lahaina
of heat and humidity that induced
men and animals to lie down mid-afternoons
and sleep—between the mill's lunch shift whistles—
were not great, but mediocre for most things
and superlative for doing or not doing anything
useful, ugly, or good. Just for staying out of trouble.
There was time and space for a child to grow up in
playing between scrabbly hibiscus bushes,
and hopping over rutty roads
that smelled of five-day-old urine, all on one side
of the canefield tracks, ground once blanketed
with warrior dead and sorcerer's bones.

At the shore, the white newcomers lived
crossing themselves at sunrise and sunset
in a paradise "discovered," jubilating
as Captain Cook who also had found the unfound natives
and their unfound shore naked and ready for instant use.

Mill Camp's
beginnings are beginnings
one may grow to respect if not honor
because they are a man's beginnings.

But let's not make sentiment
the coin for the cheap treatment
some got—and others enjoyed handing out.
Let's call the fair, fair.

What may have been good, good enough
because it was there,
like space waiting for time to fill it up
(while we were looking elsewhere);
nevertheless, plantation worlds
enjoyed their own tenors:
ghettos of mind, slums of the heart.

 VINCE WANNASSAY *(1936–2017), Umatilla,* was a poet, writer, artist, and community worker. After some years on skid row he began writing and published in many anthologies, including *Dancing on the Rim of the World: An Anthology of Contemporary Northwest Native American Writing* (1990). He mentored many people in the Native community in the Portland, Oregon, area.

FORGOTTEN COYOTE STORIES

A LONG TIME AGO
WHEN I WAS A KID

I LIVED WITH MY
UNCLE AND AUNT

MY UNCLE RODE WITH
    JOSEPH
WHEN HE WAS A KID . . .
I MEAN MY UNCLE NOT JOSEPH

UNCLE USE TO TELL US KIDS
      COYOTE STORIES

SOME WERE FUNNY, SOME WEREN'T

MY MOTHER TOOK US, FROM UNCLE & AUNT

SHE PUT US IN A CATHOLIC BOARDING SCHOOL.
AT SCHOOL I TOLD SOME OF THE
      COYOTE STORIES.

      THE SISTERS SAID "DON'T BELIEVE
      THOSE STORIES"..
BUT BELIEVE US.....

ABOUT A GUY
      WHO WAVES A STICK ... AND THE SEA OPENS
      ****
WALKS ON WATER
      ****
WHO DIES AND COMES BACK ... TO LIFE AGAIN
      ****
WHO ASCENDS UP INTO THE SKY ....

I USED TO BELIEVE ALL THOSE
      STORIES
I DON'T ANYMORE.

NOW I WISH.....I COULD
      REMEMBER THOSE
COYOTE STORIES.....UNCLE TOLD ME

DUANE NIATUM *(1938–)*, *Klallam,* is a poet, fiction writer, and editor. After serving in the United States Navy, Niatum earned a PhD from the University of Michigan. Along with his creative works, Niatum served as an editor for Harper & Row's Native American Authors series. Niatum has been the recipient of many awards and accolades, including the Governor's Award from the State of Washington, the Lifetime Achievement Award from the Native Writers' Circle of the Americas, and grants from the Carnegie Fund for Authors and PEN.

Chief Leschi of the Nisqually

He awoke this morning from a strange dream—
Thunderbird wept for him in the blizzard.
Holding him in their circle, Nisqually women
Turn to the river, dance to its song.

He burned in the forest like a red cedar,
His arms fanning blue flames toward
The white men claiming the camas valley
For their pigs and fowl.
Musing over wolf's tracks vanishing in snow,
The memory of his wives and children
Keeps him mute. Flickering in the dawn fires,
His faith grows roots, tricks the soldiers
Like a fawn, sleeping black as the brush.

They laugh at his fate, frozen as a bat
Against his throat. Still, death will take
Him only to his father's longhouse,
Past the flaming rainbow door. These bars
Hold but his tired body; he will eat little
And speak less before he hangs.

Center Moon's Little Brother

I camp in the light of the fox,
Within the singing mirror of night.
Hunt for courage to return to the voice,
Whirling my failures through the meadow
Where I watch my childhood pick
Choke cherries, the women cook salmon
On the beach, my Grandfather sings his song to deer.
When my heart centers inside the necklace
Of fires surrounding his village of white fir,
Sleeping under seven snowy blankets of changes,
I will leave Raven's cave.

The Art of Clay

The years in the blood keep us naked to the bone.
So many hours of darkness we fail to sublimate.
Light breaks down the days to printless stone.

I sing what I sang before, it's the dream alone.
We fall like the sun when the moon's our fate.
The years in the blood keep us naked to the bone.

I wouldn't reach your hand, if I feared the dark alone;
My heart's a river, but it is not chilled with hate.
Light breaks down the days to printless stone.

We dance from memory because it's here on loan.
And as the music stops, nothing's lost but the date.
The years in the blood keep us naked to the bone.

How round the sky, how the planets drink the unknown.
I gently touch; your eyes show it isn't late.
Light breaks down the days to printless stone.

What figures in this clay; gives a sharper bone?
What turns the spirit white? Wanting to abbreviate?
The years in the blood keep us naked to the bone.
Light breaks down the days to printless stone.

 FRED BIGJIM *(1941–)*, *Iñupiaq,* is a poet who grew up in Nome, Alaska. Earning graduate degrees from Harvard University and the University of Washington, Bigjim has published several collections of poetry, including *Sinrock* (1983) and *Walk the Wind* (1988), as well as nonfiction and fiction works. He has also worked as an educator and an educational counselor for Native American youth.

SPIRIT MOVES

Sometimes I feel you around me,
Primal creeping, misty stillness.
Watching, waiting, dancing.
You scare me.

When I sleep, you visit me
In my dreams,
Wanting me to stay forever.
We laugh and float neatly about.

I saw you once, I think,
At Egavik.
The Eskimos called you a shaman.
I know better, I know you're
Spirit Moves.

ED EDMO *(1946–)*, **Shoshone-Bannock,** is a poet, playwright, performer, traditional storyteller, tour guide, and lecturer on Northwest tribal culture. He lectures, holds workshops, and creates dramatic monologues on cultural understanding and awareness, drug and alcohol abuse, and mental health. His poetry collection is *These Few Words of Mine* (2006).

INDIAN EDUCATION BLUES

I sit in your
crowded classrooms
learn how to
read about dick,
jane & spot
but I remember
how to get deer
    I remember
    how to beadwork
    I remember
    how to fish
    I remember
    the stories told
    by the old
but spot keeps
showing up &
my report card
is bad

PHILLIP WILLIAM GEORGE *(1946–2012)*, *Nez Perce,* was a poet, writer, and champion traditional plateau dancer. His poem "Proviso" had been translated into eighteen languages worldwide and won multiple honors, including being performed on *The Tonight Show Starring Johnny Carson* and *The Dick Cavett Show.* In addition to his poetry, George also wrote, produced, and narrated *Season of Grandmothers* for the Public Broadcasting Corporation.

BATTLE WON IS LOST

They said, "You are no longer a lad."
I nodded.
They said, "Enter the council lodge."
I sat.
They said, "Our lands are at stake."
I scowled.
They said, "We are at war."
I hated.
They said, "Prepare red war symbols."
I painted.
They said, "Count coups."
I scalped.
They said, "You'll see friends die."
I cringed.
They said, "Desperate warriors fight best."
I charged.
They said, "Some will be wounded."
I bled.
They said, "To die is glorious."
They lied.

IMAIKALANI KALAHELE (*1946–*), *Kanaka Maoli,* is a poet, artist, and musician. Writing in a combination of English, Pidgin (Hawaiian Creole English), and ʻōlelo Hawaiʻi, Kalahele seeks to honor ancestral knowledge while challenging colonial injustice. In addition to his poetry and art book *Kalahele* (2002), his poems have been published in several anthologies, including *Mālama: Hawaiian Land and Water* and *ʻōiwi: a native hawaiian journal*, and his art has been exhibited throughout the Pacific. The 2019 Honolulu Bienniale recognized his prolific contributions to art in Hawaiʻi by naming the event "Making Wrong Right Now" after a line from his poem "Manifesto."

Make Rope

get this old man
he live by my house
he just make rope
every day
you see him making rope
if
he not playing his ukulele
or
picking up his moʻopuna
he making
rope

and nobody wen ask him
why?
how come?
he always making
rope

morning time . . . making rope
day time . . . making rope
night time . . . making rope
all the time . . . making rope

must get enuf rope
for make Hōkūleʻa already

most time
he no talk
too much
to nobody

he just sit there
making rope

one day
we was partying by
his house
you know
playing music
talking stink
about the other
guys them

I was just
coming out of the bushes
in back the house
and
there he was
under the mango tree
making rope
and he saw me

all shame
I look at him and said
"Aloha Papa"
he just look up
one eye
and said
"Howzit! What? Party?
Alright!"

I had to ask
"E kala mai, Papa
I can ask you one question?"

"How come
everyday you make rope
at the bus stop
you making rope
outside McDonald's drinking coffee
you making rope.
How come?"

he wen
look up again
you know
only the eyes move kine
putting one more
strand of coconut fiber
on to the kaula
he make one
fast twist
and said
"The Kaula of our people
is 2,000 years old
boy
some time . . . good
some time . . . bad
some time . . . strong
some time . . . sad
but most time
us guys
just like this rope

one by one
strand by strand
we become
the memory of our people

and
we still growing
so
be proud
do good

and
make rope
boy
make rope."

MICHAEL McPHERSON *(1947–2008)*, *Kanaka Maoli,* was a poet, publisher, editor, and lawyer. Interested in cultivating and maintaining a literature that was uniquely Hawaiian, McPherson wrote poetry, founded Xenophobia Press, and published the journal *HAPA.* In 1988, McPherson received a certificate of merit from the Hawai'i House of Representatives, acknowledging his work and scholarship on Hawaiian literature. As a lawyer, McPherson worked on Native Hawaiian claims in environmental law and Hawaiian land use.

Clouds, Trees & Ocean, North Kauai

In Hā'ena's cerulean sky today
the cirrus clouds converge upon
a point beyond the summer horizon, all
hurtling backward: time
drawn from this world as our
master inhales.

The ironwoods lean down their dark needles
to the beach, long strings of
broken white coral and shells that ebb
to the north and west, and wait
dreaming the bent blue backs of waves.

MAHEALANI PEREZ-WENDT *(1947–), **Kanaka Maoli,*** is a poet, writer, and activist. Her poetry was recognized through the University of Hawai'i's Elliot Cades Award for Literature in 1993. She is the author of the poetry collection *Uluhaimalama* (2007) and her poems have been published in numerous anthologies. Perez-Wendt also has an extensive history of community engagement, formerly serving as executive director of Native Hawaiian Legal Corporation, serving as the first Native Hawaiian board member of the Native American Rights Fund, and working extensively with prison issues and sovereignty restoration.

ULUHAIMALAMA

We have gathered
With manacled hands;
We have gathered
With shackled feet;
We have gathered
In the dust of forget
Seeking the vein
Which will not collapse.
We have bolted
The gunner's fence,
Given sacrament
On blood-stained walls.
We have linked souls
End to end
Against the razor's slice.
We have kissed brothers
In frigid cells,
Pressing our mouths
Against their ice-hard pain.
We have feasted well
On the stones of this land:
We have gathered
In dark places

And put down roots.
We have covered the Earth,
Bold flowers for her crown.
We have climbed
The high wire of treason–
We will not fall.

 WAYNE KAUMUALII WESTLAKE *(1947–1984)*, *Kanaka Maoli,* was born on Maui and raised on the island of Oʻahu. With Richard Hamasaki, he created and edited the literary journal *Seaweeds & Constructions* from 1976 to 1983. His posthumous collection, *Westlake: Poems by Wayne Kaumualii Westlake (1947–1984)*, edited by Mei-Li M. Siy and Richard Hamasaki (University of Hawaiʻi Press, 2009), includes nearly 200 poems, many previously unpublished.

HAWAIIANS
EAT
FISH
EAT
HAWAIIANS
EAT
FISH
EAT
HAWAIIANS
EAT
FISH
EAT
HAWAIIANS
EAT
FISH

DANA NAONE HALL (*1949–*), *Kanaka Maoli*, founded Hui Alanui o Mākena, an organization that successfully prevented the destruction of the Piʻilani Trail, a part of the road that once encircled Maui built by the *aliʻi nui* Piʻilani in the sixteenth century; and she has been at the forefront to protect *iwi kupuna* (ancestral remains) at Honokahua and other sacred burial sites. In addition, she is the editor of *Mālama: Hawaiian Land and Water* (1985). Her book *Life of the Land: Articulations of a Native Writer* (2017), a collection of poetry and memoir focused on her activism, won an American Book Award in 2019.

Hawaiʻi '89

for Leahi

The way it is now
few streams still flow
through loʻi kalo
to the sea.
Most of the water
where we live
runs in ditches alongside
the graves of Chinese bones
where the same crop has burned in the fields
for the last one hundred years.

On another island,
a friend whose father
was born in a pili grass
hale in Kahakuloa,
bought a house on a concrete
pad in Hawaiʻi Kai.
For two hundred thousand
he got window frames
out of joint and towel racks
hung crooked on the walls.

He's one of the lucky ones.
People are sleeping in cars
or rolled up in mats on beaches,
while the lū'au show hostess
invites the roomful of visitors
to step back in time
to when gods and goddesses
walked the earth.
I wonder what she's
talking about.

All night, Kānehekili
flashes in the sky
and Moanonuikalehua changes
from a beautiful woman
into a lehua tree
at the sound of the pahu.

It's true that the man
who swam with the sharks
and kept them away
from the nets full of fish
by feeding them limu kala
is gone,
but we're still here
like the fragrant white koki'o
blooming on the long branch
like the hairy leafed nehe
clinging to the dry pu'u
like the moon high over Ha'ikū
lighting the way home.

ANDREW HOPE III *(1949–2008)*, *Tlingit,* was a poet and a Tlingit political activist. Born in Sitka, Alaska, Hope was the cofounder of the Tlingit Clan Conference as well as Tlingit Readers, a nonprofit publishing house. He married Iñupiaq poet Elizabeth "Sister Goodwin" Hope. Inspired by the work of Tlingit poet Nora Marks Dauenhauer, Hope used his poetry to help the Tlingit language remain alive in written form.

SPIRIT OF BROTHERHOOD

They sing Onward Christian Soldiers
Down at the ANB Hall
Every year in convention
The kids don't like that song
They don't like missionary history
We shove that in the closet nowadays
The church had little to do with
ANB adopting this battle song
William Paul, Sr. introduced it
after he heard it at Lodge 163 of A.F. and A.M.
Portland, Oregon
The Masonic Lodge influence
The song bothers me
That's no secret
But
My people went into the church to survive
I don't know what the pioneer days were like
Up here in gold rush Alaska
I listen to the Black church and think about the
music of the Black spirit
the gospel of Sam Cooke and the Soul Stirrers
Otis Redding and the others
That spirit catches you
When you walk into the meeting and feel like family
You'll know what I'm saying

HAUNANI-KAY TRASK *(1949–), Kanaka Maoli,* is a prolific poet, scholar, and political activist and a leader of the Hawaiian sovereignty movement. She is the author of two scholarly monographs, *Eros and Power: The Promise of Feminist Theory* (1984) and *From a Native Daughter: Colonialism and Sovereignty in Hawai'i* (1993), a foundational text in Hawaiian and Indigenous studies, and has written many influential essays. She has two poetry books, *Light in the Crevice Never Seen* (1999) and *Night Is a Sharkskin Drum* (2002). She is a professor emeritus of Hawaiian studies at the University of Hawai'i at Mānoa, where she cofounded the Kamakakūokalani Center for Hawaiian Studies.

An Agony of Place

there is always this sense:
    a wash of earth
    rain, palm light falling
    across ironwood
    sands, fine and blowing
    to an ancient sea

i hear them always:
    with fish hooks and nets
    dark, long
    red canoes
    gliding thoughtlessly
    to sea

and the still lush hills
    of laughter
    buried in secret
    caves, bones of love
    and ritual, and sacred
    life

a place for the manō
the pueo, the ʻōʻō
for the smooth flat pōhaku
for a calabash of stars
     flung over the Pacific

and yet
our love suffers
with a heritage
of beauty

in a land of tears

where our people
go blindly
servants of another
race, a culture of machines

grinding vision
from the eye, thought
from the hand
until a tight silence
descends

wildly in place

Night Is a Sharkskin Drum

Night is a sharkskin drum
    sounding our bodies black
        and gold.

    All is aflame
the uplands a shush
    of wind.

From Halemaʻumaʻu
        our fiery Akua comes:
E Pele ē,

    E Pele ē,

        E Pele ē.

Koʻolauloa

  I ride those ridge backs
down each narrow
cliff   red hills
  and birdsong in my
head   gold dust
on my face   nothing

whispers but the trees
  mountains blue beyond
my sight   pools of
icy water at my feet

  this earth glows the color
of my skin   sunburnt
natives didn't fly

  from far away
but sprouted whole through
velvet *taro*   in the sweet mud

  of this *ʻāina*
their ancient name
is kept   my *piko*
safely sleeps

famous rains
flood down
in tears

I know these hills
my lovers   chant them
  late at night

owls swoop
  to touch me:

ʻaumākua

EARLE THOMPSON (1950–2006), *Yakima,* was born in
Nespelem, Washington. His creative works have won writing com-
petitions, such as the one held at Seattle's annual Bumbershoot
festival, and they have been included in various publications, including *Blue
Cloud Quarterly.*

MYTHOLOGY

My grandfather placed wood
in the pot-bellied stove
and sat; he spoke:

"One time your uncle and me
seen some stick-indians
driving in the mountains
they moved alongside
the car and watched us
look at them
they had long black hair
down their backs and were naked
they ran past us."

Grandfather shifted
his weight in the chair.
He explained,
"Stick-indians are powerful people
they come out during the fall.
They will trick little children
who don't listen
into the woods
and can imitate anything
so you should learn
about them."

Grandfather poured himself
some coffee and continued:
"At night you should put tobacco
out for them
and whatever food you got
just give them some
'cause stick-indians
can be vengeful
for people making fun of them.
They can walk through walls
and will stick a salmon up your ass
for laughing at them
this will not happen if you understand
and respect them."

My cousin giggled. I listened and remember
Grandfather slowly sipped his coffee
and smiled at us.
The fire smoldered like a volcano
and crackled.
We finally went to bed. I dreamt
of the mountains and now
I understand my childhood.

DIAN MILLION *(1950–)*, *Tanana Athabascan,* received her PhD from the University of California, Berkeley. Million's *Therapeutic Nations: Healing in an Age of Indigenous Human Rights* focuses on the politics of mental and physical health, with attention to how it informs race, class, and gender in Indian Country. She teaches American Indian Studies at the University of Washington.

THE HOUSING POEM

Minnie had a house
which had trees in the yard
and lots of flowers
she especially liked the kitchen
because it had a large old cast iron stove
and that
the landlord said
was the reason
the house was so cheap.

Pretty soon Minnie's brother Rupert came along
and his wife Onna
and they set up housekeeping in the living room
on the fold-out couch,
so the house warmed and rocked
and sang because Minnie and Rupert laughed a lot.

Pretty soon their mom Elsie came to live with them too
because she liked being with the laughing young people
and she knew how the stove worked the best.
Minnie gave up her bed and slept on a cot.

Well pretty soon
Dar and Shar their cousins came to town looking for work.
They were twins

the pride of Elsie's sister Jo
and boy could those girls sing. They pitched a tent under
the cedar patch in the yard
and could be heard singing around the house
mixtures of old Indian tunes and country western.

When it was winter
Elsie worried
about her mother Sarah
who was still living by herself in Moose Glen back home.

Elsie went in the car with Dar and Shar and Minnie and Rupert and got her.
They all missed her anyway and her funny stories.
She didn't have any teeth
so she dipped all chewable items in grease
which is how they're tasty she said.
She sat in a chair in front of the stove usually
or would cook up a big pot of something for the others.

By and by Rupert and Onna had a baby who they named Lester,
or nicknamed Bumper, and they were glad that Elsie and Sarah
were there to help.

One night the landlord came by
to fix the leak in the bathroom pipe
and was surprised to find Minnie, Rupert and Onna, Sarah and Elsie, Shar
    and Dar
all singing around the drum next to the big stove in the kitchen
and even a baby named Lester who smiled waving a big greasy piece of dried
    fish.

He was disturbed
he went to court to evict them
he said the house was designed for single-family occupancy
which surprised the family
because that's what they thought they were.

GLORIA BIRD *(1951–), Spokane,* is a poet and a scholar whose honors include the Diane Decorah Memorial Poetry Award from the Native Writers' Circle of the Americas. Her work frequently discusses and works against the harmful representations and stereotypes of Native peoples. As one of the central figures of Northwest Native poetry, Bird taught at the Institute of American Indian Arts in Santa Fe and was a cofounder of the Northwest Native American Writers' Association.

In Chimayo

The one-room adobe skeleton sat on a hill overlooking a field that would not grow anything but adobe brick. We packed holes around the vigas in winter, built a fire to "sweat" the walls insulating us for moving in.

Sr. Lujan sold the land as dried and Mexican as he, would sell what lay on the land: the rusted equipment of his father, the cellar dug into the dirt, and the bridge we crossed to reach the land he's sold.

His fat lawyer spoke with hands as coarse and brown as burnt fish asking for the price of the bridge belonging to Sr. Lujan, one hundred dollars to not be bothered any longer, Sr. Lujan whispering, *"es verdad"* next to him.

In Chimayo a crucifix is planted higher up on a ridge watching over what sacrifices were made of Chimayo all year. From my knees, I watched brighter stars journey the path of sky the cross did not fill through the night of my labor, rocking for comfort not found through an open window.

Early morning I lay on the floor to give birth, a veil of rain falling. *Hina-tee-yea* is what he called it in his elemental language. Four days later, named our daughter also, fine rain, child of the desert mesas, yucca, and chamisal.

Across the arroyo, the news would remind Manuelita of her grief, *y su hijito* lost the month we moved in. That spring, centipedes sprinkled sand from the warming vigas where they were hidden.

IMAGES OF SALMON AND YOU

Your absence has left me only fragments of a summer's run
on a night like this, fanning in August heat, a seaweeded song.
Sweat glistens on my skin, wears me translucent, sharp as scales.

The sun wallowing its giant roe beats my eyes back red and dry.
Have you seen it above the highway ruling you like planets?
Behind you, evening is Columbian, slips dark arms

around the knot of distance that means nothing
to salmon or slim desiring. Sweet man of rivers,
the blood of fishermen and women will drive you back again,

appointed places set in motion like seasons. We are like salmon
        swimming against the mutation of current to find
our heartbroken way home again, weight of red eggs and need.

ELIZABETH "SISTER GOODWIN" HOPE (1951–1997), *Iñupiaq*, served on the Institute of Alaska Native Arts board and was a member of the Native American Writers' Circle of Alaska. She was married to Tlingit poet Andrew Hope III. She published a book of poems called *A Lagoon Is in My Backyard* in 1984.

PIKSINÑAQ

when popcorn
first came up north
north to Kotzebue sound
little iñuit
took it home from school
long long ago when
the new century first woke up

Aana sat on neat
rows of willow branches
braiding sinew into thread

Uva Aana niggin
una piksinñaq
for you grandmother
eat this
it is something that bounces

after Aana ate it
the little iñuit girls
giggled hysterically
for sure now, they said
old Aana is going to bounce too

for hours
Aana sat hunched over
with her eyes squinched shut
she grasped onto neat rows
of willow branches
waiting for the popcorn
to make her bounce around

 DAN TAULAPAPA McMULLIN *(1953–), Samoan (Amerika Sāmoa)*, a *fa'afafine* poet, visual artist, and filmmaker, was raised on Tutuila Island in the villages of Maleola and Leone. He has garnered national acclaim, receiving awards like the Poets & Writers Award from the Writers Loft and earning a spot on the American Library Association Rainbow Top Ten List. Along with his poetry, his visual artwork has been exhibited worldwide, including at the Metropolitan Museum of Art in New York City, New York University's Asian/Pacific/American Institute, and the United Nations.

The Doors of the Sea

There was a ship
went into the sea
over the body of my brother
I am just a boy
he was not much older than me
the goddess is good and cruel
wants her share of life, like us
sparkling dust of birds far away whom we follow, the stars
the blood red dust of life
as my brother's face
disappeared beneath us
beneath the ship which carried us and the goddess
to where we do not know
leaving the war of my grandfather
the smell of smoke following us
our keel, my brother, knocking down the doors of the sea
the tall, and the wild waves coming, crashing
under the keel of my brother's name
far from the sound of places we were leaving
the roads we followed
marching past my uncle's crooked mountain forts
while his men called out at us
with our long hair
on our shoulders
first by my brother's name
who was this girl with him, leave her with us
she is my brother, he said
not glancing at me
our songs we sang in the warm rain for the goddess
blessed be her name
her cloak the wild wood pigeons turning
her crown the lone plover's crying
where now are you brother?

JOE BALAZ (*1953–*), *Kanaka Maoli,* is a poet in both American English and Pidgin (Hawaiian Creole English) and an editor. Invested in preserving Hawaiian oral traditions as well as Pidgin writing, Balaz wrote *After the Drought* (1985), and *OLA* (1996), a collection of visual poetry; edited *Hoʻomānoa: An Anthology of Contemporary Hawaiian Literature* (1989); and recorded an album of Pidgin poetry, *Electric Laulau* (1998). In 2019 he published *Pidgin Eye,* a collection of poems written over the previous thirty years.

Charlene

Charlene
wun wahine wit wun glass eye

studied da bottom
of wun wooden poi bowl

placed in wun bathtub
to float just like wun boat.

Wun mysterious periscope
rising from wun giant menacing fish

appeared upon da scene.

Undahneath da surface
deeper den wun sigh

its huge body
lingered dangerously near da drain.

Wun torpedo laden scream
exploded in da depths

induced by Charlene

who wuz chanting
to da electric moon

stuck up on da ceiling.

Silver scales
wobbled like drunken sailors

and fell into da blue.

No can allow
to move da trip lever on da plunger

no can empty da ocean

no can reveal da dry porcelain ring
to someday be scrubbed clean.

Charlene
looked at all da ancestral lines

ingrained on da bottom of da round canoe
floating on da watah

and she saw her past and future.

Wun curious ear wuz listening

through wun empty glass
placed against da wall

and discovered
dat old songs wuz still being sung

echoing like sonar
off of da telling tiles.

 DIANE L'X̱EIS' BENSON (1954–), *Tlingit,* is a poet, perform-
ing artist, speaker, and scholar. Utilizing poetry, Benson performed
her one-woman shows nationally and internationally, most nota-
bly, "Mother America Blues" and "My Spirit Raised its Hands." Her work
addressing violence and injustice issues through performance art, speak-
ing, and teaching earned her community service awards, as well as a Bonnie
Heavy Runner Victim Advocacy Award, a Goldie Award from the Golden
Crown Literary Society, and nominations for the Pushcart Prize in poetry
and the Herb Alpert Award in the Arts. Benson serves as faculty for the
Department of Alaska Native Studies and Rural Development at the Uni-
versity of Alaska Fairbanks.

Ax̱ Tl'aa

For those whose
children were taken from them

My aunt gives me
a picture of my mother
A woman
    Whose voice
    drifted waterlogged
    onto a California
    beach

And cried silent

POTLATCH DUCKS

Sleek,
We sneak just so,
past the tall blades of grass
across the flats of Minto

Canoe glides with no sound
our paddles dipping water like
ancient spirits in dance

Ducks abundant
we'll take plenty to the
village, but mother earth
urges play and off come our shirts
young man's long hair flying
paddle high, woman's long hair
laying, teasing the open sky

Heading on with
potlatch ducks to the village edge,
I can hardly breathe,
as if the ancient ones
are watching, and are about to
sneeze

GRIEF'S ANGUISH

Uncle sharpened his harpoon for
fishing. It felt like war. Her pain
was heard in her movement. Listen.
Listen, she is hanging clothes in the
rain. Listen. I think he will come
back from fishing. But her son never does.
And uncle sharpens his harpoon. But

he's gone fishing. A debt will be paid
today you see. A debt will be paid.
An eye for an eye. That is the way
he sees it.
　　　　I wait until sunset. By the attic.
Top of the stairs. I wait. For tomorrow
comes needling light at blades of grass begging
to feel freedom's scarred feet.

 ROBERT DAVIS HOFFMAN *(1955–)*, *Tlingit,* is a poet, carver, and multi-media artist. Davis considers himself a neo-traditionalist Tlingit artist and storyteller, working in both non-traditional and traditional modes. His collection of poetry, *Soul Catcher*, was published in 1986.

At the Door of the Native Studies Director

In this place years ago
they educated old language out of you,
put you in line, in uniform, on your own two feet.
They pointed you in the right direction but
still you squint at that other place,
that country hidden within a country.
You chase bear, deer. You hunt seal. You fish.
This is what you know. This is how you move,
leaving only a trace of yourself.
Each time you come back
you have no way to tell about this.

Years later you meet their qualifications—
native scholar.
They give you a job, a corner office.

Now you're instructed to remember
old language, bring back faded legend,
anything that's left.
They keep looking in on you, sideways.
You don't fit here, you no longer fit there.
You got sick. They still talk of it,
the cheap wine on your breath
as you utter in restless sleep
what I sketch at your bedside.
Tonight, father, I wrap you in a different blanket,
the dances come easier, I carve them for you.
This way you move through me.

ELIZABETH WOODY (1959–), *Confederated Tribes of Warm Springs,* a poet and an illustrator, was born in Ganado, Arizona. After attending the Institute of American Indian Arts in Santa Fe, she received her BA from Evergreen State College and her master's in public administration from Portland State University. She is the recipient of several awards and accolades; her first book of poetry, *Hand into Stone,* received the American Book Award, and she was named the Poet Laureate of Oregon for 2016–18.

WEAVING

for Margaret Jim-Pennah and Gladys McDonald

Weaving baskets you twine the strands into four parts.
Then, another four. The four directions many times.
Pairs of fibers spiral around smaller and smaller sets of threads.
Then, one each time. Spirals hold all this design
airtight and pure. This is our house, over and over.
Our little sisters, Khoush, Sowitk, Piaxi, Wakamu,

the roots will rest inside.
We will be together in this basket.
We will be together in this life.

TRANSLATION OF BLOOD QUANTUM

31/32 Warm Springs–Wasco–Yakama–Pit River–Navajo
1/32 Other   Tribal Roll number 1553

THIRTY-SECOND PARTS OF A HUMAN BEING
SUN   MOON   EVENING STAR   AT DAWN CLOUDS   RAINBOW   CEDAR
LANGUAGE   COLORS AND SACRIFICE   LOVE   THE GREAT FLOOD
THE TORTOISE   CARRIES THE PARROT   HUMMINGBIRD   TRILLIUM
THE CROW   RAVEN   COYOTE   THE CONDOR   JAGUAR   GRIZZLY
TIMBER WOLF   SIDEWINDER   THE BAT   CORN   TOBACCO   SAGE
MUSIC   DEATH   CONSCIOUSNESS OF THE SPIDERWEB
    RESURRECTED PROPHETS
RECURRENT POWER OF CREATION IS FUELED BY SONG

Like the lava, we have always been indomitable in flowing
purposes. A perpetuity of *Ne-shy-Chus* means we are rooted
in ancestral domain and are *Free*, with any other power
reserved in the truce of treaty, 1855, or any other time.
We kept peace. Preserved and existed through our *Songs,
Dances, Longhouses,* and the noninterruption of giving Thanks
and observances of the Natural laws of Creating by the Land
itself. The *Nusoox* are as inseparable from the flow of these
cycles. Our *Sovereignty* is permeated, in its possession
of our individual rights, by acknowledgment of good
for the whole
and this includes the freedom of the *Creator* in these teachings
given to and practiced by *The People*. We are watched over
by the mountains, not Man, not Monarchy,
or any other manifestations

of intimidation by misguided delusions of supremacy
over the Land or beings animate or inanimate.

SHERMAN ALEXIE (1966–), *Spokane,* is an award-winning
and nationally recognized poet, novelist, and short-story writer,
whose honors include an American Book Award, the National
Book Award for Young People's Literature, and a National Endowment for
the Arts fellowship. Alexie founded Longhouse Media, a nonprofit organi-
zation that teaches Native American youth how to use media for cultural
expression and social change.

THE SUMMER OF BLACK WIDOWS

The spiders appeared suddenly
after that summer rainstorm.

Some people still insist the spiders fell with the rain
while others believe the spiders grew from the damp soil like weeds with
    eight thin roots.

The elders knew the spiders
carried stories in their stomachs.

We tucked our pants into our boots when we walked through the fields of
    fallow stories.
An Indian girl opened the closet door and a story fell into her hair.
We lived in the shadow of a story trapped in the ceiling lamp.
The husk of a story museumed on the windowsill.
Before sleep we shook our blankets and stories fell to the floor.
A story floated in a glass of water left on the kitchen table.
We opened doors slowly and listened for stories.

The stories rose on hind legs and offered their red bellies to the most
    beautiful Indians.
Stories in our cereal boxes.
Stories in our firewood.
Stories in the pockets of our coats.
We captured stories and offered them to the ants, who carried the stories
    back to their queen.
A dozen stories per acre.
We poisoned the stories and gathered their remains with broom and pan.

The spiders disappeared suddenly
after that summer lightning storm.

Some people will insist the spiders were burned to ash
while others believe the spiders climbed the lightning bolts and became a
    new constellation.

The elders knew the spiders
had left behind bundles of stories.

Up in the corners of our old houses
we still find those small, white bundles
and nothing, neither fire
nor water, neither rock nor wind,
can bring them down.

THE POWWOW AT THE END OF THE WORLD

I am told by many of you that I must forgive and so I shall
after an Indian woman puts her shoulder to the Grand Coulee Dam
and topples it. I am told by many of you that I must forgive
and so I shall after the floodwaters burst each successive dam
downriver from the Grand Coulee. I am told by many of you
that I must forgive and so I shall after the floodwaters find
their way to the mouth of the Columbia River as it enters the Pacific

and causes all of it to rise. I am told by many of you that I must forgive
and so I shall after the first drop of floodwater is swallowed by that salmon
waiting in the Pacific. I am told by many of you that I must forgive and so I
    shall
after that salmon swims upstream, through the mouth of the Columbia
and then past the flooded cities, broken dams and abandoned reactors
of Hanford. I am told by many of you that I must forgive and so I shall
after that salmon swims through the mouth of the Spokane River
as it meets the Columbia, then upstream, until it arrives
in the shallows of a secret bay on the reservation where I wait alone.
I am told by many of you that I must forgive and so I shall after
that salmon leaps into the night air above the water, throws
a lightning bolt at the brush near my feet, and starts the fire
which will lead all of the lost Indians home. I am told
by many of you that I must forgive and so I shall
after we Indians have gathered around the fire with that salmon
who has three stories it must tell before sunrise: one story will teach us
how to pray; another story will make us laugh for hours;
the third story will give us reason to dance. I am told by many
of you that I must forgive and so I shall when I am dancing
with my tribe during the powwow at the end of the world.

DG NANOUK OKPIK (1968–), *Iñupiaq*, was born in Anchor-
age, and her family is from Barrow, Alaska. She earned an MFA
from the University of Southern Maine's Stonecoast program and
her poetry has been widely acclaimed, with *Corpse Whale* (2012) winning
an American Book Award. She was the recipient of the Truman Capote Lit-
erary Trust Scholarship, is an alumna of the Institute of American Indian
Arts, and lives in Santa Fe.

THE FATE OF INUPIAQ-LIKE KINGFISHER

But no one can
stop
a bird spear set
in motion,

made of notched bone,

feathered arrows pinnate

around the shaft,

with hair fringe
as it strikes

piercing depilated skin.

Some humans weave themselves

with lime grass,
into large orbs.

Others make goosefeet baskets

of seaweed or with narrow leaves,

or collect matches or tobacco.

The lamp soot burns like gas.

On Clovis point a circular icy reef,

my existence becoming a flicker

like the orange scales of a kingfisher.

We pirouette, diving, diving,
                                          deep.

No Fishing on the Point

Look at my/her engraved chin   made by deep lines of soot-ink.
      See the grove across her/my face.
A bull caribou   tramples my shoulders,   pins

her/me to the roof rock,   tethers my backstrap.   Boxed   in ice
cellars,   bowhead meat ferments,   freezes
to jam.

A shotgun blasts the sky to alert the plywood shacks
of migrating bowheads. The CB voice alerts: *"AAAIIGGIAARR"*
the house pits and Quonset huts which line the shore of ice laden waters,
      gray dorsal fins
rise on the Beaufort Sea. A chore-girl in rags, she/I sit/s lotus-legged,
      weaving baleen
baskets.

            Here, brother watches   and waits for
                      the correct time   to strike,
right above the   blow hole.
      Here, it is clean kill. Blood water all around us.
      Here, a woman far away crying for the whale's soul.

But, the men still heave to the beach

another day and a half. Pulling, winching,

pulling, dragging.

She/I cut/s opaque flesh and black meat with a jagged *ulu*,
carve *muktuk*, tie dark and white ribbons on each
gunnysack to mark the body parts. She/I slice/s the dorsal fin, give it to my
    brother
for ceremony, barter a bag of whalebones for fuel to heat the aged and
    chilled cement
barracks.

On *Birnirk* for thousands
of years called Point Barrow.
Now here,   a duck site a place of trade, where a DEW line
crosses
an old military port of call   for sighting air attacks,
where they want
to claim the sea for roads.   She's/I've watched the currents,
migrations, felt the rough movements
of the ice, which brings   feasts,   and   famine.

CHRISTY PASSION (*1974–*), *Kanaka Maoli,* is a poet and a critical-care nurse. Passion has been the recipient of several literary awards, including Hawaiʻi Pacific University's James A. Vaughn Award for Poetry, the *Atlanta Review* International Merit Award, the Academy of American Poets Award, and the Eliot Cades Award for Literature. In addition, her collection of poetry, *Still Out of Place* (2016), earned the Ka Palapala Poʻokela Honorable Mention for Excellence in Literature.

Hear the Dogs Crying

A recording of her voice, an old woman's voice
full of gravel and lead steeped through
the car radio. She spoke of gathering limu
visitors on ships, and dusty roads in Wai'anae.
In the distance you could almost hear
the dogs crying, the mullet wriggling in the fish bag.
Nostalgic for a tūtū I never knew,
I feel the ocean pulse inside me
waves rolling over, pushing me till I leap
from this car through the congested H-1
across the noise and ashen sky
emerge beneath the rains in Nu'uanu.
I move past the fresh water ponds
past the guava trees towards homes
with flimsy tin roofs where
my father, already late for school,
races up Papakōlea with a kite made
of fishing twine. Framed in a small kitchen
window, tūtū scrapes the meat from awa skin
for dinner tonight, wipes her hands on
old flour bags for dish cloths.
She is already small and wants to forget
I may be too late—

I have tomatoes and onion from the market, tūtū,
my hand is out, my plate is empty
and some bones for the dogs to stop their crying
do you know my name?
I am listening for your stories to call me in
my hand is out, my plate is empty
for your stories to show me the way
tūtū, do you know my name?

BRANDY NĀLANI McDOUGALL *(1976–), Kanaka Maoli,* is a poet, scholar, editor, and publisher from Kula, Maui. She is an associate professor specializing in Indigenous studies in the American Studies department at the University of Hawaiʻi at Mānoa. She is the author of *The Salt-Wind: Ka Makani Paʻakai* (2008), a poetry collection, and the scholarly monograph *Finding Meaning: Kaona and Contemporary Hawaiian Literature* (2016), which won the 2017 Beatrice Medicine Award for Scholarship in American Indian Studies. She is the editor of several anthologies and, with Craig Santos Perez, cofounded Ala Press, which publishes Indigenous Pacific literature.

He Mele Aloha no ka Niu

I'm so tired of pretending
each gesture is meaningless,

that the clattering of niu leaves
and the guttural call of birds

overhead say nothing.
There are reasons why

the lichen and moss kākau
the niu's bark, why

this tree has worn
an ahu of ua and lā

since birth. Scars were carved
into its trunk to record

the moʻolelo of its being
by the passage of insects

becoming one to move
the earth, speck by speck.

Try to tell them to let go
of the niu rings marking

each passing year, to abandon
their only home and move on.

I can't pretend there is
no memory held

in the dried coconut hat,
the star ornament, the midribs

bent and dangling away
from their roots, no thought

behind the kāwelewele
that continues to hold us

steady. There was a time
before they were bent

under their need to make
an honest living, when

each frond was bound
by its life to another

like a long, erect fin
skimming the surface

of a sea of grass and sand.
Eventually, it knew it would rise

higher, its flower would emerge
gold, then darken in the sun,

that its fruit would fall, only
to ripen before its brown fronds

bent naturally under the weight
of such memory, back toward

the trunk to drop to the sand,
back to its beginnings, again.

Let this be enough to feed us,
to remember: ka wailewa

i loko, that our own bodies
are buoyant when they bend

and fall, and that the ocean
shall carry us and weave us

back into the sand's fabric,
that the moʻopuna taste our sweet.

Ka ʻŌlelo

O ke alelo ka hoe uli o ka ʻōlelo a ka waha.
The tongue is the steering paddle of the words uttered by the mouth.
—ʻŌlelo Noʻeau

ʻekahi

Think of all the lost words, still unspoken,
waiting to be given use, again, claimed,
or for newly born words to unburden
them of their meanings. There are winds and rains

who have lost their names, descending the slopes
of every mountain, each lush valley's mouth,
and the songs of birds and mo'o, that cope
with our years of slow unknowing, somehow.
It was not long ago that 'ōlelo
was silenced, along with its *dying race*,
who lived, then thrived, reverting to the old
knowing words. English could never replace
the land's unfolding song, nor the ocean's
ancient oli, giving us use again.

'elua

Like the sea urchin leaves, pimpling its shell
as its many spines let go, turn to sand,
my great-grandfather's Hawaiian words fell
silent, while his children grew, their skin tanned
and too thin to withstand the teacher's stick,
reprimands demanding English only.
The ban lasted until 1986,
after three generations of family
swallowed our 'ōlelo like pōhaku,
learned to live with the cold, dark fruit under
our tongues. This is our legacy—words strewn
among wana spines in the long record
the sand has kept within its grains, closer
to reclaiming our shells, now grown thicker.

'ekolu

Ka 'Ōlelo has a lilting rhythm
arising from the coastal mountains' moans
as they loosen their salted earth, succumb
to the ocean and its hunger for stone.
It carries the cadence of nā waihī,
born from the fresh rain in nā waipuna
and flowing past the fruiting 'ulu trees,

wiliwili, kukui, and koa.
It holds the song my grandfather longs for
most, as he remembers his father's voice,
and regrets not asking him to speak more
Hawaiian, so that he may have the choice
to offer words in his inheritance,
knowing his 'ohā will not be silenced.

'ehā

Think of all the old words that have succumbed,
their kaona thrown oceanward for English
words we use like nets to catch the full sum
of our being, finding too little fish
caught in the mesh, even as we adjust
the gauge, reshaping them to suit our mouths.
I must admit I love the brittle crust
my clumsy tongue's foreignness forms; it crowns
the dark, churning pith of prenatal earth
rising in the volcano's throat, unspoken
for now, founding my wide island of words.
And kaona, a ho'okele's current,
circles during my wa'a's slow turn inward,
steering my tongue through each old word learned.

'elima

As the 'ape shoot, whose delicate shoots
shoot forth their young sprouts, and spread, and bring forth
in their birth, many branches find their roots
in the dark, wet 'ōlelo the earth bore.
My unripe tongue taps my palate, my teeth,
like a blind ko'e that must feel its way
through the liquids, mutes and aspirates of speech,
the threading of breath and blood into lei:
"E aloha. 'O wai kou inoa?"

I ask, after the language CD's voice.
"'O Kekauoha ko'u inoa,"
my grandfather answers, "Pehea 'oe?"
So, we slowly begin, with what 'ōlelo
we know; E ho'oulu ana kākou.

 JOAN KANE (1977–), *Iñupiaq*, was born in Anchorage, Alaska. She attended Harvard University and earned her MFA from Columbia University. Kane's accolades and honors include the 2014 Indigenous Writer in Residence fellowship at the School for Advanced Research, judge for the 2017 Griffin Poetry Prize, recipient of the 2018 John Simon Guggenheim Foundation fellowship, along with fellowships and residences from the Native Arts and Cultures Foundation, the Rasmuson Foundation, and the Alaska State Council on the Arts.

VARIATIONS ON AN ADMONITION

I have played with the skulls of seals
And feigned them to be children.

I will tell you of the black spot
Constantly before me–

I had tried hard to make land,
But the coast has altogether vanished.

I ask that you keep your eyes shut
Until the sound of the swarm

Above has passed, that you mind not
A certain brightness. After all,

I have whittled you into life-size–
I will divide you into many men

With time for me to gather
The bones of all sorts of animals

And stir life into them.

NUNAQTIGIIT

(people related through common possession of territory)

The enemy misled that missed the island in the fog,
I believe in one or the other, but both exist now
    to confuse me. Dark from dark.

Snow from snow. I believe in one—

Craggy boundary, knife blade at the throat's slight swell.

From time to time the sound of voices
                as through sun-singed grass,

or grasses that we used to insulate the walls of our winter houses—
walrus hides lashed together with rawhide cords.

So warm within the willows ingathered forced into leaf.

I am named for your sister Naviyuk: call me *apoŋ*.

Surely there are ghosts here, my children sprung
    from these deeper furrows.

The sky of my mind against which self-
                  betrayal in its sudden burn
    fails to describe the world.

We, who denied the landscape
                    and saw the light of it.

Leaning against the stone wall ragged
I began to accept my past and, as I accepted it,

I felt, and I didn't understand:
                    I am bound to everyone.

LEHUA M. TAITANO (*1978–*), **CHamoru**, born in Guåhan, is a queer poet, fiction writer, and cofounder of Art 25. Her chapbook *appalachiapacific* won the 2010 Merriam-Frontier Award for short fiction. She is also the author of two poetry collections, *A Bell Made of Stones* (2013) and *Inside Me an Island* (2018).

Letters from an Island

Hi Everyone. Maria Flores to Shelton Family, 1982.

Hi everyone
I hope you are all fine
as for us we are
just fine
you ought to know how
I fill of writing
I'm not that good so please
excuse me I just make
this cookies for my girl
to remember the old lady
I think the baby can't
try it I have a gift and
her m__ one m____

and I've other for Leah
and the shoes for Lehua
and the blouse I've buy
lady the mama is just
are 500 the blouse is 6 or
I hope you all like it
please write to me if you
recived it did you recived
the one that Lanie mail it
I ask Lanie and she said
she just mail it the other
day I want to thank you
for the meat
it really good
Mary give me a ring
but it fit on my small
finger please
don't tell her
that I'm giving you something
tell Mary if she want me
to come I'm ready
just
send my ticket

 CEDAR SIGO *(1978–), Suquamish.* His published works include *Stranger in Town* (2010), *Language Arts* (2014), and *Royals* (2017). Raised on the Suquamish Reservation near Seattle, Washington, Sigo later studied at the Jack Kerouac School of Disembodied Poetics at Naropa University. He is the editor of Joanne Kyger's *There You Are: Interviews, Journals, and Ephemera* (2017).

A Small Secluded Valley

Your portraits are all thin indians
Half their faces edging out the fog
Where sparks rain onto our temple, where I enter
to write the names of my poems for the night, Daybreak Star
and The Sun, both of which
                                I never got around to
For want of love and allegiance in every second, my regrets
you interrupted. Offset in the kind light as a crown.
(Evan's walking around sounds behind a closed door)
Nice to see you, to walk a bit and stop, as on a river,
its lava shut under in a tunnel of love, regardless
the visions hike up overnight and flames trail off like
the finest spider's thread slipping my mind.

After Self-Help

All my rooms are alien
Towers of books tilt & crumble
                          at the least extended breath
A matinee beyond recall
Brown birds pale breasted darting through
Too Late Hello Later
Kiss the lights and they change
                       out over the Stardust
Cities are huge machines for sorting poets
Skating down the cellophane-enfolded hills
Even cast off lines have their own pull and rhyme
Man at leisure ripped out of my mind
Lonesome after mine own kind
Hot black—soft white—warm reds
Mine a thinking man's cartoon western
Mine the one who enters the stories
Mine the evergreen tears brushed with coral
The boat in the box is mine and mine the full sky

CATHY TAGNAK REXFORD *(1978–)*, *Iñupiaq*, is a poet and playwright. The author of *A Crane Story* (2013), illustrated by Sini Salminen, she has received fellowships from the First Peoples House of Learning and the Rasmuson Foundation. Her play *Whale Song* premiered at Perseverance Theatre in Juneau, Alaska in 2019.

The Ecology of Subsistence

No daylight for two months, an ice chisel slivers
frozen lake water refracting blue cinders.

By light of an oil lamp, a child learns to savor marrow:
cracked caribou bones a heap on the floor.

A sinew, thickly wrapped in soot, threads through
the meat on her chin: a tattoo in three slender lines.

One white ptarmigan plume fastened to the lip of
a birch wood basket; thaw approaches: the plume turns brown.

On the edge of the open lead, a toggle-head harpoon
waits to launch: bowhead sings to krill.

Thickened pack ice cracking; a baleen fishing line
pulls taut a silver dorsal fin of a round white fish.

A slate-blade knife slices along the grain of a caribou
hindquarter; the ice cellar lined in willow branches is empty.

Saltwater suffuses into a flint quarry, offshore
a thin layer of radiation glazes leathered walrus skin.

Alongside shatters of a hummock, a marsh marigold
flattens under three black toes of a sandhill crane.

A translucent sheep horn dipper skims a freshwater stream;
underneath, arctic char lay eggs of mercury.

Picked before the fall migration, cloudberries
drench in whale oil, ferment in a sealskin poke.

A tundra swan nests inside a rusted steel drum;
she abandons her newborns hatched a deep crimson.

 DONOVAN KŪHIŌ COLLEPS (1978–), *Kanaka Maoli*, was born in Honolulu, Hawai'i, and was raised on the 'Ewa plains of O'ahu. A PhD candidate in English at the University of Hawai'i at Mānoa, he is also a production editor at the University of Hawai'i Press.

KISSING THE OPELU

For my grandmother

I am water, only because you are the ocean.

We are here, only
because old leaves have been falling.

A mulching of memories folding
into buried hands.

The cliffs we learn to edge.
The tree trunk hollowed, humming.

I am a tongue, only because
you are the body planting stories with thumb.

Soil crumbs cling to your knees.
Small stacks of empty clay pots dreaming.

I am an air plant suspended, only
because you are the trunk I cling to.

I am the milky fish eye, only
because it's your favorite.

Even the sound you make
when your lips kiss the opelu
socket is a mo'olelo.

A slipper is lost in the yard.
A haku lei is chilling in the icebox.

I am a cup for feathers, only
because you want to fill the hours.

I am a turning wrist, only
because you left the hose on.

Heliconias are singing underwater.
Beetles are floating across the yard.

 CRAIG SANTOS PEREZ *(1980–)*, **CHamoru,** is a poet,
scholar, educator, editor, and publisher who has won several awards
and honors for the four books of poetry in his series *from unincorpo-*
rated territory, including the PEN America Literary Award for Poetry (2011),
an American Book Award (2015), a Lannan Literary Award (2016), and
the Elliot Cades Award for Literature (2017). He cofounded, with Brandy
Nālani McDougall, Ala Press, a publishing company that specializes in
Indigenous Pacific literature. He is an associate professor of creative writing
in the English department at the University of Hawai'i at Mānoa.

GINEN THE MICRONESIAN KINGFISHER [I SIHEK]

[our] nightmare : no
birdsong—
the jungle was riven emptied
of *[i sihek]* bright blue green turquoise red gold
feathers—everywhere : brown
tree snakes avian
silence—

the snakes entered
without words when [we] saw them it was too late—
they were at [our] doors sliding along
the passages of *[i sihek]*
empire—then

the zookeepers came—
called it *species survival plan*—captured *[i sihek]* and transferred
the last
twenty-nine micronesian kingfishers
to zoos for captive breeding *[1988]*—they repeated *[i sihek]*
and repeated :

"if it weren't for us
your birds   [i sihek]
would be gone
forever"

what does not change /

last wild seen—

ISHMAEL HOPE *(1981–)*, **Tlingit** and **Iñupiaq,** grew up surrounded by both Tlingit and Iñupiaq cultures. He is the son of poets Andrew Hope III and Elizabeth "Sister Goodwin" Hope. In conjunction with his poetry, Hope has coordinated festivals, performed as an actor, and been a lead writer for the video game *Never Alone (Kisima Innitchuna)*, which visualizes traditional Iñupiaq lore.

Canoe Launching into the Gaslit Sea

Now, as much as ever, and as always,
we need to band together, form
a lost tribe, scatter as one, burst
through rifle barrels guided
by the spider's crosshairs. We need
to knit wool sweaters for our brother
sleeping under the freeway,
hand him our wallets and bathe
his feet in holy water. We need
to find our lost sister, last seen
hitchhiking Highway 16
or panhandling on the streets of Anchorage,
couchsurfing with relatives in Victoria,
or kicking out her boyfriend
after a week of partying
in a trailer park in Salem, Oregon.

Now, as much as ever, and as always,
we need to register together,
lock arms at the front lines, brand
ourselves with mutant DNA strands,
atomic whirls and serial numbers
adding ourselves to the blacklist.
We need to speak in code, languages
the enemy can't break, slingshot

garlic cloves and tortilla crumbs,
wear armor of lily pads and sandstone
carved into the stately faces of bears
and the faraway look of whitetail deer.
We need to run uphill with rickshaws,
play frisbee with trash lids, hold up
portraits of soldiers who never
made it home, organize a peace-in
on the walls of the Grand Canyon.
We need to stage earnest satirical plays,
hold debate contests with farm animals
at midnight, fall asleep on hammocks
hanging from busy traffic lights.

Now, as much as ever, and as always,
we need to prank call our senators,
take selfies with the authorities
at fundraisers we weren't invited to,
kneel in prayer at burial grounds
crumbling under dynamite.
We need to rub salve on the belly
of our hearts, meditate on fault lines
as the earth quakes, dance in robes
with fringe that spits medicine, make
love on the eve of the disaster.

CARRIE AYAĠADUK OJANEN (*1983–*), *Iñupiaq,* grew up in Nome, Alaska. Her family is a part of the Ugiuvamiut tribe, whom the federal government relocated to Nome. She received her MFA from the University of Montana. Her debut poetry collection, *Roughly for the North,* was published in 2018.

Fifth Saint, Sixth & Seventh

Gabriel, sing great-grandpa's song,
head thrown back, black hair gleaming
gray at your temples. So handsome, you,
great-uncle—my Uvah—I imagine my Aupa
looked like you when he was younger,
deep, dark skin and half-moon smile
gleaming, you laugh the same laugh—huh huh huh huh!

Did your heart break, as his, leaving the island—
he stayed an extra winter, left his eldest children
in Nome for school, lived on Ugiuvak—the place for winter—with Auka
and their smallest children—
Mom, age four, was there—and that 16mm
camera recording the last winter
of his traditional life.

Recording that last winter to convince the BIA to send another teacher.

The film was ruined by the August storms.
They wouldn't have watched it anyway.

Those fuckers.

O God, reading Aupa's accounts ruptures

everything forever.

Aupa never sings.

But sing, Gabriel, sing, sing grandpa's song.

Mom and Aya Margaret will stand up to dance.
We welcome everyone to dance with us.

—

You all broke, I know, everyone shattered

Auka and Aupa and their sad kitchen life,
eyes graying the straight, dusty streets of
Nome.

Everybody lost themselves in drink for years.
Some are still lost.

—

Sing, Gabriel, sing.

How beautiful our women are—
wearing floral ugithqoks,
dancing—that passionate precision—
your Frances, Auka, Marie, Mom, Margaret, Caroline, Marilyn,
and your granddaughters—in a line—motions memorized.

And then, the song is over.
They move back to their seats.

Please, Uvah, as we always do,
sing the song again, a second time,
and a second time they will stand up to dance.

 ABIGAIL CHABITNOY (1987–), *Koniag* and *Tangirnaq*,
earned her MFA from Colorado State University, where she was
a Crow-Tremblay fellow. A winner of the 2017 Locked Horn Press
Poetry Prize, she published her first poetry collection, *How to Dress a Fish*,
in 2019. Of Germanic and Aleut descent, she is a Koniag descendant and
member of the Tangirnaq Native Village in Kodiak, Alaska, and grew up in
Pennsylvania.

Anatomy of a Wave

It had everything and nothing to do
with mettle

    fire before flint before

How many bodies will a lead ball move

    through?

How many men can one stand in a row?

    When the tide went out, they had nowhere to run

      but that was many years ago, and if they have not died they live

happily still.

    But you and I know that's not how the story goes.

I wake more ghosts each morning:

      when I was born my mother and father

      planted a tree west of the garden.

      We ripped it out when I left home—

      its roots never took,

      its limbs harbored mold in the sticky east wind.

We used to think a weak spine
was inherited

        but consider the shark

how some will stop swimming

in their sleep.

How does the forecast change?

We make weather with our teeth.
Why should I be afraid of the sea?
Let the toothed skin lie

if it asks too many bones.

Wait for the waves

to start skipping,

Tie down the drifters and stretch the stomach before the fall.

Don't turn your back on the water.

What else grows on an island

without trees?

The need to make

makes body—

Others have seen water act this way before,
it was many years ago,
how many bodies a single wave can carry,
how many relatives, casually.

They tied their boats to the tops of trees
so the water wouldn't lose them,
so the story goes.

Some say it was a boat that killed them, Vasiley and Akelina. Bad heart,
     traumatized. Accidently.
I'm telling you what happens. Nikifor missed the boat.

Imagine what it might be like

          when the waters come

to be a fish

          to be twelve strong, to be six, two hundred, or forty

          sharks swimming toward you—

 NOʻU REVILLA (*1987–*), *Kanaka Maoli* and *Tahitian,* is a
queer poet, educator, editor, and performing artist from Kahului,
Maui. Her chapbook *Say Throne* was published in 2011. She served
as poetry editor of the *Hawaiʻi Review* and organized the first AlohaʻĀina
Zine workshop in solidarity with the protectors of Mauna Kea in 2015. She
earned her PhD in English from the University of Hawaiʻi at Mānoa, where
she is now an assistant professor of English, teaching creative writing.

SMOKE SCREEN

> *for every hard-working father who ever worked*
> *at HC&S, especially mine*

Was he a green, long sleeve
jacket & god-fearing man?
On the job, bloodshot.
Marrying metal in his heavy
gloves, bringing justice to his father,

who was also a smoking man.
No bathroom breaks, no helmets, no safe words.
He whistled sugarcane through his neck,
through his unventilated wife,
his chronic black ash daughters.
This is what a burn schedule looks like.
And if believing in god was a respiratory issue,
he was like his father.
Marrying metal to make a family.
At home he smoked before he slept.
In the corner with the door
ajar, cigarette poised like a first-born:
well-behaved, rehearsed.
Curtains drawn, bedrooms medicated.
He was always burning into something.
Part-dark, part-pupils.
For my father, the night was best alone.
When only he could see through
the world and forgive it.

 MICHAEL WASSON (*1990–*), *Nimíipuu, Nez Perce*, completed his MFA at Oregon State University and currently teaches conversation-based English courses off the coast of Japan. He is the author of *Self-Portrait with Smeared Centuries* (Éditions des Lisières, 2018), translated into French by Béatrice Machet, and *This American Ghost* (2017). His awards include a Native Arts and Cultures Foundation Artist Fellowship in Literature and the Adrienne Rich Award for Poetry.

A Poem for the háawtnin' & héwlekipx [The Holy Ghost of You, the Space & Thin Air]

'inept'ipéecwise cilaakt: (I am wanting to) hold a wake / (I am wanting to) hold the body

Had this body been made
                        of nothing

but its bright skeleton & autumn-

blown skin
            I would shut my eyes

into butterfly wings
    on a mapped earth. Had the gods

even their own gods, I could re-

learn the very shape
            of my face in a puddle of sky-

colored rain. Extinction is
                        to the hands

as the lips are
            to the first gesture

the tongue carves into the slick mouth

just before
            prayer. In every way

the world fails
                to light the soft inner

machine & marrow

    of the bones in motion — I imagine

smudging my tongue along a wall
                       like the chest

I dare to plunge in-
           to, the Braille of every node

blooming out
          as if the first day-

light of wintered
         snowfall. This night —

like any fleshed boy I dream
         of a lyre strung

with the torn hair of *hímiin* &
                in place

of my dried mouth — there
           it is. Whispers

in the blue-black dark after *c'álalal*

c'álalal reach out
        toward my teeth to strum

this wilting instrument. &
           once awake, I'm holding

its frame to build
        a window back in-

to the world. Had this body

been held after all

        these years, I would enter

you to find my frozen self

& touch. Like the gutted animal

        we take

in offering. & live.

JAMAICA HEOLIMELEIKALANI OSORIO *(1991–), Kanaka Maoli,* is a poet, performance artist, scholar, and activist from Pālolo, Oʻahu, who is widely known for her spoken-word poetry. She has performed across five continents and was invited to the White House to perform by President and Mrs. Barack Obama in 2009. She was awarded a Ford Foundation fellowship in 2017, earned her PhD in English in 2018, and is now an assistant professor of Indigenous Politics at the University of Hawaiʻi at Mānoa.

KUMULIPO

What happens to the ones forgotten
the ones who shaped my heart from their rib cages
i want to taste the tears in their names
trace their souls into my vocal chords so that i can feel related again
because i have forgotten my own grandparents' middle names
Forgotten what color thread god used to sew me together with

There is a culture
Somewhere beneath my skin that i've been searching for since i landed here
But it's hard to feel sometimes
Because at Stanford we are innovative

the city of Macintosh breeds thinkers of tomorrow
and i have forgotten how to remember

But our roots cannot remember themselves
Cannot remember how to dance if we don't chant for them
And will not sing unless we are listening
but our tongues feel too foreign in our own mouths
we don't dare speak out loud
and we can't even remember our own parents' names
so who will care to remember mine if I don't teach them

i want to teach my future children
how to spell family with my middle name—Heolimeleikalani
how to hold love with Kamakawiwo'ole
how to taste culture in the Kumulipo
please
do not forget me
my father
Kamakawiwo'ole
who could not forget his own
Leialoha
do not forget what's left
cuz this is all we have
and you won't find our roots online

We have no dances or chants if we have no history
just rants
no roots
just tears
this is all i have of our family history
and now it's yours

'O Ma'alolaninui ke kāne 'o Lonokaumakahiki ka wahine
Noho pū lāua a hānau ia 'o Imaikalani he Kāne
'O Imaikalani ke kāne 'o Keko'okalani ka wahine
Noho pū lāua a hānau ia 'o Pa'aluhi Kahinuonalani he kāne

'O Pa'aluhi Kahinuonalani ke kāne 'o Pi'ipi'i Keali'iwaiwai'ole ka wahine
Noho pū lāua a hānau iā'o Charles Moses Kamakawiwo'ole 'o
    Kamehameha ke kane
'O Hainaloa ke kāne 'o Niau ka wahine
Noho pū lāua a hāneu ia 'o Kaluaihonolulu ka wahine
'O Kaluaihonolulu ka wahine 'o Nako'oka ke kāne
Noho pū lāua a hānau ia 'o Kapahu he wahine
'O Kapahu ka wahine 'o Kua ke kāne
Noho pū lāua a hānau ia 'o Daisy Keali'i'aiawaawa he wahine [Koholālele]
'O Charles Moses Kamakawiwo'ole'o Kamehameha ke kāne 'o
        Daisy Keali'iai'awa'awa ka wahine
Noho pū lāua a hānau ia 'o Eliza Leialoha Kamakawiwo'ole he wahine
    [Kukuihaele]
'O Eliza Leialoha Kamakawiwo'ole ka wahine 'o Emil Montero Osorio ke
    kāne [Hilo]
Noho pū lāua a hānau 'ia 'o Elroy Thomas Leialoha Osorio he kāne
'O Manūawai ke kāne 'o Keao ka wahine [South Kona & Kohala]
        Noho pū lāua a hānau ia 'o Sarah Pi'ikea Papanui he wahine
'O Sarah Pi'ikea Papanui ka wahine 'o Kam Sheong Akiona
ke kāne
Noho pū lāua a hānau ia 'o Nani Kaluahine Kimoe Akiona he wahine
'O Nani Kaluahine Kimoe Akiona ka wahine 'o LeRoy Adam Anthony Kay
ke kāne
Noho pū lāua a hānau ia 'o Clara Ku'ulei Kay he wahine
'O Elroy Thomas Leialoha Osorio ke kāne 'o Clara Ku'ulei Kay ka wahine
Noho pū lāua a hānau ia 'o Jonathan Kay Kamakawiwo'ole Osorio he kāne
'O Jonathan Kay Kamakawiwo'ole Osorio ke kāne 'o Mary Carol Dunn ka
    wahine
Noho pū lāua a hānau ia 'o Jamaica Heolimeleikalani Osorio

do not forget us
mai poina

SOUTHWEST
AND WEST

"I'M HERE TO MAKE A POEM"

Deborah A. Miranda

WRITING THE INTRODUCTION to this section feels like writing a love letter about a collection of love letters. For these poets, home is the land currently called California, Nevada, Colorado, New Mexico, and Arizona, embraced by the Pacific Ocean and bordered by desert, mountains, a river, a gulf—and by an artificial boundary where ancestral crossings were once the norm.

As we journey through this poetic space, languages ripple like mountain ranges: Diné, Western Apache, Yaqui. Spanish seeps in, legacy of early colonization left behind like a worn scar; English gets pulled and stretched into Indigenous syntax and rhythms, as older languages like Keres, Cahuilla, Esselen, Mojave, Kumeyaay, Yurok, Chumash, Yuman, and Koyongk'awi push up against English like submerged rivers, slowly and relentlessly indigenizing the footprint of another colonial invader.

Walking through these poems is also a kind of homecoming. In a literal sense, our bodies carry traces of where we were born and raised: oxygen isotopes from the water we drank as children are stored within the buds of our teeth, formed before birth or during childhood. The poems in this volume carry, within their words and white spaces, indelible traces of the place where we emerged. They tell the stories inside of us, our histories, dreams, struggles, pain, joy, moments of peace and clarity. At the same time, these poems bear us forward into what comes next, the futures we rise to meet or take in our hands, carve out for coming generations.

Despite all stereotypes to the contrary, Indians do not only exist in, and only honor, the past; we also work toward and build our futures. "And realms our tribes were crushed to get / May be our barren desert yet," Arsenius Chaleco, Yuma, writes in "The Indian Requiem"—seemingly an elegy about defeat. But the closing lines reveal the speaker's intention to endure *beyond* the end of Euro-Americans; "*our* barren desert," he says. Despite the ways this earth may be dishonored and violated by settlers, Chaleco's poem is an

"Indian requiem" for *colonization*, not for Indigenous cultures. *We* will be here for the healing to come.

Still, endurance isn't easy. Simon Ortiz, Acoma Pueblo, expresses the pain of constant occupation in his poem "Indian Guys at the Bar": "I don't know if my feet can make it; / my soul is where it has always been; / my heart is staggering somewhere in between." Ortiz, along with Natalie Diaz, Tommy Pico, Adrian C. Louis, and others in this collection, illustrates the ways alcohol and trauma have been weaponized to separate the people from the land. This brutal separation is a weight carried by these hard-working poets, and it breaks our hearts even as it empowers us toward the truth about the realities of heroic recovery.

Other poems, like Koyongk'awi Linda Noel's "Lesson in Fire," rise to reaffirm the depth of Indigenous knowledge: passed on from father to daughter are not just the mechanics of building "a good fire," but the way to "tend" that fire so that the gifts inside wood are released. The knowledge that wood possesses literally warms the air the speaker breathes in, passing on different kinds of lessons, teaching her wonder and gratitude. The thickly forested homelands of Noel's Northern California people reside in this poem. Georgiana Valoyce-Sanchez (Chumash, Tohono O'odham, and Pima) speaks of the ocean's presence for California coastal tribes in "The Dolphin Walking Stick," which serves as an elegy for her father. "As he walks / strings of seashells clack softly / as when ocean waves tumble / rocks and shells and / the gentle clacking song / follows each wave / as it pulls back into / the sea," Valoyce-Sanchez writes, creating an ocean on the page as music for her father's story.

Tribal people of the Southwest and West have survived many efforts by Euro-Americans to appropriate the land and remove Indigenous lives from the organic ebb and flow of migrations, cyclical and seasonal movements, and trade routes—all ways of being in relationship with this planet. Strangely enough, when faced with the wide-open spaces of this part of the continent, the Euro-American's first response was to erect fences! "The Wall" by Anita Endrezze (Yaqui) best illustrates the ridiculous nature of artificial boundaries and the violence of racist politics. Responding to the clueless campaign promise of a politician, Endrezze's list of possible building materials begins with "saguaros,/ butterflies, and bones/ of those who perished/ in the desert." Next, her construction materials grow to include the debris of capitalism: "A Lego wall or bubble wrap" where "dreams will be terrorists." Parody, sarcasm, cynicism, and whimsy, along with chocolate and "hummingbird warriors," become her mortar, leading us to the stunning image of a "2,000 mile altar"—and beyond. Part warning, part prophecy, this poem asserts that Indigenous people on both sides of that border will outlive any wall.

Several poets write specifically of queer or two-spirit Indigenous experiences. Julian Talamantez Brolaski's poem addresses the presence of "twospirits at the/ winyan camp" at Standing Rock, North Dakota, while groaning over queer stereotypes and erasure of people of color at the Stonewall demonstrations in New York City in 1969, as portrayed in the 2015 film *Stonewall*; "and now people are treating standing rock like burning man," they add, noting more erasures. Still, "I'm here to make a poem," the author sings. Crisosto Apache's poem "Ndé'isdzán" ("two of me") visually illustrates the intersection of two genders, the collision and creation of a third, "twins born in a water-suit." Elements of earth, water, and air work together here, imagining a kind of spiritual DNA that is loving and fiercely beloved. In "Earthquake Weather," Janice Gould says of her lover, "When September comes with its hot/ electric winds,/ I will think of you and know/ somewhere in the world/ the earth is breaking open." The conflation of lover and earth could not be more profound—a connection that cannot be denied even in the midst of transformation.

Diné poets form an impressive core in this part of Indian Country; Tacey M. Atsitty, Rex Lee Jim, Luci Tapahonso, Laura Tohe, Esther G. Belin, Hershman R. John, Sherwin Bitsui, Orlando White, Bojan Louis, and Jake Skeets *represent*! The presence of Diné language in their poems is no less than a miracle, given the decimation of Indigenous languages in the Americas. Most readers of Jim's "Saad" or Tapahonso's "This is How They Were Placed for Us" won't understand Diné; *but some will*, and oh, the pleasure and empowerment of seeing one's language in a published book! As Sherwin Bitsui says of his poem from *Flood Song*, "the Navajo would understand it. But also the sound of it, . . . makes the sound of dripping water . . . splashing. The audience member who might not understand it literally can appreciate the sound of another language." In the same way, the poets of western and southwestern parts of the United States remind non-Natives of the long historical presence of Indians in this place and send a vital message to Native and dominant language speakers alike: Indigenous languages are living, valid, valuable methods of creating literary works.

Like those isotopes stored in our bodies that preserve and carry traces of our birthlands, this writing carries something indelible: Each poem moves across the page, into the eyes and minds and hearts of readers. This is an art indistinguishable from living.

Nimasianexelpasaleki. *My heart is happy.*

 ARSENIUS CHALECO (*1889–1939*), *Yuma,* was born in California on the Fort Yuma Indian Reservation. He attended the Phoenix Indian School in Arizona, where he trained as a blacksmith. After graduating, Chaleco farmed his own ten acres of land in Imperial County, California. In 1923, he served as interpreter for the Yuma Delegation, dictating a petition for the U.S. Secretary of the Interior at the convention of the Mission Indian Federation at Riverside, California. "The Indian Requiem" appears to be Chaleco's only surviving poem, originally published in *The Indian Teepee* in 1924.

The Indian Requiem

In the loose sand is thrown
The warrior's frame, now mouldering bone.

Ah, little thought the strong and brave
Who bore the lifeless chieftain forth,
Or the young wife who, weeping gave
Her first born, (years wasted now)
That through their graves would cut the plow.

Before the fields were sown and tilled,
Full to the brim our rivers plowed.
The melody of waters filled
The fresh and boundless wood.

Torrents dashed and rivulets played,
And fountains spouted in the shade.

These grateful sounds are heard no more.
The springs are silent in the sun,
And rivers, through their blackened shores,
With lessening currents run.

They waste us—ah, like April snow
In the warm noon, we shrink away,
And fast they follow as we go
Towards the setting day.

But I behold a fearful sign
To which the white man's eyes are blind,
Their race may vanish hence like mine
And leave no trace behind,

Save ruins o'er the region spread,
And tall white stones above the dead.
And realms our tribes were crushed to get
May be our barren desert yet.

CARLOS MONTEZUMA (WASSAJA) (1866–1923), *Yavapai-Apache,* was a poet, physician, and activist. As a child, he was kidnapped and sold as a slave but was adopted by his "owner," who provided a powerful education. Montezuma went on to become the first male American Indian doctor and a tireless advocate for Native issues. He worked for the Bureau of Indian Affairs hospitals and fought for Indian rights. He spent the last years of his life publishing *Wassaja,* a journal advocating for Indian rights—especially for the territory and people of his homeland.

Indian Office

If the Indian Office is in existence for the best interest of the Indians, why
    does it not work FOR THE BEST INTEREST OF THE INDIANS?

Is working on the Indians as Indians, FOR THE BEST INTEREST OF
    THE INDIANS?

Keeping the Indians as Wards, is that FOR THE BEST INTEREST OF
    THE INDIANS?

Is caging the Indians on reservations FOR THE BEST INTEREST OF
    THE INDIANS?

Does opening the Indian lands for settlers work FOR THE BEST
    INTEREST OF THE INDIANS?

Are the Reimbursement Funds (Government Mortgage) FOR THE BEST
    INTEREST OF THE INDIANS?

Are dams built on reservations FOR THE BEST INTEREST OF THE
    INDIANS?

Giving five or ten acres of irrigation land to the Indian and taking the rest of
    his land away for land-grabbers, is that FOR THE BEST INTEREST
    OF THE INDIANS?

Is selling the Indians' surplus (?) land FOR THE BEST INTEREST OF
    THE INDIANS?

To dispose of the Indians' mineral lands, is that FOR THE BEST
    INTEREST OF THE INDIANS?

Selling the timber land of the Indians, is that FOR THE BEST
    INTEREST OF THE INDIANS?

To discriminate and keep back the Indian race from other races, is that
    FOR THE BEST INTEREST OF THE INDIANS?

Are Indian schools for the papooses FOR THE BEST INTEREST OF
    THE INDIANS?

Is keeping the Indians from opportunities FOR THE BEST INTEREST
    OF THE INDIANS?

Is doing everything for the Indians, without their consent, FOR THE
    BEST INTEREST OF THE INDIANS?

Keeping the Indians from freedom and citizenship, is that FOR THE
    BEST INTEREST OF THE INDIANS?

Is keeping six thousand employees in the Indian Service FOR THE BEST
INTEREST OF THE INDIANS?

For you to have sole power over the Indians, is that FOR THE BEST
INTEREST OF THE INDIANS?

Speak as we may, there is not one redeeming feature in the Indian Bureau
FOR THE BEST INTEREST OF THE INDIANS. WASSAJA is
emphatic in claiming the Indian Office has done all the harm that has
come to the Indians; it is now doing great harm to the Indians, and it
will suck the life-blood out of the Indians and that is not FOR THE
BEST INTEREST OF THE INDIANS.

DON JESÚS YOILO'I *(1904–1982)*, *Yaqui,* was born in Potám, a small Yaqui village outside Sonora, Mexico. He fought in the Yaqui Battalion during the Mexican Revolution; afterward, he worked in Arizona and Texas on railroads and in cotton fields. Around 1920 Yoilo'i returned home and collaborated with the elder deer singers in the Rio Yaqui area; he later mentored others in the way of the deer songs and *pahko* arts.

YAQUI DEER SONG

Ka ne huni
　　　into ne inia aniat
　　　　　ne na ne welamsisimne
Kia ne ka ne huni
　　　into ne inia aniat
　　　　　ne na ne welamsisimne

Kia ne ka ne huni
　　　into ne inia aniat
　　　　　ne na ne welamsisimne

Kia ne ka ne huni
        into ne inia aniat
                ne na ne welamsisimne

Ayaman ne
        seyewailo saniloata fayalikun
                weyekai
Kia ne yevuku yolemta wikoli
        ne yo yumatakai
Yevuku yolemta vaka hiuwai
        ne yo yumatakai
Ka ne huni
        into ne inia aniat
                ne na ne welamsisimne

Never again I,
        will I on this world,
                I, around will I be walking.
Just I, never again I,
        will I on this world,
                I, around will I be walking.

Just I, never again I,
        will I on this world,
                I, around will I be walking.
Just I, never again I,
        will I on this world,
                I, around will I be walking.

Over there, I,
        in an opening in the flowered-covered grove,
                as I am walking.
Just I, Yevuku Yoleme's bow
        overpowered me in an enchanted way.
Yevuku Yoleme's bamboo arrow
        overpowered me in an enchanted way.

Never again I,
     will I on this world,
          I, around will I be walking.

                   Don Jesús Yoilo'i
                   Yoem Pueblo
                   May 9, 1981

FRANK LAPENA (*1937–2019*), *Nomtipom Wintu,* a poet, singer, essayist, visual artist, and performance artist, earned his BA degree at California State University Chico and his MA from Sacramento State University, where he served as professor of Art and Ethnic Studies and director of Native American Studies for more than thirty years. Working across the fields of art, from singing to writing to visual, dance, and performative art, LaPena was a founding member of the Maidu Dancers and Traditionalists, dedicated to the revival and preservation of these Native arts.

THE UNIVERSE SINGS

Spring days
and winter nights
have beautiful
flowers shining
they make themselves
visible
by whispering
in the color
of blue pollen

Their fragrances
are footprints
lightly traveling
on the milky way

Once I was given
a bracelet of
golden yellow flowers
on velvet darkness

Reenie said that
a mouse was painted
in the color of the sun
and that he danced for joy
on seeing flowers
blossom into stars
dancing across the universe
and singing,
singing, singing.

 GEORGIANA VALOYCE-SANCHEZ (1939–), *Chumash,
Tohono O'odham,* and *Pima*, was born and raised in California.
She is an elder on the governing council of the Barbareño Chumash
Council and a board member of the California Indian Storytelling Associ-
ation. Her poems have been anthologized widely, including in *The Sound of
Rattles and Clappers, Through the Eye of the Deer,* and *Red Indian Road West.*
She recently retired from the American Indian Studies Program at Califor-
nia State University, Long Beach after twenty-eight years.

THE DOLPHIN WALKING STICK

He says
sure you look for your Spirit
symbol   your totem
only it's more a waiting
watching
for its coming

You listen
You listen for the way it
feels   deep inside

Sometimes something comes
that feels   almost
right
the way that swordfish
kept cropping up with
its long nose

but no
and so   you wait
knowing it is getting
closer   knowing
it is coming

And when that dolphin
jumped out of the water
its silver blue sides all shiny
and glistening with rainbows
against the white cloud sky
and the ocean so big
and deep
it went on
forever
I knew it had come

My father rests his hand upon
the dolphin's back
the dolphin's gaze serene
above the rainbow band
wrapped around the walking stick

He leans upon his brother friend
and walks across the room

As he walks
strings of seashells clack softly
as when ocean waves tumble
rocks and shells and
the gentle clacking song
follows each wave
as it pulls back into
the sea

The sea

So long ago
the Channel Islands filled
with Chumash People like
colonies of sea lions
along the shore   so many
people
it was time for some to
make the move
across the ocean to
the mainland

Kakunupmawa   the sun
the Great Mystery
according to men's ideas
said   don't worry
I will make you a bridge
the rainbow
will be your bridge   only
don't look down
or you will fall

Have faith

So the chosen ones began
the long walk across
the rainbow
they kept their eyes straight
toward where the mainland was
and all around them
was the ocean   sparkling
like a million scattered crystals
so blue-green and singing
lovely and cool
some looked down
and fell
into the
deep
to become
the dolphins
they too
the People

My father turns to look at me

Someone told me that story
long before I ever heard it
            It's those old ones
he says   pointing up to the ceiling
as if it were sky

They sent the dolphin to me

I always loved the sea

PAULA GUNN ALLEN (*1939–2008*), *Laguna,* was born in Cubero, New Mexico. She received her PhD from the University of New Mexico and taught at several universities, retiring from the University of California, Los Angeles as a professor of English, Creative Writing, and American Indian Studies. Allen was the author of six poetry collections, including *Life is a Fatal Disease, Skin and Bones,* and *America the Beautiful.* She is widely known for her scholarship in Native literature and feminism.

Laguna Ladies Luncheon

on my fortieth birthday

Gramma says it's so depressing—
all those Indian women,
their children never to be born
and they didn't know
they'd been sterilized.
See, the docs didn't want them
bothered, them being so poor and all,
at least that's what is said.
Sorrow fills the curve of our breasts,
the hollows behind the bone.
Three closet Indians
my mother, my grandmother and I
who nobody sterilized. Our
children are grown.
We do not dare to weep
over coffee in this elegant place;
quiet, we hold their grief unborn.
My mother says it's the same
as Nazi Germany.
A medical holocaust.
Now I'm officially
an old woman, she says,
I can tell them that.

SIMON ORTIZ (1941–), *Acoma,* was born in Albuquerque, New Mexico, and raised at Acoma Pueblo. As a young man, he served in the U.S. armed forces. Ortiz has more than two dozen volumes of poetry, prose fiction, children's literature, and nonfiction work translated and anthologized all over the world, including *Out There Somewhere, Woven Stone,* and *From Sand Creek.* Winner of the Lifetime Achievement Award from the Native Writers' Circle of the Americas, he is retired from his position as an endowed chair at Arizona State University.

My Father's Song

Wanting to say things,
I miss my father tonight.
His voice, the slight catch,
the depth from his thin chest,
the tremble of emotion
in something he has just said
to his son, his song:

We planted corn one Spring at Acu—
we planted several times
but this one particular time
I remember the soft damp sand
in my hand.

My father had stopped at one point
to show me an overturned furrow;
the plowshare had unearthed
the burrow nest of a mouse
in the soft moist sand.

Very gently, he scooped tiny pink animals
into the palm of his hand
and told me to touch them.
We took them to the edge

of the field and put them in the shade
of a sand moist clod.

I remember the very softness
of cool and warm sand and tiny alive mice
and my father saying things.

INDIAN GUYS AT THE BAR

My head is drawing closer to the bar again
when someone says,

"Damn, my wife just lost her job,
I don't know what to do."

"Sometimes I drink;
other times I think I'm just crazy."

"Hey, here comes Jim. God, he's ugly."

"That's okay, brother, sit down.
Chippewas are always like that."

"Yeah, Chippewas were made to be like that."

The words jerk through me;
they vibrate and wobble for a long time.

"If them Pueblos ever learn to work,
they'll be okay."

"It's a cultural trait with them,
climb cliffs and throw rocks,
too tired to work."

"I heard three Indian guys got stabbed
downtown outside the Winstins.
Someone was watching them from the Federal Building
from the sixth floor where the BIA is."

Silence is sometimes the still wind;
sometimes it is the emptiness.

"I went to see my parole officer;
he said to behave or we'll send you back to the res."

"Man, when I was about to get out,
I heard the guard yell, '0367 Griego,
get your red ass in gear, you're going home,'
I couldn't believe it; I just stood there and cried."

"I know. I know. Here, have another drink
of culture."

I don't know if my feet can make it;
my soul is where it has always been;
my heart is staggering somewhere in between.

SELECTION FROM *FROM SAND CREEK*

Don't fret now.

Songs are useless
to exculpate sorrow.
That's not their intent anyway.

Strive
for significance.
Cull seeds from grass.
Develop another strain of corn.

Whisper for rain.

Don't fret.
Warriors will keep alive in the blood.

Somehow
it was impossible
for them
to understand true safety.

Knowledge for them
was impossible
to understand as pain.
That was untrustworthy,
lost to memory.

Death was sin.

Their children
hunkered down, frightened
into quilts, listening
to wind
speaking Arapahoe words
for pain and beauty and generations.

But they refused to understand.
Instead, they protested
the northwind,
kept adding rooms.
Built fences.
Their children learned to plan.
Their parents required submission.

Warriors could have passed
into their young blood.

EMERSON BLACKHORSE MITCHELL (1945–), *Diné*, was born near Shiprock, New Mexico, where he still lives. He began writing poetry while he was in boarding school in the 1960s, using both Navajo and English. His autobiography, *Miracle Hill: The Story of a Navajo Boy*, was first published in 1967 and was reprinted in 2004 by the University of Arizona Press. He teaches at Red Mesa High School in Teec Nos Pos, Arizona, and at the Shiprock campus of Diné College.

MIRACLE HILL

I stand upon my miracle hill,
    Wondering of the yonder distance,
Thinking, When will I reach there?

I stand upon my miracle hill.
    The wind whispers in my ear.
I hear the songs of old ones.

I stand upon my miracle hill;
    My loneliness I wrap around me.
It is my striped blanket.

I stand upon my miracle hill
    And send out touching wishes
To the world beyond hand's reach.

I stand upon my miracle hill.
    The bluebird that flies above
Leads me to my friend, the white man.

I come again to my miracle hill.
    At last I know the all of me—
Out there, beyond, and here upon my hill.

ADRIAN C. LOUIS (*1946–2018*), *Lovelock Paiute,* the oldest of twelve children, moved from Nevada to Rhode Island, earning his BFA and MFA in creative writing from Brown University. Louis published extensively in both poetry and prose, winning the Pushcart Prize and the Cohen Award as well as fellowships from the Bush Foundation, the South Dakota Arts Council, and the National Endowment for the Arts. His time teaching and living in the Pine Ridge Reservation community in South Dakota heavily influenced his poetry. *Electric Snakes* was his last poetry collection.

SKINOLOGY

Yellow roses, wild roses,
their decades of growth,
a fierce fence between
the drunkenness
of my neighbors
& me.

◎

I have known
some badass Skins.
Clichéd bad-to-the-bone
Indians who were maybe
not bad but just broke,
& broken for sure.

◎

Late winter, late night,
a gentle rapping, a tapping
on my chamber door . . .
some guy selling a block
of commodity cheese
for five bucks.

◎

You climbed a tree,
sat there for hours
until some kind of voice
called you back home.
You unfolded your wings,
took to the air & smashed
into earth. They hauled
you to ER, then Detox
where they laughed
at your broken wings.

◎

Once, I thought
I saw eagles soar,
loop & do the crow hop
in the blue air while
the sun beat the earth
like a drum, but I was
disheveled & drinking
those years.

◎

Indians & the Internet.
Somewhere, sometime.
Whenever a Messiah
Chief is born, jealous
relatives will drag him
down like the old days
only instantly now.

◎

In a brutal land
within a brutal land
with corrupt leaders
& children killing themselves
we know who is to blame.
But, we are on a train,

a runaway train & we
don't know what to do.

◎

The good earth,
the sun blazing down,
us in our chones, butts
stuck in inner tubes,
floating down a mossy
green river, speechless,
stunned silent with joy
& sobriety & youth,
oh youth.

◎

She smiled at me
& got off her horse.
She smelled of leather
& sweat & her kiss has
lasted me fifty years.

◎

Bad Indians do
not go to hell.
They are marched
to the molten core
of the sun & then
beamed back to
their families,
purified, whole
& Holy as hell.

This Is the Time of Grasshoppers and All That I See Is Dying

Colleen,
this is the time of grasshoppers
and all that I see is dying except
for my virulent love for you.

The *Cowturdville Star-Times*,
which usually has a typo
in every damn column,
says the grasshoppers this year
"are as big as Buicks" and
that's not bad, but then we
get two eight-point pages
of who had dinner with whom
at the bowling alley café and
who went shopping at Target
in Rapid City and thus the high
church of Adrian the Obscure is sacked.

Even my old Dylan tapes are fading,
becoming near-comic antiques.
The grasshoppers are destroying
our yard and they're as big as
my middle finger saluting God.
The grass is yellow. The trees
look like Agent Orange has hit
but it's only the jaw-work of those
drab armored insects who dance
in profusion and pure destruction.

Sweet woman, dear love of my life,
when you're not angry and sputtering
at everything and everyone, you
become so childlike, so pure.

Your voice seems to have grown
higher recently, almost a little-girl pitch.

Today, like most days, I have you
home for your two-hour reprieve
from the nursing home prison.
We're sitting at the picnic table in
the backyard staring at the defoliation
of lilacs, brain matter, and honeysuckle.
You're eating a Hershey Bar and
a crystal glob of snot is hanging
from your nose.
I reach over, pinch it off,
and wipe it on my jeans.
You thrust the last bite
of chocolate into my mouth
as a demented grasshopper
jumps onto your ear.
You scream. I howl
with laughter until you do too.
Happiness comes with a price.

This is the time of grasshoppers
and all that I see is dying except
for my swarming love for you.

Last night on PBS some
lesioned guy being screwed to death
by legions of viral invisibility
blurted the great cliché of regret:
I wish I could be twenty
again and know what
I know now . . .

My own regrets are equally foolish.
And, I wonder, how the hell
is it I've reached a place

where I'd give what's left
of my allotment of sunsets
and frozen dinners
for some unholy replay
of just one hour in some nearly
forgotten time and place?

Darling,
in the baked soil of the far west,
I first saw the ant lions, those
hairy little bugs who dug funnel
traps for ants in the dry earth.
At twelve, looking over the edge
of one such funnel surrounded by
a circle of tiny stones in the sand,
I aimed a beam of white light
from my magnifying glass
and found I could re-create
a hell of my own accord.

Poverty and boredom
made me cruel early on.
The next summer while digging
postholes I found a cache of
those grotesque yellow bugs
we called Children of the Earth
so I piled matches atop them
and barbecued their ugliness.
I was at war with insects.

In my fifteenth summer I got
covered with ticks in the sagebrush
and that fall I nervously lost my cherry
in a cathouse called the Green Front
and got cursed with crabs but that's
not what I want to sing about
at all . . . come on now.

This is no bug progression.
This ain't no insect sonata.

This is only misdirection,
a sleight of hand upon the keys
and the unholy replay of just
one hour in some nearly
forgotten time and place
that I'd like to return to
will remain myth or maybe
a holy, tumescent mystery.

And let's not call
these bloodwords
POETRY or a winter count
of desperate dreams
when reality is much simpler.

Colleen,
I swear to Christ
this is the time of grasshoppers
and all that I see is dying except
for my sparkling love for you.

 LINDA NOEL (1947–), *Koyongk'awi Maidu,* is a former poet lau-
reate of Ukiah, California. Her debut collection, *Where You First
Saw the Eyes of Coyote,* was published in 1983; since then, her work
has been featured in exhibits across California such as "Sing Me Your Story,
Dance Me Home: Art and Poetry from Native California" and in antholo-
gies such as *Reinventing the Enemy's Language: Contemporary Native Women's
Writings of North America.*

LESSON IN FIRE

My father built a good fire
He taught me to tend the fire
How to make it stand
So it could breathe
And how the flames create
Coals that turn into faces
Or eyes
Of fish swimming
Out of flames
Into gray
Rivers of ash
And how the eyes
And faces look out
At us
Burn up for us
To heat the air
That we breathe
And so into us
We swallow
All the shapes
Created in a well-tended fire

LESLIE MARMON SILKO (*1948–*), *Laguna,* was born in Albuquerque, New Mexico, and raised at Laguna Pueblo, and she graduated from the University of New Mexico. A multidimensional artist, she works in poetry, essays, fiction, painting, and film. Her literary works include *Storyteller, Ceremony, Almanac of the Dead, Gardens in the Dunes,* and *The Turquoise Ledge: A Memoir.* The recipient of a MacArthur Foundation Grant and a National Endowment for the Arts fellowship, Silko lives in Tucson, Arizona.

Where Mountain Lion Lay Down with Deer

I climb the black rock mountain
       stepping from day to day
               silently.
I smell the wind for my ancestors
      pale blue leaves
      crushed wild mountain smell.
Returning
      up the gray stone cliff
      where I descended
           a thousand years ago.
Returning to faded black stone
where mountain lion lay down with deer.
It is better to stay up here
                  watching wind's reflection
                  in tall yellow flowers.
The old ones who remember me are gone
      the old songs are all forgotten
and the story of my birth.
How I danced in snow-frost moonlight
     distant stars to the end of the Earth,
How I swam away
      in freezing mountain water
      narrow mossy canyon tumbling down
             out of the mountain
             out of deep canyon stone
       down
             the memory
             spilling out
             into the world.

Long Time Ago

Long time ago
in the beginning
there were no white people in this world
there was nothing European.
And this world might have gone on like that
except for one thing:
witchery.
This world was already complete
even without white people.
There was everything
including witchery.

Then it happened.
These witch people got together.
Some came from far far away
across oceans
across mountains.
Some had slanty eyes
others had black skin.
They all got together for a contest
the way people have baseball tournaments nowadays
except this was a contest
in dark things.

So anyway
they all go together
witch people from all directions
witches from all the Pueblos
and all the tribes.
They had Navajo witches there,
some from Hopi, and a few from Zuni.
They were having a witches' conference,
that's what it was.
Way up in the lava rock hills

north of Cañoncito
they got together
to fool around in caves
with their animal skins.
Fox, badger, bobcat, and wolf
they circled the fire
and on the fourth time
they jumped into that animal's skin.

But this time it wasn't enough
and one of them
maybe Sioux or some Eskimos
started showing off.
"That wasn't anything,
watch this."

The contest started like that.
Then some of them lifted the lids
on their big cooking pots,
calling the rest of them over
to take a look:
dead babies simmering in blood
circles of skull cut away
all the brains sucked out.
Witch medicine
to dry and grind into powder
for new victims.
Others untied skin bundles of disgusting objects:
dark flints, cinders from burning hogans where the
dead lay
Whorls of skin
cut from finger tips
sliced from the penis end and clitoris tip.

Finally there was only one
who hadn't shown off charms or powers.
The witch stood in the shadows beyond the fire

and no one ever knew where this witch came from
which tribe
or if it was a woman or a man.
But the important thing was
this witch didn't show off any dark thunder charcoals
or red ant-hill beads.
This one just told them to listen:
"What I have is a story."

At first they all laughed
but this witch said
Okay
go ahead
laugh if you want to
but as I tell the story
it will begin to happen.

Set in motion now
set in motion by our witchery
to work for us.

Caves across the ocean
in caves of dark hills
white skin people
like the belly of a fish
covered with hair.

Then they grow away from the earth
then they grow away from the sun
then they grow away from the plants and animals.
They see no life.
When they look
they see only objects.
The world is a dead thing for them
the trees and rivers are not alive
the mountains and stones are not alive.
The deer and the bear are objects.

They see no life.
They fear
they fear the world.
They destroy what they fear.
They fear themselves.

The wind will blow them across the ocean
thousands of them in giant boats
swarming like larva
out of a crushed ant hill.

They will carry objects
which can shoot death
faster than the eye can see.

They will kill the things they fear
all the animals
the people will starve.

They will poison the water
they will spin the water away
and there will be drought
the people will starve.

They will fear what they find.
They will fear the people.
They will kill what they fear.

Entire villages will be wiped out.
They will slaughter whole tribes.
Corpses for us
Blood for us
Killing killing killing killing.

And those they do not kill
will die anyway
at the destruction they see

at the loss
at the loss of the children
the loss will destroy the rest.

Stolen rivers and mountains
the stolen land will eat their hearts
and jerk their mouths from the Mother.
The people will starve.

They will bring terrible diseases
the people have never known.
Entire tribes will die out
covered with festering sores
shitting blood
vomiting blood.
Corpses for our work

Set in motion now
set in motion by our witchery
set in motion
to work for us.

They will take this world from ocean to ocean
they will turn on each other
they will destroy each other
Up here
in these hills
they will find the rocks,
rocks with veins of green and yellow and black.
They will lay the final pattern with these rocks
they will lay it across the world
and explode everything.

Set in motion now
set in motion
To destroy
To kill

Objects to work for us
objects to act for us
Performing the witchery
for suffering
for torment
for the stillborn
the deformed
the sterile
the dead.

Whirling
Whirling
Whirling
Whirling
set into motion now
set into motion.

So the other witches said
"Okay you win; you take the prize,
but what you said just now—
it isn't so funny
it doesn't sound so good.
We are doing okay without it
we can get along without that kind of thing.
Take it back.
Call that story back."

But the witch just shook its head
at the others in their stinking animal skins, fur
and feathers.
It's already turned loose.
It's already coming.
It can't be called back.

JANICE GOULD *(1949–2019)*, *Koyongk'awi Maidu,* was a poet and scholar born in San Diego and raised in Berkeley, California. She earned her PhD in English at the University of New Mexico and published five books of poetry: *Beneath My Heart, Earthquake Weather, Doubters and Dreamers, The Force of Gratitude,* and *Seed.* She was awarded grants from the National Endowment for the Arts, the Astraea Foundation, and the Roothbert Fund, as well as a Ford Foundation Diversity Fellowship. The Pikes Peak poet laureate from 2014 to 2016, Gould taught Women's and Ethnic Studies at the University of Colorado at Colorado Springs. She was an accomplished musician, playing and performing folk, classical, Flamenco, and blues, and a teacher and practitioner of Aikido Koshin Shuri.

EARTHQUAKE WEATHER

It's earthquake weather in California,
that hazy stillness along the coast
just before the Santa Anas howl
out of the east, hot and dry.

There were days in September when we drove
down the fault line south of Hayward.
We went where there were Spanish names:
Suñol and Calaveras,
la Misión de San José.
I remember seeing the cells of the padres,
their faded vestments,
the implements of wood and iron.

We were looking for another country,
something not North America:
a taste, a smell, a solitary image—
the eucalyptus on a bleached hill.
Its blue pungent leaves made you long
for another home.

That was what you wanted from me—
to be your other home,
your other country.
Being Indian, I was your *cholo*
from the Bolivian highlands.
I was your boy, full of stone
and a cold sunset.

At night, seated at your bedside,
I was remote. I often made you weep—
you in the guise of an *angelita*.
You lay on the low mattress,
a weaving beneath your head,
and watched me with your slow eyes,
your sadness.

When September comes with its hot,
electric winds,
I will think of you and know
somewhere in the world
the earth is breaking open.

 ANITA ENDREZZE (1952–), *Yaqui*, graduated from Eastern Washington University with an MA in creative writing and has published several poetry and short story collections, including *At the Helm of Twilight; Throwing Fire at the Sun, Water at the Moon; The Humming of Stars and Bees and Waves: Poems and Short Stories; Butterfly Moon;* and *Enigma*. Her paintings have been featured on the covers of books as well as in exhibitions around the world.

THE WALL

Build a wall of saguaros,
butterflies, and bones
of those who perished
in the desert. A wall of worn shoes,
dry water bottles, poinsettias.
Construct it of gilded or crazy house
mirrors so some can see their true faces.
Build a wall of revolving doors
or revolutionary abuelas.
Make it as high as the sun, strong as tequila.
Boulders of sugar skulls. Adobe or ghosts.
A Lego wall or bubble wrap. A wall of hands
holding hands, hair braided from one woman
to another, one country to another.
A wall made of Berlin. A wall made for tunneling.
A beautiful wall of taco trucks.
A wall of silent stars and migratory songs.
This wall of solar panels and holy light,
panels of compressed cheetos,
topped not by barbed wire but sprouting
avocado seeds, those Aztec testicles.
A wall to keep Us in and Them out.
It will have faces and heartbeats.
Dreams will be terrorists. The Wall will divide
towns, homes, mountains,
the sky that airplanes fly through
with their potential illegals.
Our wallets will be on life support
to pay for it. Let it be built
of guacamole so we can have a bigly block party.
Mortar it with xocoatl, chocolate. Build it from coyote howls
and wild horses drumming across the plains of Texas,
from the memories
of hummingbird warriors and healers.

Stack it thick as blood, which has mingled
for centuries, la vida. Dig the foundation deep.
Create a 2,000 mile altar, lit with votive candles
for those who have crossed over
defending freedom under spangled stars
and drape it with rebozos,
and sweet grass.
Make it from two-way windows:
the wind will interrogate us,
the rivers will judge us, for they know how to separate
and divide to become whole.
Pink Floyd will inaugurate it.
Ex-Presidente Fox will give it the middle finger salute.
Wiley Coyote will run headlong into it,
and survive long after history forgets us.
Bees will find sand-scoured holes and fill it
with honey. Heroin will cover it in blood.
But it will be a beautiful wall. A huge wall.
Remember to put a rose-strewn doorway in Nogales
where my grandmother crossed over,
pistols on her hips. Make it a gallery of graffiti art,
a refuge for tumbleweeds,
a border of stories we already know by heart.

 OFELIA ZEPEDA (1952–), *Tohono O'odham,* earned her PhD from the University of Arizona, where she was named a Regents' Professor in 2007 and has been a professor of linguistics. Her book *A Papago Grammar* is the only pedagogical text about the Tohono O'odham language. She has published several collections of poetry, including *Ocean Power: Poems from the Desert, Jewed 'I-Hoi/Earth Movements,* and *Where Clouds are Formed.* Zepeda is the recipient of a MacArthur Fellowship as well as an Endangered Language Fund grant. She is currently the head of the American Indian Studies department at the University of Arizona.

Bury Me with a Band

My mother used to say, "Bury me with a band,"
and I'd say, "I don't think the grave will be big enough."
Instead, we buried her with creosote bushes,
and a few worldly belongings.
The creosote is for brushing her footprints away as she leaves.
It is for keeping the earth away from her sacred remains.
It is for leaving the smell of the desert with her,
to remind her of home one last time.

Ocean Power

Words cannot speak your power.
Words cannot speak your beauty.
Grown men with dry fear in their throats
watch the water come closer and closer.
Their driver tells them, "It's just the ocean,
it won't get you, watch it, it will roll away again."

Men who had never seen the ocean
it was hard not to have the fear that sits in the pit of the stomach.
Why did they bring us this way?
Other times we crossed on the desert floor.
That land of hot dry air
where the sky ends at the mountains.
That land that we know.
That land where the ocean has not touched for thousands of years.
We do not belong here,
this place with the sky too endless.
This place with the water too endless.
This place with air too thick and heavy to breathe.
This place with the roll and roar of thunder always playing to your ears.

We are not ready to be here.
We are not prepared in the old way.
We have no medicine.
We have not sat and had our minds walk through the image
of coming to this ocean.
We are not ready.
We have not put our minds to what it is we want to give to the ocean.
We do not have cornmeal, feathers, nor do we have songs and prayers ready.
We have not thought what gift we will ask from the ocean.
Should we ask to be song chasers
Should we ask to be rainmakers
Should we ask to be good runners
or should we ask to be heartbreakers.
No, we are not ready to be here at this ocean.

LAURA TOHE (1952–), *Diné*, is Tsénahabiłnii, Sleepy Rock People clan, and born for the Tódich'inii, Bitter Water clan. She received a PhD in English from the University of Nebraska. A scholar, writer, poet, and librettist, and the daughter of a code talker, Tohe's books include *No Parole Today, Tséyi'/Deep in the Rock: Reflections on Canyon de Chelly,* and *Code Talker Stories.* She is professor emerita of English at Arizona State University and was named poet laureate of the Navajo Nation for 2015–2017.

WHEN THE MOON DIED

Peter MacDonald, former President of the Diné Nation, was convicted of various illegal activities and is now serving a prison sentence.

When the moon died
we watched in silent awe
the closing of her light
above the treetops.

My father's voice comes back to me:
   "It's a bad sign for us
          when it happens at night.
It hasn't rained here,"
               and we look eastward
      at the thirsty earth,
the sun bearing down
       on the cracks in the ground.
"We must not be living right."

The neighbor brought out a
camera and aimed it
at the moon.
Minutes later only a
blurred image emerged.

    "If it happens during the day,
        it's bad for the white people.
    Years ago the flu killed a lot
         of them.
    It was bad."

I returned to the typewriter while
the moon hid herself
as if in shame.

    "They say you're not supposed
       to do anything,
    don't go to bed,
    don't eat. Pregnant
       women shouldn't see it.
    Three people shot because of
      MacDonald.
    We're not living right."

When the moon died
she reminded us of

the earth ripping apart
violent tremors,
greasy oceans,
the panic of steel winds,
whipping shorelines and
thirsty fields.
Grandfather trees pulled
for profit.
The Earth is angry at the people.
We're not living right.

No Parole Today

*In 1980 prisoners rioted in the Santa Fe State Prison. After several days of
violence and bloodshed, the prison was retaken by authorities.*

A shadow of smoke passed
over my dreams
I awoke trying to remember what was said
about Santa Fe and prison
the blood and emotions spilling over
I dressed and poured a cup of coffee

     then I remembered

my own scars
lying on bunk beds
and listening to
floor polishers whirling
and the bell that drove me
to sneaking behind cars and freeways

I swore then I would never
scrub no more walls
and porches at midnight

not for the woman
who sits sideways in auditorium chairs
and steals bacon from the back door
as easily as she could steal your confidence
I'm not from here
no more rubber meat and showering on cement floors
I learned early that my life
was separated by walls
and roll calls

Last night they said
a thousand men uncapped themselves behind barbed wire and smoke

 LUCI TAPAHONSO (1953–), Diné, is a professor emerita of English literature at the University of New Mexico. Her books include *A Breeze Swept Through; Blue Horses Rush In; Sáanii Daha-taał: The Women Are Singing; A Radiant Curve,* and several children's books. She was the recipient of a Native Writers' Circle of the Americas Lifetime Achievement Award and a Native Arts and Cultures Foundation artist fellowship. She was the first poet laureate of the Navajo Nation.

Blue Horses Rush In

For Chamisa Bah Edmo, Shisóí' aląąji' naaghígíí

Before her birth, she moved and pushed inside her mother.
Her heart pounded quickly and we recognized
the sound of horses running:
     the thundering of hooves on the desert floor.

Her mother clenches her fists and gasps.
She moans ageless pain and pushes: This is it!

Chamisa slips out, glistening wet, and takes her first breath.
     The wind swirls small leaves
     and branches in the dark.
Her father's eyes are wet with gratitude.
He prays and watches both mother and baby—stunned.

This baby arrived amid a herd of horses,
     horses of different colors.

White horses ride in on the breath of the wind.
White horses from the east
where plants of golden chamisa shimmer in the moonlight.

She arrived amid a herd of horses.

Blue horses enter from the south
bringing the scent of prairie grasses
from the small hills outside.

She arrived amid a herd of horses.

Yellow horses rush in, snorting from the desert in the west.
It is possible to see across the entire valley to Niist'áá from Tó.
Bah, from here your grandmother went to war long ago.

She arrived amid a herd of horses.

Black horses came from the north.
They are the lush summers of Montana and still white winters of Idaho.

Chamisa, Chamisa Bah. It is all this that you are.
You will grow: laughing, crying,
and we will celebrate each change you live.

You will grow strong like the horses of your past.
You will grow strong like the horses of your birth.

Hills Brothers Coffee

My uncle is a small man.
In Navajo we call him, "shidá'í,"
      my mother's brother.

He doesn't know English but
      his name in the white way is Tom Jim.
      He lives about a mile or so
      down the road from our house.

One morning he sat in the kitchen,
drinking coffee.
      I just came over, he said,
      the store is where I'm going to.

He tells me about how my mother seems to be gone
every time he comes over.
      Maybe she sees me coming
      then runs and jumps in her car
      and speeds away!
      He says smiling.
We both laugh—just to think of my mother
      jumping in her car and speeding.

I pour him more coffee and
      he spoons in sugar and cream until
      it looks almost like a chocolate shake
      then he sees the coffee can.
      Oh, that's the coffee with the man in the dress
      like a church man.
      Ah-h, that's the one that does it for me.
      Very good coffee.

I sit down again and he tells me
      some coffee has no kick.

Bu this one is the one.
It does it good for me.

I pour us both a cup and
  while we wait for my mother,
   his eyes crinkle with the smile and he says
   yes, ah yes, this is the very one
   (putting in more sugar and cream).

So I usually buy Hills Brothers coffee
  once or twice a day
   I drink a hot coffee and

  it sure does it for me.

This Is How They Were Placed for Us

I

Hayoołkáałgo Sisnaajiní nihi neł'iih łeh.
Blanca Peak is adorned with white shell.
Blanca Peak is adorned with morning light.
She watches us rise at dawn.
Nidoohjeeh shá'áłchíní, nii łeh.
Get up, my children, she says.

She is the brightness of spring.
She is Changing Woman returned.
By Sisnaajiní, we set our standards for living.
Bik'ehgo da'iiná.

Because of her, we think and create.
Because of her, we make songs.
Because of her, the designs appear as we weave.
Because of her, we tell stories and laugh.
We believe in old values and new ideas.
Hayoołkáałgo Sisnaajiní bik'ehgo hózhónígo naashá.

II

This is how they were placed for us.
Ałní' ní' áago Tsoo dził ánii łeh, "Da'oosą́, shá'áłchíní."
In the midday sunlight, Mount Taylor tells us,
"It's time to eat, my little ones."

She is adorned with turquoise.
She is adorned with lakes that sparkle in the sunlight.
Jó 'éí biniinaa nihitah yá'áhoot'ééh.
Tsoo dził represents our adolescence.
Mount Taylor gave us turquoise to honor all men,
thus we wear turquoise to honor our brothers,
we wear turquoise to honor our sons,
we wear turquoise to honor our fathers.
Because of Tsoo dził, we do this.

We envision our goals as we gaze southward.
Each summer, we are reminded of our own strength.
T'áá hó' ájít' iigo t'éiya dajinii łeh.
Tsoo dził teaches us to believe in all ways of learning
Ałní' ní' áago Tsoodził bik'ehgo hózhónígo naashá.

III

This is how they were placed for us.
E'e'aahjigo, Dook'o'oosłííd sida.
To the west, the San Francisco Peaks are adorned with abalone.
Each evening she is majestic.
She is adorned with snow.
She is adorned with the white light of the moon.

The San Francisco Peaks represent the autumn of our lives.
Asdzání dahiniłníí doo.
Dinééh dahiniłníí doo.

In the autumn of our lives,
they will call us woman.

In the autumn of our lives,
they will call us man.

The San Francisco Peaks taught us to believe in strong families.
Dookʼoʼoosłííd binahjiʼ danihidziił.
The San Francisco Peaks taught us to value our many relatives.
Eʼeʼaahjígo Dookʼoʼoosłííd bokʼehgo hózhónígo naashá.

IV

This is how they were placed for us.
Chahałheełgo Dibé Nitsaa, "Daʼołwosh, sháʼáłchíní," níi łeh.
From the north, darkness arrives—Hesperus Peak—
urges us to rest. "Go to sleep, my children," she says.
She is adorned with jet.
She is our renewal, our rejuvenation.
Dibé Nitsaa binahjiʼ laanaa daniidzin łeh.
Hesperus Peak taught us to have hope for good things.

Haigo sáanii, dahiniłníí doo.
Haigo hastóíí, dahiniłníí doo.
In the winter of our life, they will call us elderly woman.
In the winter of our life, they will call us elderly man.
In the winter of our life, we will be appreciated.
In the winter of our life, we will rest.
Chahałheełgo Dibé Nitsaa bikʼehgo hózhónígo naashá.

This is how the world was placed for us.
In the midst of this land, Huerfano Mountain
is draped in precious fabrics.
Her clothes glitter and sway in the bright sunlight.
Gobernador Knob is clothed in sacred jewels.
She wears mornings of white shell.
She wears the midday light of turquoise.
She wears evenings of abalone, the light of the moon.
She wears nights of black jet.

This is how they were placed for us.
We dress as they have taught us,
adorned with precious jewels
and draped in soft fabrics.

All these were given to us to live by.
These mountains and the land keep us strong.
From them, and because of them, we prosper.

With this we speak,
with this we think,
with this we sing,
with this we pray.

This is where our prayers began.

 DEBORAH A. MIRANDA (1961–), **from** *Ohlone/Costanoan-Esselen* **and** *Chumash people,* was born in Los Angeles, California, and grew up mostly in Washington State. She earned her PhD in English from the University of Washington. Her mixed-genre book *Bad Indians: A Tribal Memoir* received the PEN Oakland/ Josephine Miles Literary Award; her poetry collections include *Indian Cartography, The Zen of La Llorona,* and *Raised by Humans.* Miranda is currently the Thomas H. Broadus Professor of English at Washington and Lee University.

I Am Not a Witness

I found Coyote, Eagle, and Momoy
in a book, but cannot read
the Chumash words. I found
photographs of bedrock slabs pocked by
hundreds of acorn-grinding holes,

but the holes are empty, the stone
pestles that would curve to my grip
lie dead behind museum glass.
Mountains and rivers and oaks rise
in Spanish accents: San Gabriel,
Santa Ynez, Robles.
These are not real names.

Some of our bones rest in 4000 graves
out back behind the Mission.
Some of our bones are mixed into mud
to strengthen cool thick walls
where smallpox and measles came and stayed.
Some of our bones washed down the river
whose name I do not know
past islands I cannot name
to the sea where
I have never sailed.

Mixed-blood, I lay claim by the arch
of my eyebrows, short nose, dark hands.
I am not a witness. I am left behind, child
of children who were locked in the Mission
and raped. I did not see this:
I was not there—but I am here.
Where is the place that knows me?

MESA VERDE

The earth is salmon-colored here, cracked
into plates like the shell of a giant turtle.
It is a place I've seen in a dream.
Our faces tingle with the heat of sun,
the fiery way we look at one another.
When we drive down the steep road
back to the highway, you stop
the car so I can gather a stalk of some
rosy blossom, unknown, unidentified.
Your hands gently cup the waxy petals,
fingertips outlining leaves as if you know
how to stroke color and scent, coax forth
a name like a blood secret. The aroma
of honey, nectar, hangs in dry air.
Tiny gold ants crawl on the hairy stem,
seek the deep center, enter it.
As we drive on, I leave the branch behind.
The ants will find their way home carrying
a burden so sweet it needs no name,
a story to tell about being taken up,
removed, finding the intricate paths back.

REX LEE JIM (1962–), *Diné*, was born and raised in Rock Point, Arizona, on the Navajo reservation. He is born of the Red House People and born for the Red Streak Running into Water People. He earned his MA from Middlebury College. His books include *Saad Lá Tah Hózhóón: A Collection of Diné Poetry, Dúchas Táá Kóó Diné,* and *Áhí Ni' Nikisheegiizh.*

SAAD

Hodeeyáádą́ą́' honishłǫ́
Adáádą́ą́' honishłǫ́
Dííjį́ honishłǫ́
Yiską́ą́go honishłǫ́
Ahóyéel'áágóó honishłǫ́
      Saad shí nishłį́
      Saad diyinii shí nishłį́
      Saad diyinii díí shí nishłį́

Shee nitsáhákees
Shee tsohodizin
Shee ni'dit'a'
Shee yáti'
Shee nahat'á
Shee iiná
      Saad shí nishłį́
      Saad diyinii shí nishłį́
      Saad diyinii díí shí nishłį́

Ts'ídá t'áá ał'ą́ą́ ánisht'éego honishłǫ́
Shinahjį' nitsáhákees ał'ą́ą́ át'é
Shinahjį' tsodizin ał'ą́ą́ át'é
Shinahjį' sin ał'ą́ą́ át'é
Shinahjį' saad ał'ą́ą́ át'é
Shinahjį' nahat'á ał'ą́ą́ át'é
Shinahjį' iiná ał'ą́ą́ át'é
      Saad shí nishłį́
      Saad diyinii shí nishłį́
      Saad diyinii díí shí nishłį́

Iiná ałtaas'áí yisht'į́
Ó'ool'į́įł ałtaas'áí yisht'į́
Yódí ałtaas'áí yisht'į́
Nitł'iz ałtaas'áí yisht'į́

Díí biniiyé nohokáá' dine'é baa ádinisht'ą
Nohokáá' dine'é diyinii
Nohokáá' dine'é ílíinii
Nohokáá' dine'é jooba'ii
Díí biyi'déę' hahosiists'įįhgo
Iiná doo nídínééshgóó k'ee'ąą yilzhish
Díí biniiyé nohokáá' dine'é baa ádinisht'ą
      Saad shí nishłį́
      Saad diyinii shí nishłį́
      Saad diyinii díí shí nishłį́

Ahóyéel'áágóó honishłǫ́
Yiską́ągo' honishłǫ́
Dííjį́ honishłǫ́
Adą́'dą́ą́ honishłǫ́
Hodeeyáádą́ą́' honishłǫ́
      Saad shí nishłį́
      Saad diyinii shí nishłį́
      Saad diyinii díí shí nishłį́

VOICE

In the beginning I am
Yesterday I am
Today I am
Tomorrow I am
Forever I am
      Voice I am
      Sacred voice I am
      Sacred voice this I am

People think with me
People pray with me
People sing with me

People speak with me
People plan with me
People live with me
>Voice I am
>Sacred voice I am
>Sacred voice this I am

I come in many forms
Because of me people think differently
Because of me people pray differently
Because of me people sing differently
Because of me people speak differently
Because of me people plan differently
Because of me people live differently
>Voice I am
>Sacred voice I am
>Sacred voice this I am

I value different ways of living
I value different ways of doing
I value different soft goods
I value different hard goods
These are reasons why I gave myself over to the earth surface people
A holy people
A respected people
A compassionate people
When I sound from within them,
Without falling apart, life ceaselessly expands
These are reasons why I gave myself over to the earth surface people
>Voice I am
>Sacred voice I am
>Sacred voice this I am

Forever I am
Tomorrow I am
Today I am

Yesterday I am
In the beginning I am
     Voice I am
     Sacred voice I am
     Sacred voice this I am

 MARGO TAMEZ (1962–), *Lipan Apache,* was born in Austin, Texas. She received her MFA in creative writing from Arizona State University and her PhD in American Studies from Washington State University. Her books include *Alleys and Allies, Naked Wanting,* and *Raven Eye.* Currently, Tamez is an associate professor in Indigenous Studies at the University of British Columbia.

My Mother Returns to Calaboz

> *The Lower Rio Grande, known as the Seno Mexicano (the Mexican Hollow or Recess), was a refuge for rebellious Indians from the Spanish presidios, who preferred outlawry to life under Spanish rule.*
> —Americo Paredes, With His Pistol in His Hand

The fragmented jawbones
and comblike teeth of seagulls
sometimes wash up from the gulf
to the levee of the river
and gather striated along the berms
where my grandfather irrigated sugarcane.

My mother, returned after forty years away,
walks there often,
hassled by INS agents
when she jogs by the river.
They think she runs away from them,

that she is an illegal,
trespassing from Mexico.
Used to the invasion,
she asks them how they assume,
how *exactly* do they know
if she came from here, or there?
I am an indigenous woman,
born in El Calaboz, you understand?
she says loudly in Spanish,
and they tear out,
the truck wheels spinning furiously,
sand sprayed into the humid air.

When I was a girl walking on the levee,
I thought I saw gull teeth
chomping at the soil wall.
The air was dank steam,
the scent of sand, roots,
and something alive beneath the soil,
deeper and older than memory.
When I immersed my hand inside
the cloudy water,
it became a fluid form,
soft, something becoming,
something ancient.

The air is still heavy with heat and damp,
but smells like diesel and herbicides.
The scene reminds me of failed gestations.
My reproduction, the plants', and the water's,
each struggling in the same web of survival.

When I was a girl, my grandfather taught me
to put a small clump of soil in my mouth,
and to swallow it. I watched him.
Then I did.
I used to watch the gliding and swerves

of uprooted reeds in the river's unhurried flow
to the Gulf.
I reached with all my body,
stomach on the bank of the levee,
hands and arms stretched out like an acrobat
to touch and grasp their slender stems.
Once, my feet pressed into the soupy bog,
and stepping up was the sound of gurgles,
like seaweed breathing.

Now, I think I'd like to be running with my mother
when she tells off *la migra*.
Listen to the bubbling duet of water and plant life,
listen to their sound,
closely.
Again and again.

 ESTHER G. BELIN (*1968–*), *Diné,* multimedia artist and poet, was born in Gallup, New Mexico; grew up in Los Angeles, California; and now lives in Durango, Colorado. She earned degrees from the Institute of American Indian Arts, in Santa Fe; the University of California Berkeley; and Antioch University. Her first book, *From the Belly of My Beauty,* won the American Book Award; her second collection, *Of Cartography,* was published in 2017.

ASSIGNMENT 44

Bind   Tie   Bind   Tie   Bind   Tie   Small   Bind-ed
  -ing   Wood Water
    Binding   Fire(in)Sky
~~Binding~~   the   Sky ~~Binding~~   Skies
~~Binding~~ the   Skies(Waters)
  Bound   and   unraveled   and   bound
And   (of)Wood   and Skies and bound and
  Unravelling   the   Sky
        ~~Unravelling~~   Sky
        ~~Unravelling~~   ~~the~~(in)   (Waters)~~Skies~~
Unravelling   our(Fire)   and   Skies
    and Bind   (-ed, -ing)   Tie   Bind   Tie   Bound

Assignment 44
Analyze the above conversation. Read it aloud. Read it loudly. Weave a
thread through it. Bind your bundle of sayings, be mindful of loose strands.
Smooth down frayed edges. Smudge with fire or water.

Extra Credit: Take the relocated points from the previous diagram and use
them as an entryway.

FIRST WOMAN

Emerged from the everlasting clay at the bottom
of Cañon Diablo

Now she walks down Cerrillos toward the plaza
the clay still part of her
bundled in velveteen inside her knapsack
ready for the first display window with the right price

She walks on
wanting to hail a ride
yet wanting her limbs to mark the pavement
ever so lightly with blood and flesh and
   quarter-century-plus-old bones
and usually Coyote picks up her scent and comes
   sniffin' around

Yá'átééh' abíní
Aoo', yá'átééh, First Woman says
wishing she just walked on
but he knew her tongue
paused to look with both eyes
wide open
bright like sunny-side-up eggs
With big teeth and smile Coyote asks, háágóóshá'?
Plaza'góó and before he can respond First Woman adds,
Shí k'ad dooleeł, hágoónee'
First Woman turns halfway to get the side ways view
dark hair catching the sun skews her image
and sure enough Coyote
still there
chuckles and says, hazhó'ígo, hazhó'ígo . . .

First woman breathes
focusing the fire within her
tending her own heat
back then
the fire was her first child
Her body
a wood-burning stove
giving her cravings for chili
hot and spicy, rich with flavor and settling with heat
later taking it back with nightmares or itchy breasts or
   sore tailbones
Her womb
a cauldron

boiling or simmering
her temperature still a little offset
and First Woman
breathes in the morning
and exhales the scent of wily Coyote
breathes in the white
light rays of the new morning
and coffee still hot enough to sip
and tailpipe exhaust
as she crosses the railroad tracks ever closer toward the plaza

HERSHMAN R. JOHN (1970–), *Diné,* was born in California and grew up on the Navajo reservation in Sand Springs, Arizona. He earned his MFA from Arizona State University. John's poetry collection, *I Swallow Turquoise for Courage,* was published by University of Arizona Press in 2007; his writing appears in numerous anthologies including *Nuclear Impact, Family Matters, Teaching as a Human Experience,* as well as literary journals. John teaches at Phoenix College and Arizona State University.

A Strong Male Rain

The air dances with wet sand off golden dunes.
The horse begins to get excited
From the whispers of rolling thunder in the distance.
A tidal wave of dust swallows the sky.
A heavy rainstorm is coming.

Slowly he crawls across the sky, angry.
He's large and bumpy with thick, strapping gray muscles.
This storm cloud is male, that's what Grandma says.
"When the clouds gather anger, they cry thunder and rain.
          This is Male Rain."

The sudden winds kick up sand into my eyes. I blink.
In a drying puddle from yesterday's storm, I see Darcy's face.
Darcy, a Jewish girl from Phoenix—
A friend also afraid of the Male Rain.
Her brother Ean brought on her fears.

Grandma brought on mine.
She told us kids to sit still and don't talk during a storm
Or we'd get struck by lightning.
When Darcy was young, she used to sit at the window
And watch the lightning show during monsoon season.

Ean walked to his sister by the window.
He grinned his teen-age teeth and said,
"You know, if you stand too close to the window,
          A *Kugelblitz* will get you."
"A *Kugelblitz?*" she questioned.
"Yeah, a ball of lightning to chase you."
She never watched the light show again.
Instead during stormy nights, she silently cried in bed.
Little Jewish tears added to the monsoon's rain.
She told me this story one rainy night.

I told her about the Male Rain and what not to do during a storm.
She told me about Ean and his tale of the *Kugelblitz*.
I guess Jews and Navajos aren't all that different.
We were both afraid of thunderstorms.
We have other past storms we were afraid of too.
She had the Holocaust
And I had America.

Lightning flashes. . . . Thunder follows. . . .
I begin whipping my horse, trying to escape the storms.

CRISOSTO APACHE *(1972–), Mescalero Apache, Chiricahua Apache, and Diné of the 'Áshįįhí (Salt Clan)* born for the Kinyaa'áanii (Towering House Clan), was born in Mescalero, New Mexico. He earned an MFA from the Institute of American Indian Arts in Santa Fe and debuted his first poetry collection, ~~GENESIS~~, in 2018. He lives in Denver and teaches writing at various local colleges, where he continues to advocate for Native American two-spirit–identified people.

Ndé' Isdzán ["two of me"]

—my note to selves

isdzán / woman	haastiń / man
he crosses two links	she crosses two links
intertwine into helix	a helix intertwines
a twin water-born suit	twins born in a water-suit
inside synchronous sun	synchronous moon inside
solar pollex extends	lunar forelimb extends
his deterrent dirt road	her itinerant interstate
atop a white mountain	into white gypsum basin
he fills a dual purpose	she nestles inside it all
he lusts uncontrollably	she absolves eternally
from oceanic derivative	from continental impasse
he calls concerting giants	she infuses vesper currents
of monozygotic origin	fusing each obtuse head
he recognizes star birth	she identifies twin stars
he a soft drizzle	she a rainstorm
a turquoise flaw	a vague shell white
of stone into stone	of water into water
a unisex-binary-copy of	a copy-binary-unisex
transfusing powerful	transfuse of power
of entropy existence	though viscous cells
transfer of M2F	transfer of F2M
a myopic resolve	ignores center clash
of genetic boundary	nearly kinetic entrance
these parts of me	remain conflicted
these parts of me	are not gradual
Y chromosome	or X chimera
haastiń / her (I)	isdzán / his

enter (sexual) sections
c o l l i d e

SHAUNNA OTEKA McCOVEY (1972–), *Yurok* and *Karuk*, grew up on the Yurok and Hoopa Valley reservations, and in Karuk Country in Northern California. She earned degrees in social work (Humboldt State University and Arizona State University) and in First Nations environmental law (Vermont Law School). Her book of poetry, *The Smokehouse Boys*, was published in 2005; she also contributed to *Eating Fire, Tasting Blood: An Anthology of the American Indian Holocaust* and *Mni Wiconi/Water Is Life: Honoring the Water Protectors at Standing Rock and Everywhere in the Ongoing Struggle for Indigenous Sovereignty.* McCovey taught social work at Humboldt State and is currently compact negotiator for the U.S. Department of the Interior–Indian Affairs, Office of Self Governance.

I Still Eat All of My Meals with a Mussel Shell

Creation stories
thespiritbeings
have long been disputed
emergedfrom
by theories of
theground
evolution and
atKenek
strait crossings.

Because our rivers
halfbreedshave
were once filled
agodthatis
with gold
neitherIndian
our women were violated
orwhite
in the worst imaginable way.

Only a few
prayersgo
still know
unheardwhen
the formula that
notspokenin
will bring the salmon
ournativetongues
up the river.

If you cannot see
Istilleat
between the lines
allofmymeals
then your collected facts
witha
will never constitute
musselshell
knowledge.

 SHERWIN BITSUI (*1975–*), *Diné,* was born in White Cone,
Arizona, and graduated from the Institute of American Indian Arts
in Santa Fe. He has authored three collections of poetry, *Shapeshift,*
Flood Song, and *Dissolve.* He has been awarded an American Book Award, a
Whiting Award, a Truman Capote creative writing fellowship, and a Lannan
Literary Fellowship. He teaches at the Institute of American Indian Arts'
MFA program and at Northern Arizona University.

from *Flood Song*

tó

tó

tó

tó

tó

tó

from *Dissolve*

This mountain stands near us: *mountaining*,
it mistakes morning with mourning
when we wear slippers of steam
              to erase our carbon footprint.

Wind's fingers wearing yours
you unravel a plow of harvested light,
notice its embers
              when scrubbed on drowned faces—

                        repel fossilized wind.

The Caravan

The city's neon embers
stripe the asphalt's blank page
where this story pens itself nightly;
where ghosts weave their oily hair
into his belt of ice,
dress him in pleated shadows
and lay him fetal
on the icy concrete—
the afterbirth of sirens glistening over him.

We drain our headlights
on his scraped forehead
and watch the December moon
two-step across his waxen eyes;
his mouth's shallow pond—
              a reflecting pool
              where his sobs leak into my collar.
One more, just one more, he whispers,
as he thaws back into the shape of *nihitstilí*
bruised knees thorning against his chest.

We steal away,
our wheels moan
through sleet and ash.

Death places second, third,
and fourth behind us.

At home on the Reservation:
Father sifts dried cedar leaves
over glowing embers,
Mother, hovering
above cellphone light, awaits:
    He's okay,
    never went out,
    watched a movie instead.

But tonight,
my speech has knives
that quiver at the ellipses
of neon Budweiser signs
blinking through the fogged windshield,
and I text:
    I've only rescued a sliver of him,
    he's only twenty-five
    and he smells like blood and piss,
    his turquoise bracelet snatched for pawn,
    by the same ghost who traded his jacket
    for a robe of snow and ice,
    before inviting him
    back into the Caravan
        for *one more, just one more.*

ORLANDO WHITE *(1976–)*, *Diné*, is from Tółikan, Arizona. He is of the Naaneesht'ézhi Tábaahí and born for the Naakai Diné'e. He holds an MFA from Brown University and has published two collections of poetry, *Bone Light* and *LETTERRS*. The recipient of the San Francisco Poetry Center Book Award and a Truman Capote creative writing fellowship, White teaches at Diné College in Tsaile, Arizona.

To See Letters

Everything I write requires this: Alphabet.

It was a notion I did not know when I was six years old. In kindergarten I was more interested in the image of a letter on a flash card. I noticed its shape distinguishing itself from its background. Then, with my eyes I tore the O in half. In the moment I felt language separate from its form.

I recall my mother playing a word puzzle. She'd circle a line of letters amongst many other letters scattered on the page. She treated each word carefully never touching the pen to the letters. Then, she would give me the pen. I would circle random letters. She'd smile and give me a hug.

My mother once told me that my step-dad found a picture of my real father. He ripped it up. To this day, I still do not know who my father is.

I always called my step-dad, David. And he called me by my middle name, Orson. To him it was better than looking at me and calling me "son." I am still ashamed of my middle name.

He tried to teach me how to spell.

I showed him homework from my first grade class. It was a list of words assigned for me to spell. He looked at me as he was sharpening a pencil with his knife. I remember the way he forced my hand to write. How the pencil stabbed each letter, the lead smearing. I imagined each word bruising as I stared at them.

The words reminded me of the word puzzle.

But without images it meant nothing at all.

He said, "Spell them out."
I could not. "Then sound them out first!"

I recall a day, like many other days in grammar school, when an older boy made fun of me because I could not speak proper English. I always mispronounced words, and I would wonder how to spell them.

I still could not move the pencil in my hand. I saw the letters lined up on paper, but I wanted to circle them.

He shouted out, "Spell them out you little fucker! I am going to hit you if you don't."

I remember the shape of his fist.

No one was around, not even my mother. It was as close to intimacy as I got with my step-dad. I did not say anything to anyone. He bought me toys as an act of contrition. I forgave him.

When David hit me in the head, I saw stars in the shape of the Alphabet. Years later, my fascination for letters resulted in poems.

EMPTY SET

Vacant folio,   middle of an unwritten;

coaxial *o* rolls out from its shape:

          unoccupied but

designed by   inaudible flashes of *colorless*.

In the depths of paper, underneath

text; what was before   a blank,

another layer of spotless pulp. Circle

out of its dermis ink: human bulb, skull light.

Where the substance of thought

enlightens   the narrative of bone,

skeleton according to speech;

          of being alive within an empty set.

Like the shape of   sound before

ink forms, before structured print

writhes through and out. Curly brackets

enclose sibilant: an *s*, a phonetic infection.

But a writer corrects what it hears, forgets

in there where   ink absorbs paper, evolves

into written fungic. A spore of alphabet cannot

be sterilized with revision;   so one creates

a circumference   around the letter

to entrap, to press   its outbreak of silence.

CASANDRA LÓPEZ *(1978–), Cahuilla/Tongva/Luiseño,* has an MFA from the University of New Mexico and is the author of a poetry collection, *Brother Bullet.* Lopez teaches at the Northwest Indian College and is a cofounder of the journal *As/Us: A Space for Women of the World.* Currently, Lopez is working on a memoir titled "A Few Notes on Grief."

A New Language

My words are always
        collapsing

upon themselves, too tight
        in my mouth. I want a new
language. One with at least
        50 words for grief

and 50 words for love, so I can offer
        them to the living
who mourn the dead. I want

a language that understands
        sister-pain and heart-hurt. So
when I tell you Brother

is my hook of heart, you will see

the needle threading me to
        the others, numbered
men, women and children
        of our grit spit city.

I want a language to tell you
        about 2010's
37th homicide. The unsolved:
        a man that my city turned
to number,
        sparking me

back to longer days when:
        Ocean is the mouth
of summer. Our shell fingers
                drive into sand, searching—we find

tiny silver sand crabs,
        we scoop and scoop till we bore and go
in search of tangy seaweed.

We are salted sun. How we brown
        to earth. Our warm flesh flowering.

In this new language our bones say
        sun and *sea*, reminding us of an old
language our mouths have forgotten, but
        our marrow remembers.

JULIAN TALAMANTEZ BROLASKI (1978–), *Mescalero and Lipan Apache,* were born in California and received their PhD at University of California Berkeley. They are a two-spirit and transgender poet and musician, author of *gowanus atropolis, Advice for Lovers,* and *Of Mongrelitude,* and coeditor of *NO GENDER: Reflections on the Life & Work of kari edwards.* Along with poetry and writing, they are a cofounder of the Indigenous Peoples' Committee at Pratt Institute.

Stonewall to Standing Rock

who by the time it arrived
had made its plan heretofore
stonewall   it had not a penny
thats not true it had several pennies

can you make a sovereign nation a national park how condescending
instead just tell them to honor the treaty

what can poetry do it
cant not not do nothing
it must undulate w/ the 2:30 pm dance music the sole
patrons at stonewall

there was a shooting in ohio today
the music made me feel a little anxious it was
hard thumping dance music a notch
upwards of 100 bpm notoriously the beat of life
the optimum tempo for cpr
I consider downloading a metronome real quick to test it to tap it out but
I don't want to be 'anywhere near' my phone
meaning it's in my bag on the stool 2 feet from me

there is an amy winehouse video on no sound at least
I think it is amy winehouse
she is at a funeral black and white
there is a stuffed bird slightly obscuring my view of the tv
it looks like a kind of tall pigeon w/ mottled brown
and russet with a white ringlet necklace and black dots
is it a carrier pigeon I wonder I sent
a text to jocelyn at standing rock several texts

are you still on the road
ariana and i r gonna go out there in december
sending love to you

tried calling bt yr mailbox is full
send a sign when u can xoxo

howdy. thinking of u w love.
hope all is well. send smoke
signal telegram carrier pigeon
send love to my twospirits at the
winyan camp.

last night we prayed for her and for zephyr and l. frank &
the twospirits especially at standing rock
there's no sign of that struggle here but they are selling tshirts commemorating
the other and the six days of riots
led by transwomen of color they later tried to whitewash in that terrible movie
like it was all these hot angry upright downright forthright white gays so ready
for the revolution
and now people are treating standing rock like burning man

a drink called goslings
videos by the pigeon misaligned with the music
the smell of booze in the air made both of us recoil slightly I saw
or felt it

I'm here to make a poem I was already paid for when I had less than $2 in
my bank account (and I joked I would go right to the bar and buy every-
body drinks) not even enough for a subway ride and I used the 58 cents I'd
gotten for busking for the first time alone in the long hallway between the
library at bryant park and the orange line trains by the ovid quote 'gutta
cavat lapidem' water (or a drop of water really) hollows out
a stone. lapidum a stone or rock ariana once described cd wright's style
          as lapidary
I loved this as a description of writing like the hieroglyphics are
literally lapidary and I told my grandmother about it as we
were driving from mescalero to albuquerque she knew all about the
plants and the names for all the rockforms mesas or buttes or
ziggurats and I said how do

you know all these she said by long observation and
I used to study geology in college I wanted to major in it
but they wouldn't allow women
to major in the hard sciences then so she
began to study religion
tho she already had medicine

ricky martin on the beach
or is it someone younger sexier
the grand canyon splitting apart
is it an ad is it a video
even the sands at the beach
are bouncing with the beat
the tempo has stayed very similar this whole time a tick
up I suspect from 100bpm

 BOJAN LOUIS (*1981–*), *Diné,* was born in Window Rock, Arizona, in the Navajo Nation. He was the inaugural Virginia G. Piper fellow-in-residence at Arizona State University, former editor for *RED INK: An International Journal of Indigenous Literature, Arts, & Humanities,* and co-founder of the journal *Waxwing.* His debut poetry collection, *Currents* (2017), won the American Book Award. Louis is an assistant professor in creative writing and American Indian Studies at the University of Arizona.

If Nothing, the Land

i. the toughest sheriff in the world

There is no other bad than what I say's bad.
It's tough-living on this land. Miles of desert,
undeveloped; the interstates, mostly unmanned,
are threads unspooled down broad hallways.
Beyond their edge: the space is *dead,*
a rogue trailer or redskin reservation.
Backward problems
of methamphetamine and rape. Those doors

have their own police, their own dumb justice.
I concern my posse with invasion. Paperless
beaners. Rust that ruins a polish.
Inedible animals doing no man any good,
unless buried to cease the flies and the stink.

ii. flock of Seagals

If not thousands then millions of hours
I've played *bang-bang*; nabbed bad guy
brownies in kung fu-grip shoot-em-ups.
Who's better fit to patrol kids in tiny pants
than a convicted man? Limits,
like borders, stretch thin and tear. If anyone
can get a gun then shouldn't everyone
have one at the ready, like in the glory days:

a round up of savages, spics, and spooks out
to devalue our kids, good at killing their own.
I learned from watching birds nestled within
cacti: though there might be many, a single bird
more makes another cavity, an eventual collapse.

iii. come mierda para el desayuno

Chickens dismantle, like pit crews can
a vehicle, scorpions quickly.
Urged forward by pickers hens bob
and amble over fallen oranges, bruised grapefruit;
seek pincers, stingers, exoskeletons;
their work urgent and efficient.
Back at the coop stubborn roosters fight,
bloody, and unfeather each other

until the losers peck frail chicks from the clutch,
strew limp bodies beneath fluorescent light.
The hens return, squawk and circle the carcasses,
until the migrants transfer them in sacks
meant for citrus to anonymous holes on the land.

TACEY M. ATSITTY (*1982–*), *Diné*, is Tsénahabiłnii (Sleep Rock People) and born for Ta'neeszahnii (Tangle People). Her maternal grandfather is Tábąąhí (Water Edge People) and her paternal grandfather is Hashk'áánhadzóhí (Yucca Fruit Strung-Out-In-A-Line People). Atsitty earned her MFA from Cornell University. Her awards and fellowships include a Truman Capote creative writing fellowship and the Philip Freund Prize. Her first poetry collection is *Rain Scald*.

SONNET FOR MY WRIST

I tend to mistake your ribs for a hand towel,
it hangs on a nail above the washbowl, the hand towel,
ripped. There's something wearing about the end curve
of thread. When I sleep I keep my palms open. Verve:
we were lovers in a field of gray. In Navajo, we say something

rote: I'll radical when you hurt me something
close, even you waft—it's best I tether, forget flyaways
I plucked. My bones, they lay, to me, like fray. Like gaunt:
I don't crawl back for fragments, even a spinal cord
of sinew—it's not going to close. You rope
me from stray to grip: it's all for naught. I'm born
for my father, Tangle People. Our mouths in webs:
tonight my wrists part, and you chase
my insides until they dangle into pieces.

Rain Scald

When standing (in rain) for so long, you no longer hear
or feel it falling—you believe it's stopped. Step away—

look to your (skin; muck itch. It's a) shame, your hands
have gone bald from fungus. Taking you to (what's beneath scab,

to) one of those nights when you know (your gums will bleed.
To say) it's been a while or it has to do with (wrist mange

is to say rot comes so easily now, skin weep—) lapse. Step through
the whole (black of your home) and still know damp, know

(exactly when to bend your finger for) the light switch.

            '   '   '

        so familiar (in aubade)

            shame, your hands

have gone haywire. Taking you to (what's beneath rust: ranges

    they've grazed—) a time

        when you're combed through

    when you know your knuckles—

and all that rain has swallowed.

NATALIE DIAZ (1982–), *Mojave/Gila River,* was born at the Fort Mojave Indian Village in Needles, California. She attended Old Dominion University, where she played point-guard for the women's basketball team, reaching the NCAA Final Four, and earned her MFA in poetry and fiction. *When My Brother Was an Aztec,* her debut collection, was published in 2012. She is the winner of the *Narrative* Poetry Prize, a Lannan Literary Fellowship, and a MacArthur Fellowship. She is currently the Maxine and Jonathan Marshall Chair in Modern and Contemporary Poetry at Arizona State University.

IT WAS THE ANIMALS

Today my brother brought over a piece of the ark
wrapped in a white plastic grocery bag.

He set the bag on my dining table, unknotted it,
peeled it away, revealing a foot-long fracture of wood.
He took a step back and gestured toward it
with his arms and open palms —

    It's the ark, he said.
    You mean Noah's ark? I asked.
    What other ark is there? he answered.

Read the inscription, he told me,
it tells what's going to happen at the end.
What end? I wanted to know.
He laughed, *What do you mean, "what end"?*
The end end.

Then he lifted it out. The plastic bag rattled.
His fingers were silkened by pipe blisters.
He held the jagged piece of wood so gently.
I had forgotten my brother could be gentle.

He set it on the table the way people on television
set things when they're afraid those things might blow-up
or go-off — he set it right next to my empty coffee cup.

It was no ark —
it was the broken end of a picture frame
with a floral design carved into its surface.

He put his head in his hands —

> *I shouldn't show you this —*
> *God, why did I show her this?*
> *It's ancient — O, God,*
> *this is so old.*

> *Fine*, I gave in, *Where did you get it?*
> *The girl*, he said. *O, the girl.*
> *What girl?* I asked.
> *You'll wish you never knew*, he told me.

I watched him drag his wrecked fingers
over the chipped flower-work of the wood —

> *You should read it. But, O, you can't take it —*
> *no matter how many books you've read.*

He was wrong. I could take the ark.
I could even take his marvelously fucked fingers.
The way they almost glittered.

It was the animals — the animals I could not take —

they came up the walkway into my house,
cracked the doorframe with their hooves and hips,
marched past me, into my kitchen, into my brother,

tails snaking across my feet before disappearing
like retracting vacuum cords into the hollows
of my brother's clavicles, tusks scraping the walls,

reaching out for him — wildebeests, pigs,
the oryxes with their black matching horns,
javelinas, jaguars, pumas, raptors. The ocelots
with their mathematical faces. So many kinds of goat.
So many kinds of creature.

I wanted to follow them, to get to the bottom of it,
but my brother stopped me —

> *This is serious*, he said.
> *You have to understand.*
> *It can save you.*

So I sat down, with my brother wrecked open like that,
and two-by-two the fantastical beasts
parading him. I sat, as the water fell against my ankles,
built itself up around me, filled my coffee cup
before floating it away from the table.

My brother — teeming with shadows —
a hull of bones, lit only by tooth and tusk,
lifting his ark high in the air.

When My Brother Was an Aztec

he lived in our basement and sacrificed my parents
    every morning. It was awful. Unforgivable. But they kept coming
        back for more. They loved him, was all they could say.

It started with him stumbling along *la Avenida de los Muertos,*
    my parents walking behind him like effigies in a procession
        he might burn to the ground at any moment. They didn't know

what else to do except be there to pick him up when he died.
    They forgot who was dying, who was already dead. My brother
        quit wearing shirts when a carnival of dirty-breasted women

made him their leader, following him up and down the stairs—
    They were acrobats, moving, twitching like snakes—They fed him
        crushed diamonds and fire. He gobbled the gifts. My parents

begged him to pluck their eyes out. He thought he was
    Huitzilopochtli, a god, half-man half-hummingbird. My parents
        at his feet, wrecked honeysuckles, he lowered his swordlike mouth,

gorged on them, draining color until their eyebrows whitened.
    My brother shattered and quartered them before his basement festivals—
        waving their shaking hearts in his fists,

while flea-ridden dogs ran up and down the steps, licking their asses,
    turning tricks. Neighbors were amazed my parents' hearts kept
        growing back—It said a lot about my parents, or parents' hearts.

My brother flung them into *cenotes,* dropped them from cliffs,
    punched holes into their skulls like useless jars or vases,
        broke them to pieces and fed them to gods ruling

the ratty crotches of street fair whores with pocked faces
     spreading their thighs in flophouses with no electricity. He slept
          in filthy clothes smelling of rotten peaches and matches, fell in love

with sparkling spoonfuls the carnival dog-women fed him. My parents
     lost their appetites for food, for sons. Like all bad kings, my brother
          wore a crown, a green baseball cap turned backwards

with a Mexican flag embroidered on it. When he wore it
     in the front yard, which he treated like his personal *zócolo*,
          all his realm knew he had the power that day, had all the jewels

a king could eat or smoke or shoot. The slave girls came
     to the fence and ate out of his hands. He fed them *maíz*
          through the chain links. My parents watched from the window,

crying over their house turned zoo, their son who was
     now a rusted cage. The Aztec held court in a salt cedar grove
          across the street where peacocks lived. My parents crossed fingers

so he'd never come back, lit *novena* candles
     so he would. He always came home with turquoise and jade
          feathers and stinking of peacock shit. My parents gathered

what he'd left of their bodies, trying to stand without legs,
     trying to defend his blows with missing arms, searching for their fingers
          to pray, to climb out of whatever dark belly my brother, the Aztec,
          their son, had fed them to.

TOMMY PICO (1984–), *Kumeyaay*, was born and raised on the Viejas Reservation and now divides his time between Los Angeles and Brooklyn. He is the author of the poetry collections *IRL*, *Nature Poem*, *Junk*, and *Feed*. Pico has been the recipient of numerous fellowships and awards, including a Lambda Literary fellowship, a New York Foundation for the Arts fellowship, an American Book Award, and a Whiting Award. Currently, he is a contributing editor at the website Literary Hub, and he cohosts the podcast *Food 4 Thot*.

---

from *Nature Poem*

Like poison oak or the Left Eye part in "Waterfalls"
you become a little bit of everything you brush
against. Today I am a handful of raisins and abt 15 ppl on the water taxi.

When my dad texts me two cousins dead this week, one 26 the other
30, what I'm really trying to understand is what trainers @ the gym
mean when they say "engage" in the phrase "engage your core"
also "core"

restless terms batted back and forth.

Rest is a sign of necrosis. Life is a cycle of jobs. The biosphere is alive
with menthol smoke and my unchecked voicemails. I, for one, used to
believe in God
and comment boards

I wd say how far I am from my mountains, tell you why I carry
Kumeyaay basket designs on my body, or how freakishly routine it is to
hear someone died

but I don't want to be an identity or a belief or a feedbag. I wanna b
me. I want to open my arms like winning a foot race and keep my
stories to myself, I tell my audience.

Grief is sneaking cigs from the styrofoam cups on the tables next to the creamers and plates of Mary's pineapple upside-down cake, running off to the playground behind the schoolroom trailers to (try and) smoke them

We were supposed to grow old together, hold down food, run for cover, give birth.

Body the job
was to keep breathing.

JAKE SKEETS (1991–), *Diné,* is Black Streak Wood, born for Water's Edge, from Vanderwagen, New Mexico. He holds an MFA in poetry from the Institute of American Indian Arts in Santa Fe, is a member of Saad Bee Hózhǫ́: A Diné Writers' Collective, and currently teaches at Diné College in Tsaile, Arizona. He is a winner of the 2018 Discovery/*Boston Review* Poetry Contest and the 2018 National Poetry Series for his debut collection, *Eyes Bottle Dark with a Mouthful of Flowers.*

DRUNKTOWN

Indian Eden. Open tooth. Bone Bruise. This town split in two.
Clocks ring out as train horns, each hour hand drags into a screech—
iron, steel, iron. The minute hand runs its fingers
                                        through the outcrops.

Drunktown. Drunk is the punch. *Town* a gasp.
In between the letters are boots crushing tumbleweeds,
                              a tractor tire backing over a man's skull.

—

Men around here only touch when they fuck in a backseat
                go for the foul with thirty seconds left
                  hug their son after high school graduation
        open a keg
            stab my uncle forty-seven times behind a liquor store

—

A bar called Eddie's sits at the end of the world. By the tracks,
drunk men get some sleep. My father's uncle tries to get some
under a long-bed truck. The truck instead backs up to go home.

I arrange my father's boarding school soap bones on white space
and call it a poem. With my father, I come up on death
staggering into the house with beer on the breath.

—

Mule deer splintered in barbed tendon. Gray highway
veins narrow—push, pull under teal and red hills.
A man is drunk staggering into northbound lanes,
dollar bills for his index and ring fingers. Sands glitter
with broken bottles—greens, deep blues, clears, and golds.
This place is White Cone, Greasewood, Sanders,
White Water, Breadsprings, Crystal, Chinle, Nazlini,
Indian Wells, and all muddy roads lead from Gallup.
The sky places an arm on the hills around here.
On the shoulder, dark gray almost blue bleeds

into greens

                  blue greens

turquoise into hazy blue

                                 pure blue

no gray or gold

                      or oil black seeped through.

—

If I stare long enough, I see my uncle in a mirror. The bottle caps we use for eyes.

—

an owl has a skeleton of three letters
                o twists into *l*

                             the burrowing owl burrows
                   under dead cactus
                         stuffed into mouth jarred open

        feathers fall on horseweed
                     and skull bone blown open

SOUTHEAST

RENEWAL

Jennifer Elise Foerster

SOUTHEASTERN PEOPLE have long been writers. Sequoyah, whose tribute by Cherokee poet Joshua Ross is included in this region, had developed the Cherokee syllabary by 1821, the first writing system in Native North America. Muscogee and Seminole groups had developed and adopted an alphabet by 1853, coining new Mvskoke (Muscogee) words, writing constitutions, and translating English texts into Mvskoke.

This long history of writing is made apparent by the prolific works of early authors like Alexander Posey (Mvskoke, 1873–1908) and John Rollin Ridge (Cherokee, 1827–67), who was one of the earliest known Native American novelists. But we can also look to periodicals published and edited by Native people beginning in the mid-nineteenth century. The first Native press, the *Cherokee Phoenix*, was founded by Elias Boudinot in 1838. The Cherokee Female Seminary published its first periodical, *Cherokee Rose Buds*, in 1853. Throughout these early writings, many of which are represented here, I am most struck by what the poems conceal. Writings published in school periodicals had to be presented as optimistic evidence—propaganda—of the boarding school's "success," heavily monitored as these publications were by the white school administrators. While promoting "Indian education" in ways that, on the surface, seem to demoralize cultural identity and tradition, these are also poems of cultural survival and adaptation. While the poem may pronounce assimilation, read deeper and you will find resistance, wit, irony, and grief. In the 1850s, few would have recognized the unspeakable sorrow of the Trail of Tears in John Gunter Lipe's sentimental, ballad-metered "To Miss Vic," which reads on the surface as a rather common lament over a heedless lover. As Samuel Sixkiller addresses his graduating class at the Carlisle Indian Industrial School, he is at the same time addressing the administrators, those who have assembled "To help nature's children . . . [to] make pure Americans from ocean to bay." I imagine only Sixkiller's classmates understood his irony. His assertion of "the noble Red Man" as "the true, the only American" was lost to those only listening for their own reflection, a self-affirming national narrative. The reliance of this narrative on the main-tenance of a façade (i.e., Manifest Destiny as an "altruism") is one reason for Native poets being so long excluded from "American Literature."

These early poems reveal, to me, the reality of the in-betweenness that has so long characterized the indigenous Southeastern experience. The liter-ature by Native people during this catastrophic century was written against and through trauma to find a new means of surviving. The poets were living in two worlds at the crux of profound cultural, geographic, linguistic, and social change. The poetry itself reveals a negotiation of these two worlds, inte-grating contradictory beliefs in both cultural resistance and assimilation—a fierce recapitulation of tradition and, at the same time, a wielding of "new American" ideals of individualism and economic progress.

Being in-between is so much a part of the literatures of Southeastern people, but this is also what has led to its dismissal from "Native American" literature, to which standards have been, until recently, decided by everyone but Native writers. To "preserve" their idea of authentic Indianness, many cul-tural critics and canon-makers left out such writers as Alexander Posey and Mary Cornelia Hartshorne. Especially because these writers, many of whom were women—Stella LeFlore Carter, Ruth Margaret Muskrat Bronson—were writing political poems. Another reason for exclusion: Poetry is power-ful. Poetry by Native writers of the nineteenth and early twentieth centuries often engaged the same language that was stripping them of human rights: English lyric metricism and romantic themes. While we could understand this purposeful engagement as a means of asserting agency, the dominant lit-erary culture would still rebuff, insisting on its "savage vs. civilized" mythos: any writer of this kind of verse, it was assumed, had lost their "Nativeness." I shouldn't have to point out the problem here. Why would we not have writ-ten in available and contemporary forms—dirges to translate our loss, for example, or parodies of our contemporaries, as J. C. Duncan parodied Rud-yard Kipling's "The White Man's Burden" in his poem "The Red Man's Bur-den"—to speak back to the language of oppression? Positioned as we were at the crossroads, why would we not also have engaged the dominant language to stand up for our humanity, our rights? One must use all the resources one can. James Harris Guy's 1878 letter to Alfred B. Meacham is, to me, one of the best examples of poetry being wielded as a tool for political justice.

As Robert Dale Parker so deftly argues in *Changing Is Not Vanishing: A Collection of American Indian Poetry to 1930*, the poems that remain in favor with non-Native audiences as the most "authentically Indian" are transcribed (mis)translations (by non-Natives) of traditional or ceremonial songs. Such conception of "Native" poetry supports, also, the public's preferred idealization of the illiterate Native American.

Our heritage as original peoples of the Southeast has always been one of cross-cultural adaptation and diplomacy. We emerged from the Southeast Chiefdoms' collapse as numerous decentralized societies living along the rivers' confluence points, establishing alliances to maintain a balance of power in the region and, later, to form united fronts against European encroachment. We were ethnically and linguistically heterogenous among the (at least) five distinct language families indigenous to the southeast: Algonquian, Caddoan, Iroquoian, Muskogean, and Siouan. This heterogeneity of the peoples, languages, and traditions of the Southeastern tribal nations still largely defines us today.

The Southeastern region of what is currently the United States is the ancestral homelands of not only the most widely known Southeastern nations—the Cherokee, Choctaw, Chickasaw, Seminole, and Muscogee (Mvskoke or Creek)—but also countless other cultural groups—Natchez, Yuchi, Appalachee, Timucua, Koasati, Caddo, Catawba—that emerged from the Moundbuilding Centers of the Lower Mississippian Basin and its river's vast network of tributaries.

With this diversity, what we have in common is a very long story of inhabiting and living in balance with the southeastern woodlands, waterways, animals, and people. The groups indigenous to the American South are the inheritors of the Mississippian cultures, which in linear, historical time are known to have existed from 1500 B.C. until the 1600s. Our varied Southeastern emergence stories, however, go farther back, preceding the oldest known structures of civilization in what we now call the United States. Louisiana's Poverty Point, the oldest major Earthworks Center in the Western Hemisphere, is at least five thousand years old, with an effigy mound in the shape of a hawk more than 640 feet wide in wingspan. These imprints of origin, from Nanih Waiya, the Choctaw Mother Mound, to the Ocmulgee and Etowah mounds, all thousands of years old, are shared by all people indigenous to the Southeast in memory, body, and story.

What is also shared is a history of surviving through erasure and invisibility: the vibrant and diverse peoples, stories, and societies of this country's Southeastern lands are largely invisible to the "American story" of itself. The empire of Coosa, for example, which has been considered the largest chiefdom, comprised of thirty-five thousand people and spanning four hundred miles upon its encounter by Hernando de Soto in his July 16, 1540, expedition, is visible today only in a few ambiguous landforms.

For a person with indigenous roots in the Southeast who is looking for evidence of your homeland, you have to follow invisible maps. The landscape has changed, the surfaces of our histories have been written over: the longleaf pine ecosystem of Creek country's southern territory reduced from ninety million acres to three million acres in under two centuries; the river valleys of the eighteenth-century Muscogean towns now predominantly underwater as a result of twentieth-century damming practices. When we look at the maps of the Southeast, we do not see ourselves, we do not see our memories of place. But that does not mean we do not hold these memories and embody them, not only in cultural practices or ways of life, but in our poetics.

For Southeastern people, the land has always been infused with meaning. We built extensive earthworks, effigy mounds, and vast ceremonial complexes that signified our human place within the cosmos. Today, many of our stories, design motifs, architectures, and traditions of oratory reflect these ancient patterns. And while, especially in the story of Southeastern people, it is the land itself that is persistently lost, it is through land—through place—that we consistently renew. I read these poems and hear the ever-determined voice of renewal; the insistence of stories, as in "A Creek Woman Beside Lake Ontario," in which Stacy Pratt writes of "stories he keeps repeating/from inside my own body"; the survival of nature beyond the sagas of land ownership and loss, as in Moses Jumper Jr.'s "Simplicity" or Mary Cornelia Hartshorne's "Fallen Leaves"; and the power of humor, in Louis Little Coon Oliver's "Medicare" or LeAnne Howe's "Noble Savage Sees a Therapist." Humor sustains us; it also tells the truth.

Southeastern people have always been and continue to be our own agents for adaptation and change: In the face of American expansion, we formalized syllabaries and new systems of constitutional government while working with foreign landscapes to help us rebuild as nations. Likewise, Southeastern poets and orators have engaged this practice of inventive adaptation for nearly two centuries of writing, and longer when considering oral traditions. The adoption of the hymn meter is an example of one such adaptation. West African melodies and Christian Scottish hymns were introduced into many

Southeastern tribal communities in the eighteenth century and merged into a hybridized style of gospel singing. Hymns were some of the first written compositions using the Mvskoke syllabary, and it is likely that many of the hymns that make up the Mvskoke and Choctaw hymnals are also original compositions that document the experience of removal. For Mvskoke, Choctaw, Cherokee, Seminole, and Chickasaw people, call-and-response is an integral part of ceremony and celebration, as is the all-night singing, dancing, and shell-shaking that comprises most of the Green Corn traditions. Joy Harjo tells us, "In the rhythms of stomp dance are the root rhythms of blues and jazz, and of the land." Joy Harjo was the first poet I read who taught me that a poem can listen, as if to its own echo, spiraling back to its origins. Even after removal from the Southeast, where we once traveled in search of the sun, we still dance in spirals toward the coming dawn. We still dance counterclockwise and honor the fire in the center of our ceremonial circles. It is the fire that has kept our towns and people alive, traveling with us from our original homelands to help us re-establish anew when we arrived. We will always be arriving and renewing our futures.

EVENING SONG 93

From the nineteenth-century Choctaw Hymns,
"Times and Seasons."

Issa hal-a-li haa- toko Ik-sa illok isha shkee
Issa hal-a-li haa- toko Ik-sa illok isha shkee
Issa hal-a-li haa- toko Ik-sa illok isha shkee
Issa hal-a-li haa- toko Ik-sa illok isha shkee

 PETER PERKINS PITCHLYNN (*1806–1881*), *Choctaw,* helped shape the national tribal government in the nineteenth century. His father was John Pitchlynn, a white trader, and his mother was Sophia Folsom, from an influential Choctaw family. He was educated at the Choctaw Academy in Kentucky and the University of Nashville and went on to become one of the greatest chiefs of the Choctaw.

Song of the Choctaw Girl

I'm looking on the mountain,
    I'm gazing o'er the plain;
I love the friends around me,
    But wish for home again!

I hear their tones of kindness,
    They soothe my every pain;
I know they love me truly—
    I wish for that home again!

My mother's grave is yonder,
    And there it must remain;
My father's care is tender,
    I wish for home again!

My sisters and my brothers—
    Alas! it may be vain,
This longing for beloved ones—
    I wish for home again.

O, take me to my Nation,
    And let me there remain;
This other world is strange, strange—
    I wish for home again.

Give me the western forest—
    the mountain, stream and plain,
The shaded lawns of childhood—
    Give me my home again!

The free breeze of the prairie,
    The wild bird's joyous strain,
The tree my father planted—
    O, take me home again!

The sunshine and the flowers,
      My mother's grave again,
Give me my race and kindred—
      O, take me home again!

 JOSHUA ROSS *(1833–1913), Cherokee,* was the son of Andrew
Ross and Susan Lowry. His uncle was John Ross, chief of the Cher-
okees. Ross graduated from the Cherokee Male Seminary in Tah-
lequah, Oklahoma in 1855 and from Emory and Henry College in Virginia
in 1860.

SEQUOYAH

O'er Sequoyah's lonely grave
The forest oaks their branches wave;
No guide is known to point the place
Where sleeps the Cadmus of his race,
Neglected son of genius rest—
No marble pressed on thy breast;
But when the Nation fades away
Before the mighty Saxon sway;
When high upon the list of fame
In letters bright shall stand thy name;
The learned have your powers admired
And some have thought you were inspired;
Like to that might seer of old,
Before whose eye the future rolled;
Who saw great nations rise and fall
And read the writing on the wall;
Now all are loud in praising thee,
But when you lived seemed not to see,
Aught in the gift forest child

Above the common Indian wild;
So thou didst to the deep wood fly
In solitude alone to die;
No well loved hand or sister dear
To wipe away the last sad tear.

 LILY LEE (*unknown*), *Cherokee,* was a student at the Cherokee Female Seminary in Tahlequah, Oklahoma, around 1855. Since she published under a pen name, her actual identity is unknown.

Literary Day Among the Birds

Dark night at last has taken its flight,
Morn had come with her earliest light;
Her herald, gray dawn, had extinguished each star,
And gay banners in the east were waving afar.

That lovely goddess, Beautiful Spring,
Had fanned all the earth with her radiant wing;
"Had calmed the wild winds with fragrant breath,"
And gladden'd nature with an emerald wreath.

Within the precincts of the Bird Nation,
All was bustle and animation;
For that day was to witness a literary feast,
Where only Birds were invited guests.

The place of meeting was a leafy nook,
Close by the side of a sparkling brook.
Soon were assembled a merry band,
Birds from every tree in the land.

Mrs. Dove came first, in soft colors drest;
Then Mr. Canary, looking his best.
The family of Martins, dressed in brown,
And Mr. Woodpecker, with his ruby crown.

The exercises opened with a scientific song,
By the united voices of the feathered throng.
Then was delivered a brilliant oration,
By 'Squire RAVEN, the wisest bird of the nation.
Master WHIP-POOR-WILL next mounted the stage,
Trying to look very much like a sage.

Eight pretty green Parrots then spoke with art;
Though small, with credit they carried their part.
Again an oration by Mr. Quail,
Spoken as fast as the gallop of snail.
And lastly, Sir BLACKBIRD whistl'd off an address,
Of twenty odd minutes, more or less.

Then came the applause, so loud and long,
That the air echoed the joyous song.
But the sun was low, so soon they sped
To their quiet nests and their grassy beds;
And rocked by the breeze, they quietly slept,
Ere the firstling star in the blue sky crept.

JOHN GUNTER LIPE *(1844–1862)*, *Cherokee,* fought during the Civil War in the Confederate army and was killed in battle in 1862. His poem "To Miss Vic" was written for Victoria Hicks, who later married his older brother.

To Miss Vic

I stand at the portal and knock,
And tearfully, prayerfully wait.
O! who will unfasten the lock,
And open the beautiful gate?

Forever and ever and ever,
Must I linger and suffer alone?
Are there none that are able to sever,
The fetters that keep me from home?

My spirit is lonely and weary,
I long for the beautiful streets.
The world is so chilly and dreary,
And bleeding and torn are my feet.

> Tahlequah, Cherokee Nation.

 JAMES HARRIS GUY *(unknown–1885)*, *Chickasaw.* Before he died, Guy had agreed to write a book of legends and poems, but only four of his poems survive. His uncle Cyrus Harris was the first elected governor of the Chickasaw Nation.

The White Man Wants the Indian's Home

Tishomingo, C.N., I. T., June 17th, 1878
A. B. Meacham, Washington, D.C.

Dear Sir:—To-day I picked up two copies of your *Council Fire*, being the first I have seen. I am a Chickasaw Indian, and in spite of the expressed contempt by the white man, I am glad of it. Are we not equal? Surely God made us so mentally as well as physically. If we stand behind the white to-day in education, is it our fault? No! had the United States Government kept its pledges toward us, our schools would now be in full operation.

There is sorrow in the Indian's home to-day. They (the whites) say our land is "too good" for us; it is only fit for the whites. And unless brave men like you stand up for us, sooner or later we perish from the face of the earth, *because we are Indians.* I did not know before that there was a white man brave enough to stand up and say in the Capital, "the Indian has been wronged." But he has been wronged, and bitterly wronged. It speaks volumes when a Senator can in the Senate-room challenge his people to produce one single instance of an Indian treaty being carried out faithfully toward the Indians.

Will you answer this? Have the five civilized nations done anything against the United States government since the Rebellion? If not, why is that United States continually trying to gain our lands? for all these Territorial bills are nothing else but levers brought to bear on the destruction of the Indians' titles. Will you, and brave men like you, allow this? We are trying to live godly lives; but sometimes I feel like an old Chickasaw Indian to whom I was describing heaven. Among other things I told him all would be brothers; that we should all live together in peace. Judge of my astonishment when he replied, "Is the white man going there?" I told him yes. Then he said, "I do not want to go there; heaven too good for Indian; white man wants it all; so Indian have to go." And he refused to listen to me any longer. Tell your government we are not drunkards or thieves; that we are doing the best we can for ourselves.

I send you a few lines expressing the sentiment of my people:

The white man wants the Indian's home,
    He envies them their land;
And with his sweetest words he comes
    To get it, if he can.

And if we will not give our lands
    And plainly tell him so,
He then goes back, calls up his clans,
    And says, "Let's make them go."

The question in the Indian's mind
    Is, where are we to go?
No other country can we find;
    'Tis filled up with our foe.

We do not want one foot of land
    The white man calls his own;
We ask nothing at his hands,
    Save to be alone.

Send me a copy of the paper and I will forward you a dollar.—

 J. C. DUNCAN *(1860–unknown), Cherokee,* was a poet about whom not much is known, other than his one surviving political poem, "The Red Man's Burden," in which the illegible words are denoted with an X.

THE RED MAN'S BURDEN

Parody on Kipling's Poem ["The White Man's Burden"]

Look at the Redman's burden
  Place in thy Christian scales,
In the hands of Dawes Commission,
  For that is what prevails.
Yes, look at the Redman's burden,
  That caused the "exiled son"
To "face the stormy waters,"
  Seeking their golden mun.

"Half devil and half child" you call
  The aborigines,
'Tis better far to be half child
  Than be a devil all.
No "heavy harness" need be spent,
  Nor "Christians" hide in wait,
  Just keep a radical president,
And Curtis to legislate.

Behold the white man's burden
  Of gold and silver bullion,
Of Redmen's scalps and broken vows
  By hundreds, yes by millions.
Yet fill their mouths of famine xxx,
  With bombshells and with grape,
For that's the way all "Christians" do
  Like Shafter did of late.

From Florida to Havana
  One stride the goddess made,
To cheer the word "expansion,"
  And in seas of blood to wade;

The xxxxxx Philippine xxxxxx
    In less than half a stride,
And the eagle's wing o'er
    The world xx in style to xxxxx.

From side to side that eagle xxxxxxxxxxx
    Above the "image's[?]" moan,
His beak upon the frozen beach[?],
    His tail the torrid zone.
All for "Christianity's sake,"
    Quoth Kipling, in his rhyme,
Perhaps he better poems make
    Than truths every time.

Another portion yet is sought
    The North Pole, so 'tis said
The problem yet has not been wrought
    But will be live or dead.
To make a plain and easy way
    For the white part of creation,
Publicly through the presses say,
    It's an Indian reservation.

White man, shake off thy burden,
'Tis enough they pride to yoke,
Give us back our freedom,
    And return to thy British yoke.
Return our land and moneys,
    Then Christianity take,
Return to us our innocence,
    We never burned at stakes.

EVALYN CALLAHAN SHAW (*1861–unknown*), *Mvskoke,* lived in Wagoner, Indian Territory, where her father, Samuel Benton Callahan, was a leading figure in Creek politics and represented the Creek and Seminole Nations in the Second Confederate Congress.

OCTOBER

October is the month that seems
All woven with midsummer dreams;
She brings for us the golden days
That fill the air with smoky haze,
She brings for us the lisping breeze
And wakes the gossips in the trees,
Who whisper near the vacant nest
Forsaken by its feathered guest.
Now half the birds forget to sing,
And half of them have taken wing,
Before their pathway shall be lost
Beneath the gossamer of frost.
Zigzag across the yellow sky,
They rustle here and flutter there,
Until the boughs hang chill and bare,
What joy for us—what happiness
Shall cheer the day the night shall bless?
'Tis hallowe'en, the very last
Shall keep for us remembrance fast,
When every child shall duck the head
To find the precious pippin red.

ALEXANDER POSEY *(1873–1908)*, *Mvskoke,* was a poet, humorist, and journalist, who was politically involved in improving living conditions in Indian Territory. He reported for and in 1902–4 owned the *Eufaula Indian Journal,* the first Native daily newspaper, which had been founded in Eufaula, Oklahoma, in 1876. He is also known for his humorous political editorial columns written in local tribal dialect in the fictional voice of Fus Fixico. He died young by accidental drowning in the North Canadian River in 1908.

To a Hummingbird

Now here, now there;
      E'er posed somewhere
In sensuous air.
      I only hear, I cannot see
The matchless winds that beareth thee.
      Art thou some frenzied poet's thought,
That God embodied and forgot?

Tulledega

My choice of all choice spots in Indian lands!
Hedged in, shut up by walls of purple hills,
That swell clear cut against our sunset sky,
Hedged in, shut up and hidden from the world.
As though it said, "I have no words for you;
I'm not part of you; your ways aren't mine."
Hedged in, shut up with low log cabins built—
How snugly!—in the quaint old fashioned way;
With fields of yellow maize, so small that you
Might hide them with your palm while gazing on
Them from the hills around them, high and blue.
Hedged in, shut up with long forgotten ways,

And stories handed down from sire to son.
Hedged in, shut up with broad Oktaha, like
A flash of glory curled among the hills!
How it sweeps away toward the morning,
Deepened here and yonder by the beetling
Crag, the music of its dashings mingling
With the screams of eagles whirling over,
With its splendid tribute to the ocean!
And this spot, this nook is Tulledega;
Hedged in, shut up, I say by walls of hills,
Like tents stretched on the borders of the day,
As blue as yonder op'ning in the clouds!

To Allot, or Not to Allot

To allot, or not to allot, that is the
Question; whether 'tis nobler in the mind to
Suffer the country to lie in common as it is,
Or to divide it up and give each man
His share pro rata, and by dividing
End this sea of troubles? To allot, divide,
Perchance to end in statehood;
Ah, there's the rub!

 SAMUEL SIXKILLER (1877–1958), *Cherokee,* was born in the Cherokee Nation in Indian Territory and educated in Pennsylvania at the Carlisle Indian Industrial School, where he was the class poet in 1895. In his anthology *Changing Is Not Vanishing,* editor Robert Dale Parker notes that Sixkiller's grandfather, also named Samuel Sixkiller, served as high sheriff of the Cherokee Nation and captain of the United States Indian Police until he was ambushed and killed in 1886 while off duty.

To Class '95

Farewell to dear class, to friends and to strangers,
    Assembling here in our honor today,
To help Nature's children—the wildflower rangers,
    And make pure Americans from ocean to bay.

At last we have roamed from woodland to mountain;
    From the murmur of pines and the emerald sea,
To drink of the pure—that life-giving fountain,
    And bask in the sun of the noble and free.

Away from the plains where often in childhood,
    From deep slumber waked by the music of rills;
Away from the glory and pleasure of wildwood,
    Away from the perfume of flower-clad hills.

And still to our hearts, Nature clings as a brother;
    We dream of repose by the streams we yet love.
Can light and advancement, our thoughts of these smother?
    Of joys placed here by the Father above?

When shall the culture, the art and refinement
    Drive from our minds, roving thoughts of the past?
Shall broad education, or savage confinement,
    Conquer the Red Man now fading so fast?

Too soon are those features the emblems of power.
    Too soon are they leaving his countenance bold.
Alas, they shall fade or to fierce foeman cower,
    And die with the past as a tale that is told.

Sad be the day when the sun in his glory
    Shall shine on the last of the noble Red Man
Or set for this race whose life is a story,
    The true, the only American.

And now we must part, may it not be forever!
     But if on this earth we can ne'er share our love,
God grant that the ties we have here had to sever,
     May be reunited in that kingdom above.

 STELLA LEFLORE CARTER *(1892–unknown), Chickasaw,* was the daughter of U.S. Congressman Charles David Carter. Her sister, Julia Carter Welch, was also a poet. The "Alfalfa Bill" Murray mentioned in Carter's poem married a Chickasaw woman but was known as a segregationist, and a racist. He called out the National Guard forty-seven times as Oklahoma governor (1931–1935) for everything from policing the sale of University of Oklahoma football tickets to shutting down oil wells. Asked how to be successful in Oklahoma politics he said, "Never say anything good about the state of Texas."

INAUGURATION DAY

The cowboy and the farmer, in chaps and Sunday clothes,
Indian and country lawyer, and folks nobody knows,
Oil magnates, women in Paris gowns, a motley, strange array,
The high and low, the rich and poor, and in "The City" today.

All proudly pay their tribute to Oklahoma's son,
"Alfalfa Bill," they call him, in half-admiring fun.
His roughened, weather-beaten face and careless dress proclaim
That he's a real pioneer and worthy of his name.

Here is no man that men can rule; his virile, homely face
Shows scars of many battles—but of weakness not a trace.
Here is the poor man's sponsor—he has known poverty.
His rugged, fearless honesty a child could plainly see.

They say he lacks in culture—yet an eager scholar he,
Of history and jurisprudence and lore of the tepee;
A typical Oklahoman—here's to a native son!
God give him strength and wisdom to run well his race begun.

 WINNIE LEWIS GRAVITT (*1895–1974*), *Choctaw,* graduated from the University of Oklahoma. She worked as a librarian and her poems were featured in *Tushkahomman, the Red Warrior,* a newspaper of Stroud, Oklahoma, published from 1935 to 1939.

SIPPOKNI SIA

I am old, Sippokni sia.
Before my eyes run many years,
Like panting runners in a race.
Like a weary runner the years lag;
Eyes grow dim, blind with wood smoke;
A handkerchief binds my head,
For I am old. Sippokni sia.

Hands, once quick to weave and spin;
Strong to fan the tanchi;
Fingers patient to shape dirt bowls;
Loving to sew hunting shirt;
Now, like oak twigs twisted.
I am old. Sippokni sia.

Feel swift as wind o'er young cane shoots;
Like stirring leaves in ta falla dance;
slim like rabbits in leather shoes;
Now moves like winter snows,
Like melting snows on Cavanaugh.

In the door I sit, my feet in spring water.
I am old. Sippokni sia.

Black like crow's feather, my hair;
Long and straight like hanging rope;
My people proud and young.
Now like hickory ashes in my hair,
Like ashes of old campfire in the rain.
Much civilization bow my people;
Sorrow, grief and trouble sit like blackbirds on fence.
I am old. Sa Sippokni hoke.

 RUTH MARGARET MUSKRAT BRONSON (*1897–1982*), *Cherokee*, was born on the Delaware County Indian Reservation and attended Mount Holyoke College on a scholarship, graduating in 1925. She worked as head of the scholarship and loan program at the Bureau of Indian Affairs in Washington, D.C., and later as the executive secretary of the National Congress of American Indians. A specialist in American Indian Affairs, Bronson also wrote a high school textbook titled *Indians Are People Too*.

SENTENCED

(A Dirge)

They have come, they have come,
Out of the unknown they have come;
Out of the great sea they have come;
Dazzling and conquering the white man has come
To make this land his home.

We must die, we must die,
The white man has sentenced we must die,

Without great forests we must die,
Broken and conquered the red man must die,
He cannot claim his own.

They have gone, they have gone,
Our sky-blue waters, they have gone,
Our wild free prairies they have gone,
To be the white man's own.

They have won, they have won,
Thru fraud and thru warfare they have won,
Our council and burial grounds they have won,
Our birthright for pottage that white man has won,
And the red man must perish alone.

LYNN RIGGS *(1899–1954), Cherokee,* was a poet and a play-wright. He was born in Claremore, Oklahoma and attended the University of Oklahoma. Although he was a poet as well, Riggs is most famous for his play *Green Grow the Lilacs*, on which the famous musical *Oklahoma!* is based.

A Letter

I don't know why I should be writing to you,
I don't know why I should be writing to anyone;
Nella has brought me yellow calendulas,
In my neighbor's garden is sun.

In my neighbor's garden chickens, like snow,
Drift in the alfalfa. Bees are humming;
A pink dress, a blue wagon play in the road;
Guitars are strumming.

Guitars are saying the same things
They said last night—in a different key.
What they have said I know—so their strumming
Means nothing to me.

Nothing to me is the pale pride of Lucinda
Washing her hair—nothing to anyone:
Here in a black bowl are calendulas,
in my neighbor's garden, sun.

 LOUIS LITTLE COON OLIVER *(1904–1991), Mvskoke,* was Euchee of the Racoon clan from the Chattahoochee region, though he lived much of his life among the Cherokee in Tahlequah, Oklahoma. He was the recipient of the first Alexander Posey Literary Award in 1987. That same year the University of Oklahoma's English department named Oliver the Poet of Honor at Oklahoma Poets Day.

MIND OVER MATTER

My old grandmother, Tekapay'cha
     stuck an ax into a stump
     and diverted a tornado.
In minutes we would have been destroyed.
It struck the little town of Porter
     ripping up the railroad tracks,
     twisted the rails and stood them up.
There was power in that twister.
There was power in my grandmother.
Those who doubt, let them doubt.

THE SHARP-BREASTED SNAKE

(Hōkpē Fuskē)

The Muskogee's hokpi—
    fuski (Loch Ness
      Monster)
        Travelled here
          by the Camp of
            The Sac and Fox;
              Thru the alluvial
                Gombo soil, flailing
                  Thrashing-up rooting
                Giant trees;
              Ploughed deep
              With its sharp breast.
            Come to rest by
          Tuskeegi Town, buried
        its self in a lake of
       mud to rest. The
      warriors of Tustanuggi
     were ordered to shoot
    it with a silver tipped
   arrow. With a great
  roar and upheaval The
Snake moved on;
winding by Okmulgee
To enter (Okta hutchee)
South Canadian River.
Thus his ploughed
  journey, The Creeks
  called (Hutchee
    Sofkee) Deepfork
    River.
      One, Cholaka,
        observed The Snake
        had hypnotic Power.

Could draw a person
into a swirling
whirlpool. It
made a sound
Like a
Tinkling
silver
Bell.
O
k
i
s
c
e.

MEDICARE

(No strings attached)

Asthmatic and wheezing I tromped
through sandburrs and bullnettles,
white sandy soils—hot winds.
Weaved through postoak runners
    —sawtooth briars.
Stopped to rest and smoke a Camel.
Like a fugitive from the law
bypassing the clear clean roads,
        Why?
I'm a fullblooded Indian—that
        is why.
I'm going to see old Nokose
    for him to diagnose my illness.
He lives in an old and sturdy
    cabin of oak logs.
Two big Indian dogs came out
        to sniff me over.

Though their hackles are up they never
        bark.
They are part of the mysticism
        of their owner,
and their scrutiny of a stranger
        is conveyed.
There is a rapport twixt Indian and Indian
        . . . no lengthy conversations, just
        presence and silence.
Finally old Nokose began
to relate the cause of my
        illness.
Humped and seeming in a trance
he spoke of entities in the spirit
        world:
The slimeless snail, the legless ant
        the microscopic demons
        the little blue-winged hunter
        wasp.
Much beyond my understanding.
He arose and went to his
        backroom
I could hear him singing in
        a monotone.
I expected to smell an odor
        of wild beasts,
  but there was a pleasant, medicinal
whiff of mint, sage and cedar.
A white feather hung from a joist
in the center of the room
  creating a mystifying air.
Old Nokose shuffled back
        looked to the feather and said:
    "If my diagnosis has been
        right
        You will turn in approval."
It seemed so long before it moved

—twisting, slowly around.
He handed me a sheaf of herbs
          a tiny box of yellow dust.
Early morning for four weeks
          I did as he told me.
I breathe freely with no pain
. . . and for some mysterious reason
my desire to smoke is dead.
I can say I owe the man
          my life,
but would he take any money?
          NO!

MARY CORNELIA HARTSHORNE (*1910–1980*), *Choctaw.*
Hartshorne won a literary essay contest in 1929 when she was a student at Tulsa University. As a result of her essay, she was flown to Hollywood, California, to meet silent film stars Mary Pickford and Douglas Fairbanks.

FALLEN LEAVES

(An Indian Grandmother's Parable)

Many times in my life I have heard the white sages,
Who are learned in the knowledge and lore of past ages,
Speak of my people with pity, say, "Gone is their hour
Of dominion. By the strong wind of progress their power,
Like a rose past its brief time of blooming, lies shattered;
Like the leaves of the oak tree its people are scattered."
This is the eighty-first autumn since I can remember.
Again fall the leaves, born in April and dead by December;
Riding the whimsied breeze, zigzagging and whirling,
Coming to earth at last and slowly upcurling,

Withered and sapless and brown, into discarded fragments
Of what once was life; dry, chattering parchments
That crackle and rustle like old women's laughter
When the merciless wind with swift feet coming after
Will drive them before him with unsparing lashes
'Til they are crumbled and crushed into forgotten ashes;
Crumbled and crushed, and piled deep in the gulches and hollows,
Soft bed for the yet softer snow that in winter fast follows
But when in the spring the light falling
Patter of raindrops persuading, insistently calling,
Wakens to life again forces that long months have slumbered,
There will come whispering movement, and green things unnumbered
Will pierce through the mold with their yellow-green, sun-searching fingers,
Fingers—or spear-tips, grown tall, will bud at another year's breaking,
One day when the brooks, manumitted by sunshine, are making
Music like gold in the spring of some far generation.
And up from the long-withered leaves, from the musty stagnation,
Life will climb high to the furthermost leaflets.
The bursting of catkins asunder with greed for the sunlight; the thirsting
Of twisted brown roots for earth-water; the gradual unfolding
Of brilliance and strength in the future, earth's bosom is holding
Today in those scurrying leaves, soon to be crumpled and broken.
Let those who have ears hear my word and be still. I have spoken.

THE POET

Sunlight was something more than that to him.
It was a halo when it formed a rim
Around some far-off mountain peak. He called
It thin-beat leaf of gold, and stood enthralled
When it lay still on some half-sheltered spot
In gilt mosaics where the trees forgot
To hide the grasses carpeting the spot.

The sky to him was not just the blue sky,
But a deep, painted bowl with clouds piled high;
And when these clouds were tinted burning red,
Or gold and Bacchic purple, then he said:
"The too-full goblets of the gods had over-run,
Nor give the credit to the disappearing sun
Who flames before he leaves the world in dun."

Between his eyes and life fate seemed to hold
A magic tissue of transparent gold,
That freed his vision from the dull, drab, hopeless part,
And kept alive a fresh, unsaddened heart.
And all unselfishly he tried to share
His gift with us who see the harsh and bare;
Be we refused. We did not know nor care.

GLADYS CARDIFF *(1942–)*, *Eastern Band of Cherokee,* was born in Browning, Montana, and grew up in Seattle, Washington. Of Irish, Welsh, and Cherokee descent, she is the author of two collections of poetry, *To Frighten a Storm* (1976) and *A Bare Unpainted Table* (1999). Cardiff's honors and awards include a Washington State Governor's First Book Award for her first book of poetry, two awards from the Seattle Arts Commission, and the University of Washington's Louisa Kerns Award.

To Frighten a Storm

O now you come in rut,
in rank and black desire,
to beat the brush, to lash
the wind with your long hair.
Ha! I am afraid,
exceedingly afraid.

But see? her path goes there,
along the swaying tops
of trees, up to the hills.
Too long she is alone.
Bypass our fields, and mount
your ravages of fire
and rain on higher trails.
You shall have her lying down
upon the smoking mountains.

COMBING

Bending, I bow my head
and lay my hands upon
her hair, combing, and think
how women do this for
each other. My daughter's hair
curls against the comb,
wet and fragrant—orange
parings. Her face, downcast,
is quiet for one so young.

I take her place. Beneath
my mother's hands I feel
the braids drawn up tight
as piano wires and singing,
vinegar-rinsed. Sitting
before the oven I hear
the orange coils tick
the early hour before school.

She combed her grandmother
Mathilda's hair using
a comb made out of bone.
Mathilda rocked her oak wood

chair, her face downcast,
intent on tearing rags
in strips to braid a cotton
rug from bits of orange
and brown. A simple act
preparing hair. Something
women do for each other,
plaiting the generations.

LINDA HOGAN *(1947–), Chickasaw.* Born in Denver, Colorado, Hogan has authored nine collections of poetry and seven collections of prose, as well as edited two anthologies. She has received grants from the National Endowment for the Arts and the Guggenheim Foundation for her fiction and was a finalist for the Pulitzer Prize for Literature. Her awards include an American Book Award from the Before Columbus Foundation, a Lannan Literary Award, a Lifetime Achievement Award from the Native Writers' Circle of the Americas, and the PEN Thoreau Prize.

LANDING

It is the day of leaving
when spiderlings
in orders of magnitude
hatch and from inward silk
unfurl toward a new god
caught by the wind.
I walk by the silk curtain
of strands that came from a body.
It is a shining world.

I want to unravel
something from the belly of myself.
It would not be about the spider who crossed water

and brought fire back to my people,
or even the length and brightness of our river
shining like silk in the light of sun and moonlight,
but about the cave up there in the high mountains
with animals made of willow twigs.
They were there before us,
tied with the string of our grasses
as if they were saying, we are one of you, the future,
and then those first ones came down on ropes of animal hair.

They have always been the far travelers
coming down from above.
That's why our fields are full of hope
and what is a story but this,
silk, the ancestors landing
and traveling who knows where
but sometimes they take your arm
and, caught on a soft wind, you follow.

BLESSINGS

Blessed
are the injured animals
for they live in his cages.
But who will heal my father,
tape his old legs for him?

Here's the bird with the two broken wings
and her feathers are white as an angel
and she says goddamn stirring grains
in the kitchen. When the birds fly out
he leaves the cages open
and she kisses his brow for such
good works.

Work he says
all your life
and in the end
you don't even own a piece of land.

Blessed are the rich
for they eat meat every night.
They have already inherited the earth.

For the rest of us, may we just live
long enough
and unwrinkle our brows,
may we keep our good looks
and some of our teeth
and our bowels regular.

Perhaps we can go live places
a rich man can't inhabit,
in the sunfish and jackrabbits,
in the cinnamon colored soil,
the land of red grass
and red people
in the valley
of the shadow of Elk
who aren't there.

      He says the damned earth is so old
      and wobbles so hard
      you'd best hang on to everything.
      Your neighbors steal what little you got.

Blessed
are the rich
for they don't have the same old
Everyday to put up with
like my father

who's gotten old,
           Chickasaw
           chikkih asachi, which means
they left as a tribe not a very great while ago.
They are always leaving,
those people.

Blessed
are those who listen
when no one is left to speak.

THE HISTORY OF FIRE

My mother is a fire beneath stone.
My father, lava.

My grandmother is a match,
my sister straw.

Grandfather is kindling like trees of the world.
My brothers are gunpowder,

and I am smoke with gray hair,
ash with black fingers and palms.

I am wind for the fire.

My dear one is a jar of burned bones
I have saved.

This is where our living goes
and still we breathe,

and even the dry grass
with sun and lightning above it

has no choice but to grow
and then lie down

with no other end in sight.

Air is between these words,
fanning the flame.

 PHILLIP CARROLL MORGAN *(1948–), Choctaw* and *Chick-asaw,* earned his PhD in Native American literature from the University of Oklahoma. Morgan won the Native Writers' Circle of the Americas First Book Award for Poetry for his poetry collection *The Fork-in-the-Road Indian Poetry Store* (2006). He is also the author of three Native American history books.

ANUMPA BOK LUKFI HILHA

(Treaty of Dancing Rabbit Creek)

pi-pokni lawah
micha pi-mafo lawah-vt
yakni imposa-ttok
itikba peni fohki
bok boha chitoah akkahikah

fichi-ivknah-vt
ai ninak kolaha okchamali-lhiposhi
isht-alhpisa hikia okla-sahnoyechih
yakni-imposa-ttok
itikba akuchi hastula nowa
akuchi hina-chilukoah

chukfi lumah-vt hilha micha lobukachi-ttok

hvcha hinlatuk anufohkah-kiyoh
hanima okla-ilap-immih aia
lukfi lhali-tuk im-ibbak
nishkin okchi lawah yaya-ttok
hakta yakni chuka pisachukmah
anoa kiyoh pis-achi kanima im-oklah-vt
talhepa sipokni lvwa aiashe-ttok

kalampi-ttok issish bano-ttok
ahni-ttok illi-ttok
i-fonih-vt okla hummah ist ona-ttok
i-chabiha sitoha-fonih-vt
talli-tuk micha itamoa

amba chim-pisa
amtakla okchay-achi̱
im-boshulli micha im-tushtua-vt
okcha a̱lichih
kia aiena anumpa lvwa
pa il-anumpilih

chukfi luma-vt hilha micha lobukahci-ttok

Treaty of Dancing Rabbit Creek
(*Anumpa Bok Lukfi Hilha*)

many of our grandmothers
and grandfathers
kissed the earth
before loading on the boats
to travel the big muddy river

light yellow stars
in the jade green magnolia night
stood watch as the old ones
kissed the earth

before walking out into the winter
into the broken road

the rabbit danced and fell into the creek

pearl river could not understand
where his own people were going
they cupped the dirt in their hands
they cried many tears
because they would never again see
our beautiful home land where our people
had lived for thousands of years

they froze they were bleeding
they suffered   they died
their bones were carried to oklahoma
some of the bone bundles
were scattered and lost

but they see you
and live on through me
bits and pieces of them
awaken   strengthen
even with these words
we are speaking

the rabbit danced and fell into the creek

 MOSES JUMPER JR. *(1950–), Seminole,* is the son of Moses, an alligator wrestler and tribal leader, and Betty Mae, a writer and first woman to be tribal chair. He is the director of the recreation program for the Seminole Tribe of Florida, Hollywood Reservation, and is a cattle rancher and breeder of Seminole ponies. His book of poetry is *Echoes in the Wind: Seminole Indian Poetry of Moses Jumper, Jr.* (1990).

SIMPLICITY

The small tunnel which the rabbit uses for escape and travel,
The small imprints of the killdeer in the soft white sand near the pond,
The fragileness of the newborn doves and how the mother puts on an act to
    lure away approaching enemies,
The unity of the small minnows as they protect themselves by staying near
    the shoreline of the stream,
The clear whistling sound the scorpion makes to let one know he's near,
The shagginess of the owl's nest and the neatness of the hummingbird's,
The long, graceful jumps of the sleek, green frog,
The short, choppy hops of the lumpy toad,
The agileness and grace of the otter,
The awkward wing flapping of the crane,
The camouflage nest of the mobile alligator and the will to reach the water
    of her young,
The winding tunnels, that lead to nowhere, of the sly red fox,
The abundance of life in the wet season and stench of death in the dry.
The persistence of the mother hawk to nudge her young to make that flight,
I saw all these things, and many more, and I know they were right.

 LEANNE HOWE *(1951–), Choctaw,* writes poetry, fiction, non-fiction, and screenplays. She is the Edison Distinguished Professor at the University of Georgia. Howe is a United States Artists (USA) Ford Fellow as well as the recipient of a Lifetime Achievement Award by the Native Writers' Circle of the Americas, an American Book Award, and an Oklahoma Book Award. She was also a Fulbright Distinguished Scholar to Jordan. Her most recent collection of poetry is *Savage Conversations* (2019).

Noble Savage Sees a Therapist

NOBLE SAVAGE: She's too intense for me.
And I feel nothing.   No emotion.
In fact, I'm off all females
—even lost my lust for
attacking white chicks.

(Pause.)

THERAPIST: (He writes furiously on a yellow pad, but says nothing.)

NOBLE SAVAGE: People expect me to be strong.
Wise,
Stoic,
Without guilt.
A man capable of a few symbolic acts.
Ugh—is that what I'm supposed to say?

THERAPIST: (He continues writing.)

NOBLE SAVAGE: I don't feel like
Maiming
Scalping
Burning wagon trains.
I'm developing hemorrhoids
From riding bareback.
It's an impossible role.
The truth is I'm conflicted.
I don't know who I am.
What should I do, Doc?

THERAPIST: I'm afraid we've run out of time.   Let's take this up
during our next visit.

Ishki, Mother, Upon Leaving the Choctaw Homelands, 1831

Right here is where I once suckled babies into Red people
Right here we grew three sisters into Corn, Beans, and Squash
Right here we gave goods to all who hungered
Right here we nurtured abundance.

Right here my body was a cycle of giving until
Torn from our homelands by the Naholla, and
Andrew Jackson, the duteous seamster
Intent on opening all veins.

Right here there's a hole of sorrow in the center of my chest
A puncture
A chasm of muscle
Sinew
Bones

Right here I will stitch my wounds and live on
And sing,
And sing,
I am singing, still.

The List We Make

PART 1

Luis and Salvadore, the two Miwok guides for the 1848 Donner Party, were the first to be shot and eaten as food.

William Foster had become deranged, and it is understandable why, knowing what he endured. He was terrified he would die of starvation, and Foster planned on murdering the Indians for food. Luis and Salvadore promptly ran away. The party followed their tracks. It was easy. The feet of the Indians had become so raw from exposure all their toes had fallen off, marking their trail with blood. Foster figured if the Indians didn't lead them to safety, they could at least find their corpses to use as food.

By January 9th or 10th, the Indians had suffered terrible exposure to the cold, and survived on practically nothing to eat, with no fire. They couldn't last like that. They gave out near a small creek, and it was here the Forlorn Hope came upon them. Despite argument from some and the Indians' look of terror, Foster shot the two Indians with his rifle. Though they would not have lived long, the act was horrifying.*

PART 2

The waiting road
arrives
this time San Francisco
moves along the abyss
in a black car filled with dawn and
men's underwear.

Again,
a membrane binds us
and I crave all you offer
your hands,
your poet's wrists that bleed
on the page
your penis of words
that penetrates my vagina
like a wet weapon.

We drape our bodies with new surroundings,
but like moveable sets on a theater stage
we fear hammer and nails,
hunger,
death,
longing,
and consumption.

---

* From the website: The Donner Party by Daniel Lewis. http://railboy.tripod.com/donner/

We café
trying to remember who we are,
for each other, I mean.
At Dollys, wide omelets,
big cups of brown Espresso unearth
old hungers, centuries old,
beckon.
"Yes," curves us together
and we breathe in the same thin air.
We breathe in each other
and forget all that has happened.

On the road made flesh
they separate us
from our fingers and toes
separate us from our bones.
At first, we are swallowed whole
like the wafers of God
down the gullets of hungry Christians.
Everything we did, everything we didn't do
is digested in their dreams
Now they know us better than we knew ourselves.

On the lam (again) we head north to the casinos
becoming what we fear: Consumers of goods and services.
We give twenty dollars to a stranger
to teach us how
to attach chains so
we can slip past Donner Pass
where banquet chairs pose
still as icicles
patiently awaiting our return.

We race toward the Biltmore Motel
our music is hard sevens.
We lunch in the high Sierras and
You teach me to gamble.

We crash a writers' conference
A bad poet reads an "ode to appetite"
But this time we will not be dinner.

PART 3

Seven thousand feet up
though Lake Tahoe stalks us
we practice our escape by devouring a
repugnant pig like our killers once devoured us.
At the All-American Café
you in grey to my conventional black,
we dine on goose liver,
pineapple, and curried ice cream.
Where are Luis and Salvadore now?
Who the hell cares? We're following
a treasure map of flesh and blood,
the ghost camouflage of exotic appetites
that came for Luis and Salvadore
has infected us all.
And,
what of this steamy you and I?
This steam,
This you and I?
Imprisoned by a hoary's God's ravenous hunger
we have not shadow's gaze
Nor eyes and ears.
No shadowy past.
Nothing, but here and now
made manifest within a complexion of stars
Our bodies
Conjoined in the heavens
On earth as
Luis y Salvadore
Conjoined in blood,
And oddly enough
Love.

JOY HARJO *(1951–), Mvskoke,* a poet, musician, writer, playwright, and performer, was appointed the twenty-third Poet Laureate of the United States in 2019. She is the author of nine books of poetry, including her most recent, *An American Sunrise.* She has been honored with the 2017 Ruth Lilly Prize from the Poetry Foundation, the Wallace Stevens Award from the Academy of American Poets, and a Guggenheim Fellowship. Her memoir *Crazy Brave* won the PEN USA Literary Award for Creative Non-Fiction. Her music has been awarded a Native American Music Award (NAMMY) for Best Female Artist of the Year, 2009. She is cofounder with Jennifer Elise Foerster of an arts mentorship program for Mvskoke citizens.

RUNNING

It's closing time. Violence is my boyfriend
With a cross to bear
                            Hoisted on by the church.
He wears it everywhere.
There are no female deities in the Trinity.
I don't know how I'm going to get out of here,
Said the flying fish to the tree.
                    Last call.
We've had it with history, we who look for vision here
In the Indian and poetry bar, somewhere
To the left of Hell.
Now I have to find my way, when there's a river to cross and no
Boat to get me there, when there appears to be no home at all.
                            My father gone, chased
By the stepfather's gun. *Get out of here.*
I've found my father at the bar, his ghost at least, some piece
Of him in this sorry place. The boyfriend's convincing to a crowd.
Right now, he's the spell of attraction. What tales he tells.
In the fog of thin hope, I wander this sad world
We've made with the enemy's words.

The lights quiver,
                    Like they do when the power's dwindling to a
        dangling string.
It is time to go home. We are herded like stoned cattle, like children for the
bombing drill—
Out the door, into the dark street of this old Indian town
Where there are no Indians anymore.
I was afraid of the dark, because then I could see
                              Everything. The truth with its eyes staring
Back at me. The mouth of the dark with its shiny moon teeth,
No words, just a hiss and a snap.
I could hear my heart hurting
With my *in-the-dark ears.*
I thought I could take it. Where was the party?
It's been a century since we left home with the American soldiers at our backs.
The party had long started up in the parking lot.
He flew through the dark, broke my stride with a punch.
I went down then came up.
I thought I could take being a girl with her heart in her
Arms. I carried it for justice. For the rights of all Indians.
                              We all had that cross to bear.
Those Old Ones followed me, the quiet girl with the long dark hair,
The daughter of a warrior who wouldn't give up.
I wasn't ready yet, to fling free the cross
I ran and I ran through the 2 A.M. streets.

It was my way of breaking free. I was anything but history.
I was the wind.

SHE HAD SOME HORSES

She had some horses.
She had horses who were bodies of sand.
She had horses who were maps drawn of blood.
She had horses who were skins of ocean water.

She had horses who were the blue air of sky.
She had horses who were fur and teeth.
She had horses who were clay and would break.
She had horses who were splintered red cliff.

She had some horses.

She had horses with eyes of trains.
She had horses with full, brown thighs.
She had horses who laughed too much.
She had horses who threw rocks at glass houses.
She had horses who licked razor blades.

She had some horses.

She had horses who danced in their mothers' arms.
She had horses who thought they were the sun and their
bodies shone and burned like stars.
She had horses who waltzed nightly on the moon.
She had horses who were much too shy, and kept quiet
in stalls of their own making.

She had some horses.

She had horses who liked Creek Stomp Dance songs.
She had horses who cried in their beer.
She had horses who spit at male queens who made
them afraid of themselves.
She had horses who said they weren't afraid.
She had horses who lied.
She had horses who told the truth, who were stripped
bare of their tongues.

She had some horses.

She had horses who called themselves, "horse."
She had horses who called themselves, "spirit," and kept

their voices secret and to themselves.
She had horses who had no names.
She had horses who had books of names.

She had some horses.

She had horses who whispered in the dark, who were afraid to speak.
She had horses who screamed out of fear of the silence, who
carried knives to protect themselves from ghosts.
She had horses who waited for destruction.
She had horses who waited for resurrection.

She had some horses.

She had horses who got down on their knees for any savior.
She had horses who thought their high price had saved them.
She had horses who tried to save her, who climbed in her
bed at night and prayed.

She had some horses.

She had some horses she loved.
She had some horses she hated.

These were the same horses.

RABBIT IS UP TO TRICKS

In a world long before this one, there was enough for everyone,
Until somebody got out of line.
We heard it was Rabbit, fooling around with clay and wind.
Everybody was tired of his tricks and no one would play with him;
He was lonely in this world.
So Rabbit thought to make a person.
And when he blew into the mouth of the crude figure to see

What would happen,
The clay man stood up.
Rabbit showed the clay man how to steal a chicken.
The clay man obeyed.
Rabbit showed him how to steal corn.
The clay man obeyed.
Then he showed him how to steal someone else's wife.
The clay man obeyed.
Rabbit felt important and powerful.
Clay man felt important and powerful.
And once that clay man started he could not stop.
Once he took that chicken he wanted all the chickens.
And once he took that corn he wanted all the corn.
And once he took that wife, he wanted all the wives.
He was insatiable.
Then he had a taste of gold and he wanted all the gold.
Then it was land and anything else he saw.
His wanting only made him want more.
Soon it was countries, then it was trade.
The wanting infected the earth.
We lost track of the purpose and reason for life.
We began to forget our songs. We forgot our stories.
We could no longer see or hear our ancestors,
Or talk with each other across the kitchen table.
Forests were being mowed down all over the world.
And Rabbit had no place to play.
Rabbit's trick had backfired.
Rabbit tried to call the clay man back,
But when the clay man wouldn't listen
Rabbit realized he'd made a clay man with no ears.

KIM SHUCK (*1966–*), *Cherokee,* was born in San Francisco and belongs to the Northern California Cherokee diaspora. She earned her BA in art and MFA in textiles from San Francisco State University. The author of several books of poetry, including *Smuggling Cherokee* and *Deer Trails,* Shuck is also known for her award-winning weaving and beadwork. She is a recipient of a 2019 National Laureate Fellowship and is the seventh poet laureate of San Francisco.

Water as a Sense of Place

1.

The water I used to drink spent time
Inside a pitched basket
It adopted the internal shape
Took on the taste of pine
And changed me forever.

I remember
Carrying that basket from the pump,
The slow swell of the damp roots,
Sway of a walk
That made carrying it easier.

Sometimes I imagine Step's Ford,
Both in and out of flood,
Tar Creek,
Spring River
In and out of baskets.

Gram's hands
Long, smooth fingers powerful and exact
Pull and twist
Sorting spokes and splitting weavers
Constructing my idea of water.

2.

I forgot to ask for the name
Of the creek that used to run through
What is now my backyard.
They piped it under,
But with enough rain
It remembers where to go.

Returns to shift
Mud and
Retaining walls.

It is, I imagine,
Referred to somewhere downtown
By the number of its pipe.

3.

Early training holds fast.
I sleep with water to the East of me,
Wake humming or singing
And go to water.

Bareheaded
In all but the most violent rainstorms
A connection I cannot give up
My hair and lashes glittering at first then weighed down.

I throw my windows open to the rain and
Lean out into the shock of contact.
Water so thick in the air
All but my closest neighbors are erased.

Rain is not an emergency
Not in October
Not in this place
I take it in breath by breath.

CHIP LIVINGSTON *(1967–), Mvskoke,* was born and raised in Florida. He is the author of two collections of poetry, a novel, and a collection of short stories and creative nonfiction. He has received awards from the Native Writers' Circle of the Americas, Wordcraft Circle of Native Writers and Storytellers, and the Arch and Bruce Brown Foundation. He teaches at the low-residency MFA in Creative Writing at the Institute of American Indian Arts in Santa Fe and lives in Uruguay.

A Proposal

I am a young man, Fire. You
are a young man, Wood. Listen,
I will go with you. In the air,
I enter, ancient. You in the smoke.

Kingfisher just kissed you.
The green frog, he just kissed you.
The dragonfly, wood, water, stone.
Choices are frequently made through inspiration.

A cloth, a chair, a walking stick.
Various symbols to elevate you.
The little white dog made footprints.
You and I just hold up the stars.

MARIANNE AWEAGON BROYLES *(1970–), Cherokee,* grew up in Tennessee. The author of *The Red Window,* she lives in Rio Rancho, New Mexico, and works as a psychiatric nurse in Albuquerque.

Trespassing

Warning signs dot edges of woods, rocky coasts and tell us *NO*
with letters in red, black, reflective silver and gold.
They are nailed on fences, hang from ropes, or planted
in the ground—something that will never grow.

My mother used to pull them like a spoiled root vegetable
from their staked claim of land and use them for kindling
between logs to make the fire burn longer and hotter.

The next morning, only ashes and maybe an orange
ember or two remain to be soaked with water and gathered
up with a shovel and thrown back to the earth we only think is our own.

 STACY PRATT (*1975–*), *Mvskoke,* is a former English professor
and now a freelance writer and singer-songwriter living in Tulsa.

A Creek Woman Beside Lake Ontario

Here, too, a great gold snake
writhes beneath the water,
his head at the shore, looking for us.

And is that him, riding the mist
in lines like subway commuters
rising up through the ground
into an entire other day?

He's brought me east,
to Black River Bay,

and so far the land has not swallowed
up our children.

But if he shoots another arrow in the morning,
I will follow it all the way
to the sun's house before turning around.
I go where he sends me.

I never stray entirely from the circled houses,
the old bones, the ball fields,
the pots of corn hanging over fires in the night,
the stories he keeps repeating
from inside my own body.

SANTEE FRAZIER (1978–), *Cherokee,* is the author of *Dark Thirty* (2009) and *Aurum* (2019). The inaugural School for Advanced Research Indigenous Writer in Residence fellow, his additional honors include the Lannan Foundation Residency Fellowship, Syracuse University Fellowship, the Fine Arts Work Center's Archie D. and Bertha H. Walker Foundation Scholarship, and a 2014 Native Arts and Cultures Foundation Fellowship. He directs the low-residency MFA in Creative Writing at the Institute of American Indian Arts in Santa Fe.

Sun Perch

It is late, but outside the night is glowing with snow and streetlight, quiet
but for the growl and skid of the plows. Winter, Syracuse, where the feinting
snow fusses and scatters until it collapses roofs and power lines.

And now sitting in that gauzy light, nothing but the sounds of sleep, my son's
cub-like snore, I am reminded my childhood was spent in another city, alone,
a boy who knew evenings only by the gradual blackening behind buildings,
jar bugs pinging electric poles, from the street curb hearing the clink of dishes,

chuckles of supper. I remember a fish staring blankly from the center
of a round plate rimmed with almond-eyed bluebirds—wings extended,
mid-flap—the fish, perhaps lightly steamed, then wok-fried, charred
along the belly, fins crisped, mouth open from its last breath, fossilized
in a reduction of fish sauce and honey—next to the plate, a bowl of steamed
    rice.

I sat at the table waiting, not knowing how to eat the fish or rice with
    chopsticks,
smiling as best I could while in Vietnamese John explained that I lived
    three blocks away,
that I had been home alone for days. His father looked at me as he left the
    kitchen,
wearing the shirt of a machinist, "Paul" sewn in above the right pocket.
    Later, I would learn
he worked three jobs, and on his only day off, Sunday, after mass, he would
    drive
his family to some far away lake outside the city, where they would reel in
    sun perch
and net them boat side.
           The smells of cooking oil and aromatics fading, John translated
for his mother who asked me to sleepover, and I said, no thank you, smiled,
    walked
home to whatever misfortune awaited in that dark house, where the
    plumbing was empty,
my bed a palette of blankets on the living room floor. I said no, not out of
    shame,
but because I wanted to lie down and remember how I'd used my fingers to
    scrape
flesh off bones—skin tearing with it—and how I trembled when asked to
    eat the eyes,
fins and tail.
           I remember now, how in the throes of labor my wife looked at me,
how she gripped my hand when the pain ruptured up, and how through it all,
behind the brown webbing of her pupils, there was gentleness.

When our son

finally came, he could not breathe, he was blue, motionless. I remember the
    midwife

rushing him off, and minutes later hearing gasping bawl. I didn't know what
    I saw, as my son

shivered, hands gnarled, locked in cry, still blind from birth, breathing
    underneath a plastic dome.

When I think of it now—the drive to that far away lake, my first catch
    flopping in the boat,

and later jerking the hook from its mouth—the perch must have stunned at
    the sudden

uselessness of its gills, and as I watched it gasp against the hull of the boat,
    I wished

what all boys wished for, a way of remembering how air rushes from your body

after being socked in the gut, and how to sit in the dark, alone, when
    streetlight

is just enough for a boy to make shapes with his hands, a play made of light,
    light made of snow.

THE CARNIVAL

      I studied every ride on the midway—
watched them groan, twirling
      light into blur, the Ferris wheel's

last passengers pointing out
      from their seats to town's end.
These monuments that have risen

      between the hills, to be forgotten
as the lights go out. Where was she
      in this hazy night? Maybe half-lit

in Red-Oak Bar, leaning on a man,
        wedged between his thighs. I wonder
what it is to dream of autumn,

        balled up on a park bench,
the tilt-a-whirl in my gaze,
        wanting a passing car to take me to her.

Among these monuments I am too
        small to find my way to the sandbanks
where she sometimes takes a man,

        where sometimes I wander,
skipping stones, while she earns
        in the backset of a car or under

a gun rack. It is hours like these
        you learn the path of a ditch—quiet
only the huffers know. Day breaks:

        the carnies have loaded up the rides,
heading out of town in a convoy,
        leaving nothing behind, not even the grass.

JENNIFER ELISE FOERSTER (1979–), *Mvskoke,* is the
author of two poetry collections, *Leaving Tulsa* and *Bright Raft in
the Afterweather.* A graduate of the Institute of American Indian
Arts in Santa Fe, she received her PhD from the University of Denver, was a
Wallace Stegner Fellow at Stanford, and has received grants and fellowships
from the Lannan Foundation and the National Endowment for the Arts.

Relic

An atlas
on the underside of my dream.

My half-shut eyelid—
a black wing.

I dipped sharp quills
in the night's mouth—

moths swarmed
from my throat.

I pulled a feather blanket
over my skeleton
and woke—

a map of America
flapping in the dark.

Once I dreamt
of inheriting this—

my mother
who still follows crows
through the field,

my sister's small hand
tucked inside hers,

me on her breast
in a burial quilt.

Leaving Tulsa

for Cosetta

Once there were coyotes, cardinals
in the cedar. You could cure amnesia
with the trees of our back-forty. Once
I drowned in a monsoon of frogs—
Grandma said it was a good thing, a promise
for a good crop. Grandma's perfect tomatoes.
Squash. She taught us to shuck corn, laughing,
never spoke about her childhood
or the faces in gingerbread tins
stacked in the closet.

She was covered in a quilt, the Creek way.
But I don't know this kind of burial:
vanishing toads, thinning pecan groves,
peach trees choked by palms.
New neighbors tossing clipped grass
over our fence line, griping to the city
of our overgrown fields.

Grandma fell in love with a truck driver,
grew watermelons by the pond
on our Indian allotment,
took us fishing for dragonflies.
When the bulldozers came
with their documents from the city
and a truckload of pipelines,
her shotgun was already loaded.

Under the bent chestnut, the well
where Cosetta's husband
hid his whiskey—buried beneath roots
her bundle of beads. *They tell*

the story of our family. Cosetta's land
flattened to a parking lot.

Grandma potted a cedar sapling
I could take on the road for luck.
She used the bark for heart lesions
doctors couldn't explain.
To her they were maps, traces of home,
the Milky Way, where she's going, she said.

After the funeral
I stowed her jewelry in the ground,
promised to return when the rivers rose.

On the grassy plain behind the house
one buffalo remains.

Along the highway's gravel pits
sunflowers stand in dense rows.
Telephone poles crook into the layered sky.
A crow's beak broken by a windmill's blade.
It is then I understand my grandmother:
When they see open land
they only know to take it.

I understand how to walk among hay bales
looking for turtle shells.
How to sing over the groan of the county road
widening to four lanes.
I understand how to keep from looking up:
small planes trail overhead
as I kneel in the Johnson grass
combing away footprints.

Up here, parallel to the median
with a vista of mesas' weavings,
the sky a belt of blue and white beadwork,

I see our hundred and sixty acres
stamped on God's forsaken country,
a roof blown off a shed,
beams bent like matchsticks,
a drove of white cows
making their home
in a derailed train car.

 LARA MANN (1983–), *Choctaw*, is of English, Irish, Choc-
taw, French, German, Scottish, Spanish, Cherokee, Welsh, and
Mohawk descent. A native of Kansas, her first chapbook, *A Song of
Ascents and Descents*, was published in 2014 in the United Kingdom by Salt
Publishing as part of *Effigies II*, a compilation edited by Allison Hedge Coke.
Mann previously taught English and creative writing at Haskell Indian
Nations University and works in special education.

Nanih Waiya Cave

Pearl River, Mississippi

> *A very long time ago the first creation of men was in Nanih Waiya; and
> there they were made and there they came forth. [. . .] And the Choctaws
> [. . .] came out of Nanih Waiya. And they then sunned themselves on the
> earthen rampart and when they got dry, they did not go anywhere but settled
> down on this very land and it is the Choctaws' home.*
> —Isaac Pistonatubbee

A couple miles down this iron-locked road
is a low cave in a large mound. Dad throws rocks
inside the gape. We hear shallow water.
He crawls through the opening, flashlight in hand.
I am scared of underground places, can't follow.

There is room for four grown men to stand, he echoes.
I stay where I can see what's around me:
Kudzu-draped trees, old growth, in the shadows.
I can almost see what's inside them, their stories,
but they're tight-lipped and I take my lesson.

Picnic tables, grills, beer cans surround the mound.
Even though it's miles away from any town,
no sign, not on a map, just a numbered
county road, I can see people still come here.
Dad crawls out, throws a burnt log onto the ground.

I want to go inside; shuffle, head down, knees up
into the entrance but can't go any further.
Instead I grab a handful of wet cave-wall dirt,
mossy green, replace it with my hair. I clutch
this dirt-gift, nails in palms, head pulsing heat from pain.

This place he's taken me, this Shadow World,
requires both of us. We had to come
to our Source, go in, come back out renewed.
But I'm not done with this past yet, can't end it
and reemerge; my head is burning in shadow.

OUTRODUCTION

LeAnne Howe

W E BEGIN in the East and go North. As Joy Harjo has said, "to be gracious, we should begin with Northeast–Midwest, and then wind up with the Southeast." This collection of poems, born of these lands, is not an end nor a beginning.

The undertaking for our anthology of poems by ancestor-poets has been thousands of years in the making, especially considering the song chants. We've pulled together more than 240 poems from authors of Native Nations around the Western Hemisphere into a body of work that we could recognize. Native chants have no beginning and no ending as they reverberate around the universes and sing.

Here now, I am back at dirt's door, my own homeland. I hear someone softly playing a sacred song as I write. A song cords its way up through the arms of the giant elm tree growing outside my grandparents' house. I'm cradled back into the place where memories of music and poetry began for me, Ada, Oklahoma, in the 1950s. Here again I hear my grandfather's solitary fiddle whining against my great-aunts' voices in a three-part harmony. My great-uncle plays rhythm guitar. I feel as if they play and sing all Sunday afternoon into dusk, but I can't quite be sure my memory serves. I see myself waving good-bye as they drive away in an old farm truck back to Stonewall, Oklahoma. I don't want their images to fade, so I keep waving long after they are gone.

Because I am so young, time slows down and is splintered by great fissures of sorrow. I'm back where I must be in order to write about my first encounters with poetry.

Like music, poetry also came to me through my grandparents. They both wrote poems. My Cherokee grandmother composed poetry on the backs of envelopes of letters she'd received, or in the margins of her books. I still have them. She told me when she was young, they couldn't afford paper. Iva's early life was one of poverty, and great sadness. At seventeen, she married a white man. My mother was born a year later in 1917 in a one-room cabin at Stonewall. The Mvskoke Creek midwife was named Izola, so my grandmother named her newborn daughter after the Mvskoke Creek woman.

My grandmother lost her husband and their farm in the 1918 pandemic. She and her two-year-old daughter, Izola, moved from Stonewall to Ada, where she worked as a housekeeper for fifty cents a week, plus board. Her poetic voice comes from all these losses. She usually wrote poems about dying flowers, faded rose gardens in late summer, and wilting bluebells. She never wrote about love, or her children, or all the death and dying she'd witnessed as a young woman.

Grandmother didn't write poetry about "the angel of death that would come in the spirit of a bird for her friends, and husband," but she would tell those stories to me. I know more of her life and her poetry because she was also a storyteller. She and my mother would sit at the dining table in Ada after Sunday lunch and write rhyming verses. Most of my mother's poetry is lost or destroyed. But we have my grandmother's.

Grandfather Lonnie Valentine also wrote poetry in the margins of books, and in small notebooks. He included detailed recipes for curing horse colic and curing kidney disease in horses. I have them. He was my grandmother's second husband and he played the fiddle, sang songs, cured horse colic, and wrote poetry. He never talked of writing poetry and the only reason I know he did is because I found them among his things after he died, along with his deputy sheriff's badge and a pistol. Maybe he thought it wasn't manly to write poetry and patrol the west side streets of Ada known as "the bucket of blood." At that time there were many shootings in the two-story gambling houses in west Ada. Yet my grandfather's poems were about love. In 1914, he was writing about an "orange-haired girl from Kentucky." He was seventeen years old; she was fifteen. He kept their letters. Lonnie Valentine also wrote about his love for a roan horse. In his youth, before crop failures and poverty took his family's farm, he and his brothers raised quarter horses.

I still can recall the long drive out into the country to my great-uncle's house. Today I realize it was only five miles outside of Stonewall, but it seemed much farther in those days. Once there I would lie on a quilt in the yard forgetting about the heat and mosquitoes and listen to the Indians sing and play guitars while my grandfather played the fiddle.

Lonnie Valentine was born in 1897, the same year that Queen Lili'uokalani finished translating the *Kumulipo*, a Hawaiian Creation chant. Queen Liliʻuokalani's translation opens the Pacific Northwest, Alaska, and Pacific Islands section in our anthology:

> At the time that turned the heat of the earth,
> At the time when the heavens turned and changed,
> At the time when the light of the sun was subdued
> To cause light to break forth,
> At the time of the night of Makalii (winter)
> Then began the slime which established the earth,
> The source of deepest darkness.
> Of the depth of darkness, of the depth of darkness,
> Of the darkness of the sun, in the depth of night,
> > It is night,
> > So was night born

I respond with a Choctaw chant to Queen Liliʻuokalani's chant.

> Issa hal-a-li haa- toko Ik-sa illok isha shkee
> Issa hal-a-li haa- toko Ik-sa illok isha shkee
> Issa hal-a-li haa- toko Ik-sa illok isha shkee
> Issa hal-a-li haa- toko Ik-sa illok isha shkee

Because you are holding on to me I am not dead yet.

In working on our volume of two centuries of Native Nations poetry, I've come to believe that Queen Liliʻuokalani's translation of the Creation chant of the *Kumulipo* was heard all the way across the big blue waters, and all across the lands, even in the lands of the people of Indian Territory where my grandmother and grandfather were born. Maybe all peoples everywhere still respond to Queen Liliʻuokalani's beautiful call.

We are not finished yet.

ACKNOWLEDGMENTS

ALL CREATIONS begin with an intent, a spark of light. The spark for the anthology gathered us around it, all of the poetry editors, all of the assistance in the many forms. We have done the best we can and acknowledge that no project is definitive. There could be numberless anthologies issued on the same theme, and each would be distinctly different. We offer up with gratitude this gathering, for behind each poem and poet are multitudes of poets and family ancestors. Please forgive us for any omissions or failures. And even celebrate this circle of indigenous poets and poetry, that they go forth to continue to inspire those who are coming up. There are many, so many more than when the older of us began listening to and writing poetry.

We are grateful for those in our tribal nations and communities who have taken care of our oral arts, despite the destruction that has come down from disrespect and disregard of the original inhabitants of these lands. They suffered as they held tight, and here we are, fed. It is because of them that we recall our tribal ways of doing and making, given by the tribal communities in which we were raised, whether they be in our homelands or in urban communities.

So many efforts and support structures have brought this collection into being. We would like to acknowledge the Department of English at the University of Tennessee in Knoxville, especially Allen Dunn, department chair; Margaret Lazarus Dean, director of creative writing; and English Department staff including Judith Welch, Donna Bodenheimer, and Kayla Allen. We depended especially on Jeremy Reed, Joy Harjo's assistant at UTK. He was there ensuring the details during each part of the process. Allison Davis also stepped in to assist with early editing. We are grateful to the students at UTK who helped lay the groundwork. We would also like to acknowledge Stanton B. Garner Jr. for his advice.

We are grateful for the support of the Eidson Foundation at the University of Georgia for their assistance, and for James Matthew Kliewer, from the University of Georgia, for all his editing work.

Without the continued belief and support of Jill Bialosky, our inspired editor at W. W. Norton, and the supportive staff, especially Drew Weitman, we would not be placing this book into your hands, to share. We also depended on the warrior skills of agent Kathleen Anderson, and our intrepid permissions editor, Frederick Courtwright. For translation assistance we thank Margaret Noodin and Sherwin Bitsui. We would like to thank the Tulsa Artist Fellowship for their support during the final assembly of these poems. And special thanks to Allison Hedge Coke, Carolyn Dunn, Phyllis "Coochie" Cayan, and Larry Evers for helping us to locate some of these poets.

We have had much assistance as this project developed. We would like to acknowledge Emmi Whitehorse for the use of her stunning painting as cover art, and Jill Momaday for helping us contact her father, N. Scott Momaday. We also must acknowledge Scott for his trailblazing inspiration and offerings as a poet, writer, and artist. We would not be who we are as Native writers without his efforts and creations in this world. And there's Robert Dale Parker. We relied greatly on his groundbreaking scholarship that resulted in his collection of early Native poetry, *Changing Is Not Vanishing*. We would like to thank Lisa Brooks for her scholarship and the discussion of Eleazar, and her reminder that New England Native poets are a force to be acknowledged. We remember all the editors of those earlier anthologies of Native literature, the anthology ancestors.

There are many who are not named here. May your efforts find reward in this creation.

We are in service to the peoples, lands, and inhabitants of our tribal nations and are grateful for this opportunity to share the poetry that has inspired so many, and keeps us going through times that challenge us to remember those original teachings that are most often spoken and sung through poetry.

Mvto/Yakoke.

// The Editors: Joy Harjo, LeAnne Howe, and Jennifer Elise Foerster

I would like to add gratitude to my husband, Owen Chopoksa Sapulpa, whose listening and knowledge inspires me. And for my people, the Muscogee Creek Nation, the Mvskoke, especially those who take care of the songs, poetry, and stories that feed our spirits. And mvto, mvto, mvto, mvto to my sisters LeAnne Howe and Jennifer Elise Foerster for this part of the journey. And finally, with gratitude for all the editors, advisors, and helpers without whose assistance this collection would not exist. Mvto, thank you for the source of life that emerges in poetry and song to sustain us.
// JOY HARJO-SAPULPA

First, I would like to thank *Hashtali*, whose eye is the sun. I rarely begin with the sacred, but because so many of our poetry ancestors are in this collection, it feels right to acknowledge all the powers that have been with us on the journey. I would also like to acknowledge my southeastern ancestors on both sides of my tribal families, the Billys (Choctaw) and the Bennetts (adopted Cherokee family); and my sons, Joseph Craig and Randall Craig, my husband Jim Wilson, and my granddaughters Chelsey Craig and Alyssa Warren. This book would not have come into the world without the leadership of Joy Harjo. Thank you, Joy, for pulling us together. Thank you, Jennifer Elise Foerster, for holding us together. It has been my enormous pleasure to bring the book into the world.
// LeAnne Howe

With gratitude for all who receive, return to, and return us to poetry, a breath of creation; for the poets, artists, and writers of the Institute of American Indian Arts; for the essential inspiration of my family and ancestors; for all of my teachers, especially Joy Harjo and LeAnne Howe—thank you for your enduring strength and wisdom and for inviting me to work with you on this immense endeavor; and for the guidance, time, and efforts of the regional contributing editors. I am humbled to participate in this truly collective vision.
// JENNIFER ELISE FOERSTER

CREDITS

Lara Mann, "Nanih Waiya Cave" from *A Song of Ascents and Descents, Effigies II*. Copyright © 2014 by Lara Mann. Reprinted with the permission of Salt Publishing Ltd.

Shaunna Oteka McCovey, "I Still Eat All of My Meals with a Mussel Shell" from *The Smokehouse Boys and New Poems* (Sugartown Publishing, 2018). Reprinted with the permission of the author.

Brandy Nālani McDougall, "He Mele Aloha no ka Niu" from *Poetry* (July/August 2016). Copyright © 2016 by Brandy Nālani McDougall. "Sonnet (Ka ʻŌlelo)" from *Salt-Wind / Ka Makana Paʻakai* (Honolulu: Kuleana ʻŌiwi Press, 2008). Copyright © 2008 by Brandi Nālani McDougall. Both reprinted with the permission of the author.

Dan Taulapapa McMullin, "The Doors of the Sea" from *Coconut Milk*. Copyright © 2013 by Dan Taulapapa McMullin. Reprinted by permission of The University of Arizona Press.

Michael McPherson, "Clouds, Trees & Ocean, North Kauai" from *Singing with the Owls* (Honolulu: Petronium Press, 1983). Copyright © 1983 by Michael McPherson. Reprinted with the permission of Howard McPherson.

Tiffany Midge, "Teeth in the Wrong Places" from *Guiding the Stars to their Campfire, Driving the Salmon to Their Bed* (Seattle: Gazoobi Tales, 2015). Copyright © 2015 by Tiffany Midge. Reprinted with the permission of the author. "Night Caller" from *The Woman Who Married a Bear*. Copyright © 2016 by Tiffany Midge. Reprinted with the permission of The University of New Mexico Press.

Dian Million, "The Housing Poem" from *Reinventing the Enemy's Language*, edited by Joy Harjo and Gloria Bird (New York: W. W. Norton & Company, 1997). Reprinted with the permission of the author.

Deborah A. Miranda, "I Am Not a Witness" from *Indian Cartography* (Greenfield Center, New York: Greenfield Review Press, 1999). Copyright © 1999 by Deborah A. Miranda. "Mesa Verde" from *The Zen of La Llo-*

loa" from *Light in the Crevice Never Seen*. Copyright © 1994 by Haunani-Kay Trask. Reprinted with the permission of CALYX Books.

Gail Tremblay, "Indian Singing in 20th Century America" from *Indian Singing in 20th Century America*. Copyright © 1990 by Gail Tremblay. Reprinted with the permission of the author and CALYX Books.

John Trudell, "Diablo Canyon" from *Lines from a Mined Mind*. Copyright © 2008 by John Trudell. Reprinted with the permission of Fulcrum Publishing.

Mark Turcotte, "Burn" and "Battlefield" from *Exploding Chippewas*. Copyright © 2002 by Mark Turcotte. Published 2002 by TriQuarterly Books/ Northwestern University Press. All rights reserved.

Georgiana Valoyce-Sanchez, "The Dolphin Walking Stick" from *The Sound of Rattles and Clappers: A Collection of New California Indian Writing*, edited by Greg Sarris (The University of Arizona Press, 1994). Copyright © 1994 by Georgiana Valoyce-Sanchez. Reprinted with the permission of the author.

Gerald Vizenor, "Seven Woodland Crows" and "Family Photograph." Reprinted with the permission of the author. "Fat Green Flies" from *Favor of Crows: New and Selected Haiku*. Copyright © 2014 by Gerald Vizenor. Reprinted by permission of Wesleyan University Press.

Vince Wannassay, "Forgotten Coyote Stories" from *Dancing on the Rim of the World* (Tucson: The University of Arizona Press, 1990). Copyright © 1990 by Vince Wannassay. Reprinted with the permission of the Estate of Vince Wannassay.

Michael Wasson, "A Poem for the háawtnin' & héwlekipx [The Holy Ghost of You, the Space & Thin Air]" from *Poetry* (June 2018). Copyright © 2018 by Michael Wasson. Reprinted with the permission of the author.

James Welch, "Harlem, Montana: Just Off the Reservation," "The Man from Washington," and "Riding the Earthboy 40" from *Riding the Earthboy 40*. Copyright © 1971, 1976, 1990 by James Welch. Used by permission of Penguin Books, an imprint of Penguin Publishing Group, a division of Penguin Random House LLC. All rights reserved.

Kimberly Wensaut, "Prodigal Daughter" from *Yellow Medicine Review* (Winter 2007). Copyright © 2007 by Kimberly Wensaut. Reprinted with the permission of the author.

Gwen Nell Westerman, "Wicaŋȟpi Heciya Taŋhaŋ Uŋhipi (We Come from the Stars)" from *Follow the Blackbirds*. Copyright © 2013 by Gwen Nell Westerman. Reprinted with the permission of Michigan State University Press.

Wayne Kaumualii Westlake, "Hawaiians Eat Fish" from *Westlake: Poems by Wayne Kaumualii Westlake* (University of Hawaii Press, 2009). Reprinted with the permission of the Estate of Wayne Kaumualii Westlake.

Orlando White, "To See Letters" from *Bone Light*. Copyright © 2009 by Orlando White. Reprinted with the permission of The Permissions Company, LLC, on behalf of Red Hen Press, redhen.org. "Empty Set" from *LETTERRS*. Copyright © 2015 by Orlando White. Reprinted with the permission of The Permissions Company, LLC, on behalf of Nightboat Books, nightboat.org.

Tanaya Winder, "learning to say *i love you*" and "the milky way escapes my mouth" from *Words Like Love* (West End Press, 2015). Copyright © 2015 by Tanaya Winder. Reprinted with the permission of the author.

Karenne Wood, "Chief Totopotamoi, 1654" and "Hard Times" from *Markings on Earth*. Copyright © 2001 by Karenne Wood. Reprinted by permission of The University of Arizona Press.

Elizabeth Woody, "Weaving" and "Translation of Blood Quantum" from *Luminaries of the Humble*. Copyright © 1994 by Elizabeth A. Woody. Reprinted by permission of The University of Arizona Press.

Don Jesús Yoilo'i, "Yaqui Deer Song" from *Yaqui Deer Songs, Maso Bwikam*, edited by Larry Evers and Felipe S. Molina. Reprinted with the permission of The University of Arizona Press, Larry Evers, and Felipe S. Molina.

INDEX